The Path of a Kabbalist

The Path of a Kabbalist
Z'ev ben Shimon Halevi

KS Books Ltd
London

This edition published by:

www.ksbooksltd.com
E-mail: info@ksbooksltd.com

First published in 2009 by Kabbalah Society
Copyright © Z'ev ben Shimon Halevi 2009, 2024

Every effort has been made to obtain permission to reproduce copyright material but there may be cases where we have been unable to trace the copyright holder. The publisher will be happy to correct any omissions in future printings.

The moral right of the author has been asserted.

All rights reserved.
No part of this publication may be reproduced, stored in a retrieval system or transmitted, in any form or by any means, without the prior permission in writing of the publisher, nor be circulated in any form of binding or cover other than that in which it is published and without a similar condition including this condition being imposed on the subsequent purchaser.

A CIP catalogue record for this book
is available from the British Library.

ISBN: 978-1-917606-26-4

Design by Lion Dickinson

Dedicated to my Forebears

Also an acknowledgement:

So many people have been involved in my path of development that it is not possible to name all of them. Therefore I decided to give only the key individuals identities in their roles. I offer my gratitude to them and to others not mentioned. In particular I would like to thank those who have organised groups at home and abroad and been more than hospitable here in England and in several near and far places. Finally, I would like to acknowledge my invisible mentors who have watched over my progress.

By the same author:

Adam and the Kabbalistic Trees
A Kabbalistic Universe
The Way of Kabbalah
Introduction to the World of Kabbalah
The Kabbalist at Work
Kabbalah and Exodus
Kabbalah: School of the Soul
Psychology and Kabbalah
The Kabbalistic Tree of Life
Kabbalah and Astrology
The Anointed—*A Kabbalistic Novel*
The Anatomy of Fate
Kabbalistic Contemplations

By other publishers:

Kabbalah—The Divine Plan (HarperCollins)
Kabbalah: Tradition of Hidden Knowledge (Thames & Hudson)
Astrology: The Celestial Mirror (Thames & Hudson)
As Above, So Below (Stuart & Watkins)

Contents

	Preface	xiii
1.	Introduction	15
2.	History	19
3.	Family	25
4.	Childhood	31
5.	Youth	39
6.	Learning	45
7.	Education	51
8.	Exploration	57
9.	Experience	65
10.	Observation	72
11.	Intimations	79
12.	Initiation	87
13.	Changes	93
14.	Providence	99
15.	Crisis	105
16.	Discovery	111
17.	Relationships	117
18.	Visions	123
19.	Journeys	129
20.	Books	135
21.	Psychism	143
22.	Poetry	149
	Time's Lock is Broken	151
23.	Resistance	209
24.	Parallels	216
25.	Cosmos	223
26.	Group	229
27.	Practice	235
28.	Confirmation	241
29.	Sacredness	249
30.	Humour	255

31.	Visits	263
32.	Testings	269
33.	New World	275
34.	Astrology	283
35.	Opportunity	289
36.	Novel	299
37.	Fruits	305
38.	Emergence	311
39.	Meetings	318
40.	Pilgrimages	327
41.	Marriage	333
42.	Memory	338
43.	Encounters	345
44.	Hostility	353
45.	Development	359
46.	Academy	365
47.	Orient	371
48.	Home	375
49.	Reflection	381

Illustrations

1.	Portrait	xii
2.	Horoscope	14
3.	Tradition	20
4.	Soroka	22
5.	Great-grandfather	26
6.	Family	28
7.	High Wycombe	32
8.	White Ship	35
9.	Nazism	38
10.	Hiroshima	40
11.	Observation	44
12.	First Love	46
13.	War	50
14.	Art School	52
15.	Self-portrait	54
16.	Landscape	58
17.	Companions	60
18.	Illustration	62
19.	Patient	66
20.	Mother	68
21.	Operation	74
22.	Romance	76
23.	Academy	78
24.	Study	80
25.	Cast	82
26.	Father	84
27.	Props	88
28.	Example	90
29.	Workshop	94
30.	Zodiac	96
31.	I Ching	100
32.	Book Jacket	102

33.	Crisis	106
34.	Weapons	108
35.	Friend	112
36.	Tree of Life	114
37.	Anima	118
38.	Hippies	120
39.	Work	124
40.	Levels	126
41.	Toledo	130
42.	Culture	132
43.	Jacob's Ladder	136
44.	Evidence	138
45.	Inspiration	142
46.	Symbolism	144
47.	Institutions	210
48.	Revelation	212
49.	Zoroastrianism	218
50.	Shintoism	220
51.	Telescopes	224
52.	Poster	226
53.	Cat	230
54.	Mirror	232
55.	Merkabah	236
56.	Favourite	238
57.	Maggid	242
58.	Voice	244
59.	High Priest	248
60.	Moment	250
61.	Humour	256
62.	Wit	258
63.	Spinoza	262
64.	Trenches	266
65.	Soul Mates	270
66.	Redskin	276
67.	South	278
68.	Signs	282
69.	Astrolabe	284
70.	Disaster	290
71.	Test	294

72.	Converso	298
73.	Egypt	302
74.	Endurance	306
75.	Interior	308
76.	Change	312
77.	Music	314
78.	School	320
79.	Exercise	322
80.	Haven	326
81.	Wall	328
82.	Precognition	332
83.	Fulfilment	334
84.	Astrologers	340
85.	London	342
86.	Omens	346
87.	Name	348
88.	Wrecker	352
89.	Insight	354
90.	Psychology	358
91.	Options	360
92.	Connection	364
93.	History	368
94.	Japan	370
95.	China	372
96.	Science	376
97.	Imagination	378
98.	Study	380
99.	Contemplation	382
100.	Yad	384
101.	Fate	386

FIGURE 1—PORTRAIT
The author in his mid-fifties. (Photograph by Mayotte Magnus-Lewinska).

Preface

Over the years many people have asked me how I came to Kabbalah. Therefore I decided to write an account of my path, for the record.

We all have memories. On this my seventy-fifth birthday I have many to recall. Here I have set down those experiences that were relevant to my development. I make no claim to be a saint or sage, but someone who has sought to comprehend what life on Earth is about. I have had many teachers. Most of them were unconscious instruments of Providence, which marked out the course of my spiritual education. Like everyone who lives in the everyday world I have had my good and bad times, disasters and idyllic moments, as well as breakthroughs. All these events led up to understanding what my fate was about. This fact I recognised in my middle years, although my soul knew what my destiny was to be from the time before I was born. I forgot this prenatal memory in the hurly-burly of youth and learning how to be an adult in the historic epoch and place in which I had been positioned. The text that follows passes on what I have experienced and learned in order to aid and give encouragement to those who seek the inner life, especially in difficult periods when contact with the Way is almost lost in the confusion of events. Most of all, it is to show how the miraculous can occur at any moment in life to reveal, in my case, the path of a Kabbalist.

London. Winter 2008/5768
Z'ev ben Shimon Halevi

FIGURE 2—HOROSCOPE
At the centre is a picture of the author aged about nine. The Sun in Capricorn in the 12th House generates a thoughtful introvert, interested in philosophy, religion and mysticism. The Moon in Gemini in the 5th House indicates a talent for images and teaching while the Capricorn Ascendant means that I would be a practical thinker looking much the same physically throughout a long life. A degree of success is indicated but only after a long process because Saturn and the Ascending Node are in the 1st House. Uranus in the 2nd House means that I would not have a regular job but earn my living in an unusual way. The constellation of the Descending Node, Neptune, Mars and Jupiter foreshadows problems with intelligent, spiritual and forceful women. With Pluto on the Descendant these relationships will be difficult but transformative. Venus and Mercury in the 12th House indicate that these affairs would be private, while Scorpio on the Midheaven points to achievement in the esoteric field. (Author's horoscope).

1. Introduction

My earliest memory of this life is of just before I was born. I was standing before three beings. One asked me, 'So you are bored with Paradise?' I replied, 'No, but life on Earth is where the action is.' This personage then said to me, before my descent, 'Then no complaints if the going gets rough.' I never have complained, as I knew about the Divine Plan and that no event would be without significance, however irrelevant it might seem at the time. This is what kept me on target even though I sometimes lost sight of the bigger picture.

According to the kabbalistic tradition, just before being incarnated one is shown the broad outline of one's fate and the people one is likely to meet, if one stays on course. However, after being born one soon loses this knowledge, as the demands of the body and lower psyche take over and all but a dim remembrance of purpose is forgotten. It is said, by the Tradition, that for the first seven days of life one still has the cognition of an adult. This can be seen in intelligent infants with knowing eyes immediately after birth. This fades as the physical world begins to dominate the soul and the only way the now-incarnate soul can retain its connection with a higher reality is to appear to sleep. This enables the psyche gradually to get used to being in the body which is to be its Earthly vehicle.

It is said that most souls descend from the invisible worlds because of the force of psychic gravity, that is karma, known in Kabbalah as 'measure for measure'. Thus we are impelled to return to Earth to resolve some unfinished business, learn a certain lesson, evolve further or carry out a mission. These processes are related to what are called the 'Four Journeys'. The first is the descent into flesh, or putting on 'coats of skin' as the Bible speaks of it. The second is of evolution, at both the personal and collective level, and the third is to reincarnate in order to aid mankind in its development. The final journey is the ultimate ascent, the Resurrection, when all of humanity and Existence returns to the Godhead.

Most people are on the first and second journeys in which they learn how to live on Earth where every level of humanity—good, evil, foolish and wise—is to be found. In the invisible realms these orders are separated into various levels. On Earth, however, the state of Hell can be seen everywhere where there is chaos, whereas Paradise and Heaven can be observed in people who live a balanced or holy life.

About ninety percent of incarnate humanity belong to a general soul-group such as a family, tribe or nation. They are at the level of Nature. About nine percent belong to a section which is beginning to individuate, that is the second journey, while the remaining one percent is those who know what the Divine Drama is about and choose to return on the third journey to play a conscious rôle. The Greeks classified these three orders into common people, uncommon people and heroes and heroines. In Kabbalah the terms of vegetable, animal and human people are used.

The process of Self-realisation, in which each person becomes an organ of perception for the Absolute, enables God to behold God in the Mirror of Existence. Every genuine spiritual line makes this statement in one way or another in order to encourage people to fulfil their potential. This is what the Bible means in the phrase that each of us has been 'called forth, created, formed and made'. However, to be able to execute one's destiny requires much training over many lives.

According to Kabbalah each of us is a Divine, spiritual, psychological and physical entity. At death we drop the material vehicle that enabled us to function on Earth but retain our soul. This is the essence of our psychological being. In most people the spiritual and Divine possibilities are as yet unrealised. After death we spend some time in a process of Self-assessment, before going to the appropriate level in the higher Worlds. Here we rest, reflect and enjoy either the pleasures of the afterlife or appropriate punishments of Hell, if we are in denial of any major misdemeanour. Once the dynamic of the last life is spent, then the pull of karma brings us down into the best situation on Earth for us to grow. This is often with the people who may well be part of the same family or soul-group we were with during our last incarnation. In the case of the third journey, a mature soul is usually carefully positioned to be born in a specific time and place in order to carry out a special mission.

It is said, in esoteric literature, that when a man and woman are in sexual union, the soul to be born to them hovers above the couple. Many people have reported sensing a strong presence at the moment of conception. Once this occurs, the discarnate psyche becomes attached to the embryo during the pregnancy, to a greater or lesser degree, according to their level of psychological or spiritual development. Those who are relatively advanced are not locked into the foetus until the last moment before birth, although they do try on the new body from time to time, giving rise to the phenomenon of movement in the womb. At the moment of birth the psyche, which is fluidic by nature, becomes crystallised at that point. This is related to the cosmic situation, in that the microcosm of a human being responds to the state of the macrocosm. At the moment of birth the mode of fate is set. This is represented by the positions of the Sun, Moon, planets and the Zodiac in a birth chart. Records over some four thousand years, by schools of the soul, have established that a particular celestial configuration resonates in a distinct pattern to generate the person's fate. However, only those who choose to evolve fulfil their potential.

In my case, observations over the years have proved this premise to be true in that my life's journey, as mapped out in my horoscope, has been impressively accurate. I have, for example, Sun in Capricorn in the 12th House. This indicates the introspective temperament of a practical thinker who lives most of the time in a book-lined study filled with mystical, philosophical, religious and historic objects and pictures. However, I have Moon in Gemini in the 5th House, which means I have an extrovert persona and the ability to communicate ideas about esoteric subjects through writing and teaching. Moreover, with three planets and my descending Node in the 7th House of partnership, as will be indicated I have had some fascinating but difficult personal and professional relationships. Having Uranus, the unconventional planet, in the House of possessions, finance and making a living has manifested in being a freelance writer, artist and teacher with no regular income.

All this was only in potential when I was born. According to my mother, I was an almost painless birth. Upon taking my first breath, I took on a look of calm curiosity about me. This was in sharp contrast to my elder brother, whose birth was difficult for my mother because he was so perturbed at being born. At the age of eighty he has not changed very much, despite having a large loving family, but then his Jupiter conjunct Uranus in Aries is both a creative and explosive combination.

I cannot recall being born but I do recollect very sharply being in a baby cart and thinking, 'What am I doing here in an infant's body?' Perhaps it is just as well that we are made oblivious of being an adult soul in our early years, so as to be able to concentrate upon learning how to relate to our family and the outside world. To remember where we come from might be too much to bear. It is said, in Jewish folklore, that an angel tweaks our nose at birth so as to make us forget all that we knew until we are ready to remember. However, all is not quite forgotten. I recall as a young child being acutely aware that God knew all that I did, especially when I was naughty. Some time later, as a boy, when creeping out of an orchard I realised I could never be the Messiah because I was stealing apples. How could an eight-year-old have any idea what a Messiah was? No one in my family had any idea of this concept, so how had I come by it?

Another example of perhaps being an 'old soul' was when I was at school. We children were told to turn a number of cardboard boxes into a steam train. We all started by getting in each other's way until I stood back, saw how to organise the operation and began telling the other boys how to go about it. To my surprise they did what I said which made me think; Who am I, a skinny little Jewish boy, telling these tough Cockney kids what to do? Years later I realised that this was my Moon in the 5th House of command in action, backed by the Sun's Capricornian gift for organisation. This incident aroused the jealousy of a schoolboy rival who sought to dominate the class. He picked a fight. Fortunately my brother had taught me a jujitsu throw that worked and I threw the boy over my shoulder. Having lost face he ran away. This impressed me more than the other boys. In other confrontations at school, discretion was seen to be the better part of valour. My 12th House Sun saw that this was wiser and henceforth I avoided any violence by diplomatic means. These early lessons in how to deal with hostile people were to be very useful. At the age of fifty, on the beach of Rio de Janeiro, my brother's jujitsu technique saved me from being mugged. Later, critical assaults by rabbis and others had to be dealt with by tact but with firmness. Spiritual work is not, I was to learn, all light and love.

2. History

One's family, class and cultural history have an enormous influence upon life on two levels. The first is that one is born into that soul-group because of a karmic connection over many lives, while the second level is that culture moulds the mind into the mode of that time and place. This is vital if a specific mission is to be carried out successfully. Someone whose destiny is to be a doctor, inventor or writer must understand the period into which they are incarnated in order to be effective.

In spiritual work there is a factor of really knowing a tradition from within and this cannot be acquired in one lifetime. For example, people who convert from being Jewish or Christian into Buddhism or Sufism can only have a certain comprehension of the line. Moreover, they will never be fully accepted by those born into these cultures as one of them, despite all the effort put in. There are, of course, exceptions but these are rare. The reality is that one is incarnated into a particular culture for a definite reason.

As far as I can perceive, I have been born a Jew for most of my lives. I also have strong feelings about certain places and periods of history. I have a natural affinity with the Middle East but also with China. Medieval London is very familiar while Spain evokes a mixture of pleasure and fear, as a Golden Age in Toledo gave way to the Inquisition. In this life I was born to be in England because, I believe, London is the most cosmopolitan and civilised city of my time.

Being born into a relatively orthodox Jewish family I was steeped, from the start, in a culture that is at least four thousand years old. Here I learned that I was a descendant of Abraham and in a direct blood line to Levi, the son of Leah, who was the first wife of Jacob. Moses was a Levite and his clan became the priesthood, the Cohens, while the rest of the Levites were to become the administrators of the Tabernacle and the Temple. Cohens never married outside their core families and they became the aristocracy of Israel, while the Levites were the first

FIGURE 3—TRADITION
This is a wooden candlestick, one of a pair brought from Russia by my paternal grandparents. They were part of his and his now pregnant bride's wedding endowment. Every pair of candlesticks in a Jewish household represents the outer pillars of the Tree of Life. The wife, whose privilege it is to light them, symbolises the Shekinah or middle column aspect of Divinity who is welcomed into the home on the eve of Shabbat. Bread and wine are partaken of at this ceremony in which a family gathers together. Wine and bread represent the Teaching and practice of the Tradition. Although the meaning has largely been forgotten, the ritual has been carried out for thousands of years in every country where Jews are to be found.
(Drawing by the author).

scholars of the Tradition. They, too, rarely married outside the clan. This has been substantiated by the DNA patterns of the Cohens and Levites.

With the total destruction of the Israelite Kingdom only the Judeans, that is, those of the tribe of Judah, and the Levites were left. This remnant of Jacob's people were later also exiled but they kept their identity. They returned to the Holy Land, only to be dispersed again when the Second Temple and Jerusalem were destroyed by the Romans. They were sent to various corners of the Roman Empire. There they joined Jewish communities who had formed colonies along the ancient trade routes. Thus Jews were to be found all around the Mediterranean, in the Middle East and Europe as well as in Arabia, India and China. However, despite their separation from the homeland they remained a nation because of the Torah or Teaching that could not be destroyed. This bound them together through the centuries.

On my mother's side, her Levite family were probably sited originally in Germany, along the Rhine where Jews had been settled since Roman times. By the medieval period they would have spoken German as well as being versed in Hebrew, as every Jewish boy had to be able to read at thirteen from the scrolls of the Torah. This signified that he was now considered to be an adult. Such a skill, as well as being numerate in a society where the peasants and aristocracy were illiterate, made the Jews a middle class equal in level of education to many of the Christian clergy. This situation was destroyed by the Crusades in which zealous mobs, on their way to free the Holy Land from the Moslems, regarded the Jews as infidels. Hundreds of old and well-established Jewish communities were wiped out. Most of the survivors retreated to Eastern Europe where they were welcomed as very useful assets who could develop trade and run the country estates of the aristocracy, whose members spent much of their time at the Royal Court.

On my father's side, his Levite family may have been in Spain since King Solomon's time, as Jews and Phoenicians had settlements there, or arrived later as deportees after the destruction of the Jewish state by Rome. Alternatively, they may have arrived in the Iberian Peninsula with the Arabs with whom they initially had good relations. Many peoples from the Middle East settled in Spain, where the climate resembles the Levant. Here Jews flourished during the Middle Ages, until zealots of both Islam and Christendom began to persecute them as well as war with each other. This situation came to a climax in the

FIGURE 4—SOROKA
This was a small market town port on the river Dniester in Bessarabia about 170 miles north of the Black Sea. Originally a Roman settlement, it has been overrun by many conquerors because it is a river crossing point and strategic place for merchants as well as the military. Italian merchants set up a trading post during the time of Turkish rule while Spanish Jews, from Constantinople, came to settle and become the middlemen between the traders and the local population. With the establishment of a Jewish community came a synagogue. My great-grandfather was a **Melummed,** *or Hebrew teacher, whose family name was Haham, indicating a rabbinic line in the Sefardic tradition. After the Russians took over the area in 1812 the Ashkenazim, the Yiddish-speaking Jews, came in and became the largest group of Jews in the area. They called the Spanish Jews, who always married among themselves, the Sefardishers. Both Jewish communities of Soroka were wiped out in the Second World War. (A View of Soroka).*

15th century when the last Moorish Kingdom of Granada fell and the Jews were given the ultimatum of conversion to Catholicism or exile. Around one hundred thousand Jews chose to stay and become nominal Christians, who would later be hunted down by the Inquisition for remaining secret Jews. A hundred thousand or more Jews chose exile. Among these were my father's ancestors.

Spain was the place where Kabbalah was developed, prior to the Expulsion of 1492. This was because it was a meeting place of two streams of Jewish mysticism. The first came via Italy and Germany to France. This mode, originally from Palestine, was symbolic in form, based closely on the Bible and the rabbinical view of Existence. The other line came from Mesopotamia. This was rooted in the Hellenic philosophical approach which the Moslems had adopted to give a metaphysical depth to the Koran. Some Babylonian rabbinic academies had followed suit because of the great argument, then going on, about which was the superior, faith or reason. Both religions had to defend themselves against the erudition of Eastern Christians who were familiar with ancient Greek thought. Out of this conflict came the beginning of the philosophical theology which spread, via the Jewish communities of Egypt and North Africa, into Spain. Here, Arabic translations of Plato, Aristotle and Plotinus were studied by the Jewish intelligentsia. When a family of Jewish translators fled north from Andalucia to southern France, because of Moslem persecution, the rabbinic community there, already familiar with the symbolic form of the Teaching, had the Arabic texts turned into Hebrew. The philosophical approach transformed their understanding of their mystical tradition and a wider and deeper formulation of the Teaching was born.

Jews from Spain crossed the Pyrenees to study the new blend of metaphysics and symbolism. One of their number, Azriel, returned to Gerona and helped found a school of the soul which set out to reconcile religion and reason. This was possible because the Gerona mystics had contact with the local university just a street or two away from the synagogue. From here the Kabbalah, as it came to be known, spread throughout the Spanish Jewry, much to the annoyance of Isaac the Blind, Azriel's instructor, who said that such esoteric matters should not be in the public domain. However, it was too late and Kabbalah became, in time, to be considered as important as the Bible and the rabbinic commentaries of the Talmud.

When the Jews were expelled from Spain, Kabbalah went with

them. Now it was to be found in North Africa, the Middle East and especially in the town of Safed in Palestine. It also found its way into Italy, Germany and Poland as well as the Turkish Empire centred on Istanbul. My ancestors probably came to this old Byzantine capital of Constantinople, via the Greek city port of Salonika. Both were very familiar to me when I visited them. The family then moved on into the Black Sea area and up the River Dniester into what was called Bessarabia. Here they settled in a place called Soroka where Genoese merchants had a base next to a castle which protected them. The Jews were, no doubt, very useful to the Italians as they formed a permanent trading class that could deal with the local population. The Jews in this area then spoke Ladino which was a medieval version of Spanish, even as Yiddish is a medieval form of German. Here my ancestors remained until the Ashkenazim or Yiddish-speaking Jews came into the area. This Spanish background of my paternal ancestors was to be a strong influence on my psyche and my connection with the Tradition.

3. Family

In the first edition of this book, I followed my mother's family mythology in believing that Zerach Barnet, one of the founders of the orthodox Jewish conclave *Meah Shearim* by the Old City of Jerusalem, was my great-grandfather. Subsequent research has revealed that he was not a direct ancestor. What connection there is has yet to be established. My mother's Ashkenazi grandfather Michael was a Levite. So was my paternal grandfather, Joshua, whose surname was Haham denoting a scholarly line in his Spanish Jewish culture. Indeed, his father taught at the local Sefardi synagogue in Saroka in Bessarabia.

I did not know my maternal grandparents; both died before I was born. However, I did hear how my grandfather Woolf, after whom I was to be named, came from the city of Brest-Litovsk. This was both a trading centre and a seat of rabbinic learning. Jews had settled there in the 14th century and flourished, despite periods of persecution on becoming part of the Russian empire when the city's synagogues and cemetery were destroyed to make way for a fortress.

Eastern Europe, through my family, was part of my collective unconscious but it was also linked to a very clear memory of a previous life. I had a recurring vivid recollection of being a rabbinic student lying with others on the roof of a synagogue, watching Cossack horsemen riding up and down our village street setting fire to the houses. As I watched their sabres flash in the flame light, I recall saying to one of my companions: 'If only we had guns'. Firearms have always fascinated me, without any obvious reason. I suspect this repeating memory is why my mother and father were horrified when, for my bar mitzvah present, I wanted an old Napoleonic musket I had seen in a local junk shop. It still stands guard by the door of my study.

My maternal grandfather came to England which was then considered to be the wealthiest and most civilised country in the world. He was a skilled craftsman and became a master tailor, employing several people. This meant that my mother and five other children were brought up in relatively comfortable conditions. Like

FIGURE 5—GREAT-GRANDFATHER
Israel ben David was my paternal grandmother's father. He is seen here with his second wife. As a Levite he traced his blood line through his father, and his father, and so on back to Levi, the third son of Leah, the first wife of the patriarch Jacob, son of Isaac and grandson of Abraham. According to the DNA in the genes of anyone bearing the name Levi or its derivates, such as Levine, Leven or Levinson, the connection is relatively pure. Ironically, this means they are technically not Jews as they are not of the tribe of Judah. The Levites were the administrators of the Temple and the intelligentsia of the Jewish community, producing lawyers, poets and physicians. Only the Cohens, as priests, had precedence over the Levites as the aristocrats of Jewry, who have kept an even more pure DNA line. (Great-grandfather's Family, 1904).

many migrants they brought with them the customs and culture of the 'Old Country'. These were seen in the day-to-day round of meals and annual festivals. However, there was the aim of becoming as English as possible, at least outwardly, while remaining inwardly Jewish. This is an historic pattern. In 17th century Poland, the Jews dressed in the style of Polish gentry with their fur hats and dark, long coats. The orthodox Ashkenazi Eastern European Jews still wear this mode wherever they are to be found to this day.

In 1812 the Russians took over the Ottoman province in which my Sefardi ancestors lived. Over time the Yiddish-speaking Ashkenazim migrant culture became predominant. Their more Germanic outlook was in sharp contrast to the Sefardim, who were more Mediterranean-oriented and sophisticated. Poetry and philosophy were part of Sefardi life, whereas the Ashkenazim were more ritualistic and legalistically inclined. An example of Spanish-Jewish culture is the great poem of Ibn Gabirol called *Keter-Malkhut*. It defines, in poetic terms, Jacob's Ladder, a key concept of Kabbalah. Having roots in both the Ashkenazi and Sefardi worlds was to be most useful later on as I had access to both communities in Israel and elsewhere. Providence had organised this with great skill.

When my paternal grandfather finished his military service in the Tsar's Army, his family suggested he should marry a girl called Golda. They would then go to America, as employment prospects were poor and there was an atmosphere of increasing anti-Semitism in Russia. This was soon to result in a terrible massacre in Kishinev. With a basic bundle of necessities and a pair of wooden candlesticks, the couple set off for the United States where other members of the family had settled. This must have been a difficult journey through Romania, the Austro-Hungarian Empire, Germany and Holland. When the ship they were on docked, it turned out to be London, not New York. As they had no money, they had to settle in the East End in a street where people from their home town lived. This was a common pattern, with each town and province having its own London synagogue. In the year 1900 my father, Shimon, was born in London, having been conceived before leaving Bessarabia.

Having no particular skills and being a very devout Jew, my grandfather spent more time in the local synagogue than looking for a job. Wishing to keep his independence, he became a freelance ragman who collected remnants of cloths from the many tailors' workshops in the area. This meant he and his growing family could survive while

FIGURE 6—FAMILY

This photograph was taken just before the Second World War. On the extreme left back row is my uncle Jacob, then my grandfather Joshua and my grandmother Golda. Next to her is my uncle Moses, then the bride, my aunt Sarah, with her husband Hyim. Standing behind him is my uncle, also called Hyim, and then my father Shimon. Below him sits my mother Esther and then myself as a pageboy with my brother Michael sitting to my right. My cousin Baruch is the other page. All were of a Levite blood line. This group of people formed a solid core to my life in a physical, psychological and spiritual way. While later I rejected Orthodox Judaism, I did not repudiate what lay behind the Tradition. It was the spirit of Kabbalah that nurtured me, although I did not realise this at the time. (Haham-Kaufman-Kenton family portrait).

he retained his esteem as a self-employed man. This attitude affected my father and, subsequently, me. Such things, taken on largely unconsciously, can have a decisive influence upon a life.

So it was that my paternal grandparents' home, although materially poor, had a profound cultural wealth in its Sefardi and Ashkenazi traditions. These manifested in values and customs seen in such ceremonies as Bar Mitzvahs, weddings and funerals. I was steeped in this background by going weekly to the synagogue with my father and grandfather and to Sunday school where I learnt the rudiments of Hebrew. I also heard, as a child, about my grandfather's homeland which had been inhabited by Romanians, Turks, Gypsies and Jews as well as Russians, Moslems and the descendants of Huns and Tartars. This gave me a sense of distant places which I wanted to visit in the future and a wide sense of geography and history.

One story I heard that caught my imagination was about a great uncle. He once crossed the frozen river Dniester to visit relatives in the distant town of Yompala, further up the river. On his return on that spring day, when he was half way across, the ice suddenly began to crack, split up and move downstream. He was then seen by people jumping from one ice floe to another, with a strange agility, until he reached the home shore. Here he was told how people marvelled at his confident footwork. He replied that his grandfather was in front of him telling him to follow wherever he jumped. People were astounded at this account, as the grandfather had died just the day before.

This story fascinated me as I sensed, even then, that there was more to life than just making a living and keeping the Tradition. I heard the word 'Kabbalah' mentioned from time to time but always with a sense of awe. I was told that to study Kabbalah one had to be over forty, married and a scholar. This put me off for many years because something deep in my soul did not wish to become a Hebrew scholar yet again and be caught up in endless debates about the points of law. Many lifetimes, I realised later, had been devoted to this mode of rabbinic study. Now I was only interested in what life and the Universe was about. I had come from a rabbinic family, indicated by our surname 'Haham'. However, this Sefardi appellation had been converted by the British immigration officers, when my grandfather landed in London, into Kaufman, meaning 'trader', which my grandfather was not. My father changed Kaufman to Kenton, during the Second World War, as the former was too German. Anyone with such a Germanic-sounding name came under suspicion as a spy in the semi-village in which we lived.

One result of my decision to seek out the meaning of Existence was that I did not want to learn advanced Hebrew and get involved in 'learned' argument and opinion again. Moreover, having heard my father saying his prayers in the synagogue over the years and not understanding a word he said, I concluded that it did not make any sense. As a Levite he was always called up second, after a Cohen, in the synagogue to say a prayer before reading the scrolls of the Torah. This is a traditional honour but I yearned for it to be more than just a beautiful ritual. This yearning was carried on through my childhood into adulthood. It made me search elsewhere for the inner meaning of the Torah. I knew it was to be found somewhere. Such Knowledge would explain why the Universe existed, what humanity's purpose was and why I was on Earth.

I was born in 1933, the year Hitler came to power. The first impact on me of this event was the Munich crisis of 1938 when, it was believed, Europe was about to go to war. As a five-year-old child I picked up the tension, especially when my parents took my brother and me out of London and went to distant Wales because of the possibility of the city being bombed. Another encounter with the rise of dictatorship came when my parents, on a visit to France, took us to the frontier of Italy. Here I saw fascist officials strutting about in military uniforms in a most arrogant manner. Even as a child I could recognise that this was an evil omen. This cognition was supported by hearing my parents discussing appalling stories of the Nazi treatment of Jews in Germany. Much later, I realised that the selection of my time to be born was not random. It appeared to fit in with the long-term plan of my fate. I was to witness peace and war and many other crucial dramatic events, before I was ready to come to Kabbalah and my task.

4. Childhood

When the Second World War broke out in the autumn of 1939 my brother and I, like thousands of other children, were evacuated from London. This was the first time I had been away from the secure bosom of my immediate and extended family. Suddenly we were placed in a strange and seemingly hostile environment. While the wife was very kind, the man of the house we were staying at clearly did not want us. I recall him shouting and throwing some fried bread at me. It was my first encounter with anti-Semitism. While the inner Self looked on, just observing, the everyday ego was deeply shocked by such conduct. It left its mark, not only because it was so hurtful but because it resonated with the centuries of persecution Jews had experienced.

Fortunately, within days my parents found a small house in a village on the hills just above High Wycombe, a town on an ancient road midway between London and Oxford. All history was to be found in this valley through the Chiltern Hills. Here were the remains of a prehistoric settlement, a Roman villa, a Danish fortress and a medieval hostelry. There had been a bloody battle during the English Civil War on the town's common and many famous people, such as Disraeli, the 19th century Prime Minister, had mansions nearby. During the Middle Ages, two Jewish families lived in Wycombe. They were traders who probably ran a bed and kosher breakfast place for Jews travelling between London and Oxford, a day's journey in each direction. The town was strangely familiar to me, although I did not know why.

Besides the area's rich history, which appealed to my Capricornian nature, there were the fields and woods around our village. For a London boy this was Paradise. Initially the war seemed remote in this tranquil environment but, with the Blitz on London, the illusion of peace vanished as we watched the distant blaze on the eastern horizon. One night a fire-bomb missed our house by a few hundred yards while a nearby orchard was blasted by a German aircraft well off target. After this came the flying bomb that blew in our front door and an American 500-pounder that had fallen out of a damaged aircraft on its way home from a mission. Fortunately this did not explode. I and my

FIGURE 7—HIGH WYCOMBE
This is the main street of a town in the Chiltern Hills just thirty miles from London. It had prehistoric camps, a Roman villa and a medieval hostelry, besides many other historic buildings. It was a market town famous for making the classic Windsor chair. Its population was a mixture of Celts, Saxons and Danes who, in time, had become known as the British. Up to 1290 the town had Jews who traded and provided accommodation for other Jews on their way from London to Oxford and beyond. They returned after this expulsion, in the 19th century, when Prime Minister Disraeli and the banker Rothschild came to live in the area. During the Second World War many Jews came to Wycombe to escape the bombing of London. Unknown to them and the Wycombers, the town was also the headquarters of the US 8th Air Force. Had the Germans known this they would certainly have bombed the town. (Drawing by the author).

schoolfellows had a game of who would dare touch it, to the despair of the policeman who watched over this lethal weapon until the bomb disposal team came.

Was it luck or Providence that protected us? In conversation, after the war, with ex-servicemen about their experiences, I got the impression from them that a bullet, shell or bomb had to have your name on it. For some reason, many believed they would not be killed. After the war I questioned one ex-soldier very closely, to try and understand this mystery. He told me how he had been on guard overlooking the Rhine, just before the final advance into Germany, when he asked a comrade to take his place so that he could make a cup of tea. When he came back five minutes later, he found his comrade had been killed by a German sniper. Then there was a Jew who had been fighting the Japanese in the Burmese Jungle. All his squad were wiped out in an ambush but he had been saved by his Tommy gun which deflected a potentially fatal bullet. This experience transformed him into a devout Jew. To encounter such people, who were far more mature than their years, was most illuminating. I was very struck by how all were highly individuated, that is, they seemed to have a sense of destiny about them even though they were, on the surface, ordinary people. However, because of their demeanour they had a great influence upon all who met them and worked with them. One, for example, was a kindly hospital porter who was one of my early teachers, although he did not know it.

In childhood one does not expect, in such an idyllic situation as a country school, to encounter evil. It manifested in a boy who threw stones at me, because I was Jewish, and when one of the women teachers made a very unpleasant anti-Semitic remark about being too clever. This stunned me because I had been brought up to respect educated people. I heard, years after, that the boy finished up in prison. As for the teacher, her karma is unknown, unlike the vicious school bully whom I saw three decades later on a visit to Wycombe. He was a broken man pushing a milk cart. Needless to say I did not cross the road to say 'hello'. These examples of cause and effect registered in my mind, although I did not comprehend their significance until much later.

One event at junior school that left a very strong impression on me, was the story of the 'White Ship' as told by our history teacher. In 1120 a ship carrying the English King's son and daughter was wrecked on its way home off the Normandy coast, just after a successful campaign in France. All were lost, except a butcher. No one dared to tell the king, waiting at Southampton, until the nobles taught a young boy to sing a dirge before the king about the loss of royal children at sea. After realising what he was being told the king collapsed and was never known to smile again.

The story affected me very deeply because, somewhere in my soul's memory, I had heard of this tragedy in another life. This incident linked with a recalling of myself disembarking from a French ship, at the London dock called Billings Gate, in the 12th century. I clearly remember the sights and sounds of the river Thames, the smell of fish, the climb up the small hill to Cheapside in the City and asking the way to the Jewish quarter. This street still exists as the 'Old Jewry'. I had a similar experience when I was taken to Oxford as a boy. The layout of the High Street was very familiar, even though I did not recognise any of the buildings except a Saxon church. Much later in life I discovered that there was a large Jewish community in Oxford in the Middle Ages that served the University in providing lodging for the students and, no doubt, unofficial instruction in Hebrew for the scholars there.

At one point, later in this life, I gave some lectures on Kabbalah to a private group of students at Magdalene College, Oxford. This is sited on the old medieval Jewish cemetery. While, at this event, I had the feeling I had done this centuries before, it was only when I came to understand the notion of reincarnation that everything fell into place. It also explained a deep love of England and its history.

One thing I could not comprehend at the time, and neither could my parents and teachers, was that although I was a fairly bright boy I could not read or write until I was ten years old. The strange thing was that I loved books and would scan the pages hoping to learn something

---

FIGURE 8 (Right)—WHITE SHIP
At school I heard the story of the tragic loss of a Norman King's son and daughter, on their way home from a successful campaign in France. This left an indelible impression upon my mind. It was not because it was such a sad story, but that I had heard it somewhere before, long ago when I had lived in medieval England. This irrational explanation was strengthened later when I became aware of reincarnation. The feeling of being familiar with the country in the Middle Ages was confirmed when I traced the ancient road from the Jewish quarter off Cheapside in London through High Wycombe to Oxford. The names of villages, now suburbs, and the terrain aroused old memories, especially the rivers and remaining tracts of the ancient woods along the route. The story of the White Ship haunted me to such a degree that I wrote two versions of it with pictures, in colour and black and white. This figure is one of the several illustrations in this book. (Gouache by the author).

but my brain, or something deep within, was not interested in making sense of the letters. However, I loved the pictures, diagrams and maps in books and would ask my literate brother many questions. He was a pupil at the local Royal Grammar School and very articulate. The fact that I knew much about history and geography baffled my teachers, so did my loathing of mathematics. The rational explanation was the shock of being evacuated from London and being moved from school to school until I was found a permanent place. These factors, it was believed, had slowed down my development. This was in complete contradiction to my schoolmates' view, who nicknamed me the 'Walking Encyclopaedia' as regards history. How did I come to know so much about the past, I sometimes wondered?

The reason for this fierce resistance to words and numbers only dawned on me years later when I realised, when encountering rabbinic and academic scholarship, that I had had more than enough of opinions based upon texts which were often third- or fourth-hand views of various subjects. I wanted to know for myself what was behind the learned jargon. As a result, it was the magicians in folktales that fascinated me. They appeared to know something that scholars did not. The astrologers, in particular, were my polestars. This interest led me to the study of astronomy. During the war there was a total blackout. In the countryside particularly it was possible to see the sky with great clarity. I made telescopes out of old lenses and cardboard tubes, so that I could see the cluster of stars in Orion's Belt, the mountains of the Moon and the planets. One evening, while scanning the sky, I had a profound experience of being drawn up into the 'Great Deep' of the Universe. There was more to space than its vastness. This again raised the question, 'What did astrologers know that astronomers did not?' This mystery fascinated me.

While I was at the bottom of my class in most subjects, I was the best in the village school at art. This unfortunately did not get me to pass the entrance exam to get into the grammar school. I failed the academic mark and so had to go to the local secondary school. This was known to be a pretty rough place, inhabited by the pubescent offspring of the local labouring class in our area. I dreaded going into this environment, where aggressiveness was of more value than intelligence among the boys. This I knew as I saw them fighting over the pecking order, even on the village green, where the current leader was a poacher who had a sub-machine-gun stolen from an army camp. He, too, finished up in jail.

On the last day at my junior school I wept as I said goodbyes to a relatively happy childhood. It was during this period that I learnt about Nature and the seasons while fishing, sledging in the snow, stealing ripe apples from autumnal orchards, walking through dew-glistening fields and making fairy mirrors out of wet cobwebs. Up to this point I had no worries beyond getting home in time for supper. Now all this was about to end. It was like the first time I encountered death, when I saw the dead body of my beloved grandfather under a sheet in our house. It was a great shock, as what I had taken for granted suddenly came to an abrupt halt.

FIGURE 9—NAZISM
Here the eagle of dictatorship hovers over the Acropolis, which symbolises democracy. The image was taken from a Nazi cap badge given to me by a German prisoner of war in 1944. I had realised, by then, that had the Germans succeeded in invading Britain in 1940 I and my family would have been murdered. This realisation had as profound an effect on my psyche as seeing London burning from afar from our garden and having German bombs exploding nearby. However, the reality of war hit me particularly when a young British soldier told me what it was like to kill a German. His graphic account of looking at the body of a person of his own age, whom he had just shot, was horrendous and left a deep impression on me as regards war. (Drawing by the author).

5. Youth

When I left my primary school at the age of eleven in 1944, the war was in its final stages. Shortly before the Normandy landing, which marked the turning point, Jewish families in the district of High Wycombe invited Jewish-American military personnel home to spend the Passover with them. We had an officer with a German name that seemed odd to me, until I was told that many German Jews had migrated to the United States a century before. While we were going through the ceremony I sensed he was thinking of his family and what dangers lay ahead. We never heard of him again and I suspect he was killed in the liberation of Europe. This made the war become increasingly personal, as this was someone I knew.

Death became a common theme at that time as we heard about fathers and brothers being killed in action. There was, for the first few days of the Allied assault on Normandy, an intense feeling of excitement and dread. Tens of thousands were dying around the beaches. Adding to this tense atmosphere were the German prisoners of war who were brought back to England. Most looked exhausted and depressed in their dishevelled uniforms, but some were clearly delighted to be away from the fighting. While adults treated them with a certain disdain, we children were intrigued to meet these Nazi monsters who turned out to be all too human. Later, however, as the Western and Russian armies closed in on Germany, pictures of the concentration camps began to appear. These were horrific, especially those of Jews who fell into a pit they had dug before being shot.

These, I knew, were my distant cousins. If my grandfather had not left Russia I might have been one of them. Years later I reflected that I must have chosen to be incarnated in Britain in order to avoid this catastrophe. My mother and father were exactly what I needed to be protected and nurtured for the future, while six million relatives were being murdered. Later, while at art school, I met a Polish-Jewish girl who had been pulled out alive from a pile of dead children. She was determined not to let her experience mar her life and went on to live in a positive way. She was my marker for courage and determination.

FIGURE 10—HIROSHIMA

My family was having a picnic when we heard about the atomic bomb. There were mixed feelings about it, as the Japanese had been portrayed as a savage people by war propaganda. However, the terrible slaughter inflicted by them on a Chinese city, in which hundreds of thousands of civilians died, had horrified the Western world and so Hiroshima was seen as a retribution for that crime. Over the years I came to see this as a terrible collective karma for a corrupt regime. Evidence could be seen in the numbers killed of each nationality. Russia had 20 million casualties while Britain and the United States had less than a million and Germany had five million dead. I later concluded that nations, like individuals, must inevitably reap the results of their actions. As regards the six million Jews who died in the Holocaust, this was a real problem that gave me much to think about. (Drawing by the author).

From then on, whatever personal disaster I might encounter, her example made me realise how fortunate I was to be born in Britain at that time.

My secondary school was an up-to-date facility. Unfortunately, the pupils were at that primitive stage between childhood and youth. This manifested, in the boys' section of the school, in fierce competition to be top dog. Violence was not uncommon as pubescent hormones released instincts which had, as yet, no obvious sexual targets to focus upon. I witnessed one fight in which a boy actually pulled out a knife to stab his opponent. As Fate would have it, the blade hit the belt buckle of his victim and saved both their lives. Those watching recognised the gravity of the situation and pulled the top boy off. I remember reflecting on this incident and sensing that both boys had been protected from their own stupidity. But by what?, I asked myself. The precision of avoiding a fatal incident was too accurate to be considered a lucky accident.

Another phenomenon of this period was in our class, where there were twin brothers who looked like Greek gods. At the age of about thirteen, they were the perfect example of a blend between Mercury and Venus. As none of us had yet discovered girls, who were considered irrelevant, the twins became the focus of much attention as transient pubescent homosexuality affected the whole class. Unfortunately in later life their striking good looks, which had them believe they were very special, did not get them the accolade of adults or fulfil the expectation of always being the centre of things. Later, one committed suicide and the other died shortly after. This was a lesson about nothing being taken for granted, especially beauty. As Shakespeare observed, 'Golden lads and lasses must, like chimney sweeps, come to dust'.

Another character in our class was a rough but intelligent boy who often played truant. I met him years later and asked him why he never took advantage of the meagre education we were being given, as most of our school fellows were destined for dead-end jobs. He replied that he was more interested in life and spent his days studying both animal and human nature. He was now the owner of a company and employed many people. His view of life was very different from another boy whom I heard say, upon leaving school at fifteen, that he was now free, could make money and do what he liked. Alas, the reality was that without any skills he was doomed to be work-fodder and expendable when he could not keep up with his fellows. There were, of course, safe jobs like being a postman. When I worked in the Post Office one Christmas holiday, while a student, I heard a young lad say, 'I've only thirty-nine years before I get my pension'. It was then I began to understand that a life without too much effort was the aim of most people.

In another holiday job I worked in a biscuit factory, believing that I could think profound thoughts while taking trays from one machine to another. I found, however, that after three days my mind went quite blank and for the five weeks I was there I lived, like a mouse in cage wheel, the same day over and over again. Only in the evenings and weekends was it possible to consider any possibility of reflection—except that by then one was totally exhausted. The same phenomenon occurred when I worked on a farm one summer. While the environment was very pleasant there was little time for thought. These two experiences were very important in that they defined the vegetable stratum of humanity for me. This was in stark contrast to my old school friend, who became his own master and employed others. He was a classic example of the human animal level. He may have been more but I, as yet, had no idea what a fully human being meant.

Another encounter with evil in my early education was the paedophile schoolmaster in charge of our secondary school class. I had heard there was something odd about the man, but had no idea what it was until he stroked the back of my legs while checking my school work. I was further alerted when I spoke to a school fellow while he was teaching. He became very angry and called me out to the front of the class. He declared he was going to send me to the headmaster for a caning. While I knew I had broken a rule, it did not merit such a severe punishment. I was silently outraged by this injustice. So, too, was the class, who resented his tyranny. To my surprise and relief the teacher realised he had crossed the line. He suddenly told me to return to my place. I think he saw in time that his action might have repercussions, as my parents lived only a road away from the headmaster, who knew that I was an obedient, middle class boy. He might have looked into the incident if my parents had complained. This was a threat to the teacher, who was already under suspicion. I had never had a violent hand laid on me. To be caned was bad enough but the sense of disgrace would have been even greater trauma. Upon reflection, I thought that Heaven must have intervened. While this was an irrational conclusion, I had felt a screen of protection about me as I had stood in this humiliating position before the class. This was my first intimation that I was being watched over.

One of the masters at this school, whom I did like and admire, was our aging art teacher. Many such people came out of retirement during the war, to help out in schools low on staff. He was thoughtful and encouraged those with some talent to develop, which the other teachers did not because most of the boys were not interested in anything beyond sport and, now, girls. I was, at this time, fascinated by the Middle Ages and drew and painted many images that were familiar, but from what and where I did not yet know. One day, the art teacher looked over my shoulder and said: 'Don't romanticise. The castles were dark and draughty and the people who lived in them were dirty and smelly'. I was very struck by this observation. It was true, as far as I could dimly remember from some old memory. He taught me the valuable lesson of realism and not to be taken in by surface appearance which was a vital viewpoint in later life.

Around this time I came across, in an encyclopaedia, a picture of Toledo in Spain. I knew nothing about this medieval capital city and yet, as I pored long over the picture, I knew I had some connection with the place and had to go there one day. Ten years later, as an art student, I was walking its narrow streets with the feeling that every sight and sound was strangely familiar. At that point I was not consciously aware that my ancestors had left Spain five hundred years before. Nor did I know anything about Toledo being a kabbalistic centre. I was not yet ready to recognise the Tradition. I had to learn much more about everyday life, so as to have a solid base in the current world.

The next step in my training was to win a scholarship to the local art college. This took me out of the rough and tumble of the secondary school and into an atmosphere of culture. In this environment we were taught in quite a different way. Here we were encouraged to explore a wider field, as well as learn about the principles of Art. Even more important was the quality and intelligence of the college's atmosphere, which stretched my mind. At home we had classical music and books but most conversations were about family matters and my father's job managing a London clothing factory. He, however, did teach me many vital lessons. For example, if I did not mow the lawn, I got no pocket money. No effort, no reward. As an honourable and reliable man he was a fine model. My mother, like many Jewish mothers, was good and loving but a little possessive. This was reassuring when I was a child but it became a strain when I began to explore the world beyond home and the Jewish community.

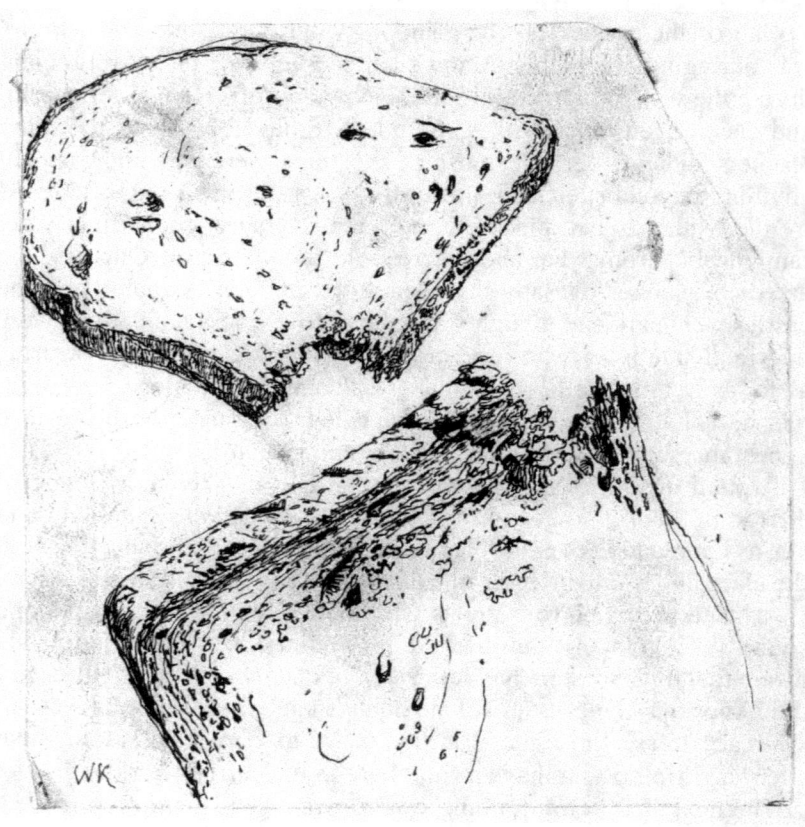

FIGURE 11—OBSERVATION
At art college we were taught to observe detail. This drawing of a piece of toast is an example of such an exercise. Such attention to minutiae taught me to observe closely not only the bigger picture but minor matters that make up the structure and dynamic of an object or situation. It is often a small element that gives a crucial clue. One must pick up on connections, in the same way as Sherlock Holmes, the master detective. An example was the fact that there were no letters between two famous poets and it was assumed they were not acquainted. The reason was that they lived a street away from each other and frequently visited. Only one astute scholar noted this vital detail. (Drawing by the author).

6. *Learning*

My class in Wycombe Junior Art College was made up of young people from a larger catchment area than the local secondary school. There were town and country students from every class and cultural heritage. At this point there were no Asians, Africans or Caribbeans but what were regarded as solid British stock, except for the one or two Jews who were always regarded as outsiders, no matter how English we tried to be. However, being ethnically conscious I was aware of subtle divisions and attitudes among my fellow students. This was fascinating, as it gave an early insight into the influence of the collective unconscious.

The Wycombe Valley was on the border between the early medieval Saxon and Danish Kingdoms. In our class we had people with Viking names, such as Skene and Guntrip, and they were indeed fair haired, blue eyed and pale of skin. The Saxons were broader in body and thick haired. In contrast there were the Celts from pre-Roman time and, more recently, the sons and daughters of Welsh migrants. These were both dark and fair but more volatile in temperament than the English. Then there were the various religious factions of High Church of England, Methodists, Baptists and Catholics, one of whom said to me in whisper: 'They persecute us as well'. I could not understand this, as he was a Christian, until he added: 'I'm a Catholic. The Protestants don't like us either'.

This awareness taught me to take into account the mindset of different people which had an enormous bearing upon their conduct. I recognised this early on as I recalled, as a child, feeling left out when my school fellows spoke about hanging up a stocking on Christmas Eve. I tried this magic ritual one Christmas but there was nothing to be found in my sock in the morning. At that point in time, it was not customary to give Jewish children presents at the festival of Hanukah, which took place around the winter solstice, like Christmas.

There had been mixed classes in our primary school but girls were of no importance to the boys, except when we had to choose the prettiest one to be May Queen. This was a puzzle for the boys

about what or who was beautiful, while to the girls it was a fierce competition. Whoever got voted Queen was to be the star for the year of the same status as the boys' Best Fighter. In the secondary school, the girls were in a separate building and therefore largely out of sight. Some of the older boys spoke about certain girls they met outside school as being 'of easy virtue'. I did not know what they meant, nor did I understand that one girl had 'one in the oven' and that a particular boy had to marry her. This was a great mystery, as sex was not taught in the lessons on biology at that time.

Most of my class at the Junior Art School were about thirteen. Some of the girls were pretty but beyond being decorative, as well as clever and talented, they were just class mates. However, there were the older girls of eighteen and over in the Senior Art department. One had an extraordinary effect on me. As we stood in lines in assembly, in the school yard one day before going to our classrooms, these senior students hung around their studio talking and even smoking, before beginning their study. One of them was an exquisite beauty, slim, elegant and obviously very intelligent. She stole my heart, in that her every movement was fascinating. She was then in the first bloom of youth and became my Anima figure and the measure for all other women in my life. She was not around for very long as she soon went off to study art in London. I never knew what became of her. This romantic image was to cause me much sorrow until I learnt that women were all too human and not goddesses.

One of the reasons for this problem is that I have three planets in Virgo in the House of partnership in my horoscope. This meant that I was attracted to delicate, beautiful, intelligent and maiden-like women. Unfortunately my descending node, or area of difficulty, is in conjunction with Mars, Jupiter and Neptune in Virgo. This also meant

FIGURE 12 (Left)—FIRST LOVE
When I was fifteen, I and my contemporaries had heard about only two kinds of love. One was sexual and the other romantic. The first was seen as immoral outside marriage by our middle-class generation. Most of us learnt about sex in the school playground and some could not believe that their parents indulged in such crude activities. In our naïvety, we turned to fantasy in our affections. This picture sums up my view of male and female relationships at the time. Besides sex being taboo, my first sweetheart was not Jewish, so she is placed in this picture in a high inaccessible tower in a medieval setting with myself as a lovesick troubadour. The ice and snow was an unconscious recognition that all passion was frozen in inhibition. This was perhaps just as well, because those who did break with custom often became teenage parents as at that time few knew about contraception. This then was seen as a great disgrace. (Painting by the author).

that the girls I was drawn to were often, in temperament, critical, powerful or dreamers. Another, less generous negative interpretation was that they could be scornful, wilful or neurotic people. A mixture of these qualities was sometimes the case, in my experience, leading to strong but difficult relationships. I concluded, over time, that these women were my karma for indiscretions in some previous incarnation. Indeed, some had very familiar figures and faces. Most remained life-long friends after our encounters because we had similar spiritual values.

As time went on, the immediate reality of practical work was manifest. We learnt to draw, use perspective, study colour, design and composition as well as develop a personal style. The boys were also taught the craft of cabinet-making, as High Wycombe was the furniture capital of Britain at that time. I made friends among the boys and learnt about Christian culture and social customs with which I was not familiar. At the beginning of our third year, after a long summer holiday when we returned for the autumn term, we boys were shocked to find that some girls turned from 'skinny lizzies', as they were called, into gorgeous females with hips and breasts. This awakened feelings that were unfamiliar in both sexes. A whole new situation emerged, which changed the dynamics of the classroom, as the mating game began.

Today, the notion of adolescent sexuality is common knowledge but then, in the late 1940s, such matters were not discussed. I learnt much about sex from my peers, often in a crude form. I knew how babies were conceived, because my brother did the job my very Victorian father could not bring himself to do. I was initially shaken by the notion of humans acting like animals but then, I did live near a farm and soon accepted how sex was part of Nature and my own new bodily processes then beginning to happen.

When it came to my first sweetheart, my cultural conditioning restrained my instincts and so I never laid a finger on her, much to her dismay. Indeed, I only kissed her many decades later to make up for the discrepancy. She eventually dropped me because, while I adored her, I made no physical advances. This was perhaps just as well because life would have become very difficult. My problem was that she was not Jewish. Our essentially innocent relationship was thus confined to occasional walks but mostly conversations, after school, before we went to our respective homes at opposite ends of the town. I could not bring myself to break a tribal rule and so I never mentioned to my family that I had a gentile girlfriend. However, when my mother met us in High Wycombe holding hands in the market place, she was very polite to my sweetheart but furious when I came home. She said I would bring disgrace on the family within the Jewish community, as such relationships had been forbidden for centuries. I took note of the warning but continued the relationship, in a more discreet way, because we had a deep connection which we maintain to this day.

The reason for my secrecy was also that I had never experienced such a delightful passion which was all-consuming, at least in my imagination. There was also the fear of pregnancy, if the relationship got out of hand. This was governed by a deep need to keep free, because I had the sense that I had some task to fulfil. This conviction was rooted in past lives, although I did not realise it consciously at the time. To refrain from conjugal intimacy, even though it went against instinct, was a conscious choice. Even so, I could not give up the relationship, even if it meant offending the Tribe. I needed a female companion who understood and loved what I would be doing. When my first love left me, to have a home and children with another, I realised it was going to be a long search for a rare kind of wife.

Of course at that age love is a youthful fantasy. I had to learn that such a passionate delusion either ended in marriage or a broken heart. As I was only sixteen and living in my parents' home I was far from considering settling down and so, while I was devastated at our parting, I knew there was no future for us. Years later, I realised that Nature is the driving force that makes young people come together in order to provide the next generation. Also, while the belief is that such loving relationships are absolutely unique, the fact is that the whole game is largely governed by one's hormones. Real relationships, soul to soul, are very rare. This I was to discover the hard way. As Providence would have it, I was enrolled by my parents in the London Art School of St. Martins. So it was that I was taken out from the local situation into a wider one in which my horizons, at every level, were radically changed.

FIGURE 13—WAR
Sometimes I would visit London and draw or paint what I saw. This is a bomb-damaged house in a smart part of the West End. It was distressing to see such fine buildings destroyed but this area was relatively less hit than the poor district of the East End where I was born. My grandparents had to be re-housed when the Blitz started but both soon died of shock upon being forced to flee their home in the centre of the Jewish community there. While their little house was not hit, several others in the same street were blasted to pieces, along with thirty thousand Londoners. It was a turning point for my family and yet a blessing for me as we moved to the beautiful Chiltern Hills. Here was the balance of a town in the valley with woods and fields above. This boyhood paradise would never have happened without the war. (Gouache by the author).

7. *Education*

St. Martins was one of the large art colleges in London and right in the centre, by the cosmopolitan district of Soho. Protestants fleeing from France in the 17th century and many refugees from the later Revolution had settled here and created a miniature Continental culture. However, in the last hundred years or so, it had became infamous as London's red-light district and the haunt of criminals, perverts and bohemians as well as artists, writers and radical thinkers. Soho had an easy-going atmosphere of sin, living alongside strict Protestantism. Here, in the cafés and restaurants, one heard talk of philosophy and politics while on Sundays the churches were filled with pious folk. By now many cultures existed in Soho including Chinese, Catholic and homosexual communities.

For a sixteen year old, who left his middle class home every day and travelled up to London on a steam train with business commuters, this was a new universe. Before, I had had to cross fields to get to school, avoiding cows, sometimes pausing to lie in the grass surrounded by wild strawberries, daisies and buttercups as I watched larks singing, ascending and dropping. Now I made my way through steam and grime into bustling streets filled with unfamiliar sights and sounds. Added to this, at St Martin's were hundreds of students from all over the world. Here there was every class of young people like myself, as well as many who were war veterans returning to finish their education.

In the school canteen, or nearby French café, we younger ones would listen to these men and women, older than their years because of their experience, talk about life and death. They spoke of what it was like to be really afraid, and the relief of survival after a dramatic episode in some distant land. In one case I heard an ex-commando tell of how he was crouching in a bomb hole, with bullets and shells passing both ways over his head, while thinking of some of his more fortunate comrades sitting in a quiet English pub on that Saturday afternoon. He asked himself what the devil was he doing where he was and how, by a miracle, he had survived? Many such stories moved me and posed the question why, amid millions who died, these individuals survived. Was it fate or just accident?

FIGURE 14—ART SCHOOL
Here we were taught how to draw. It was not enough to have talent. Without training a gift cannot develop. We were given plaster casts to practise on, as they did not move. From this discipline I learnt to draw the human body and catch the character of a face. This form of observation was to become vital, later on, when doing horoscopes or dealing with a person who came to consult me. The outer form of an individual reveals what lies below the surface. Thus, while someone might try to conceal what their inner state is, subtle clues of body language reveal what is really going on. The only difference between the artist and the psychoanalyst is what they do with their insight. All the great portrait painters were active psychologists. (Drawing by the author).

At that point I also began to observe how the motivation of each student was quite different. Many simply wanted to get an art degree, so that they could become art teachers. Others wished to go into advertising or book design. Not a few were after fame and fortune, as being a celebrity painter or sculptor was still in fashion. Photography had not yet superseded the figurative artist. There was still a market for landscapes, portraits and imaginative pictures that would sell at a high price. Abstract art was still, in the 1940s, too modern for most galleries which sold either old masters, sentimental Victorian paintings or, in the case of some, puzzling compositions that mystified buyers bought believing that they were modern masterpieces. I used to have lunch with one fellow student who later became a famous young painter. He confessed to me that he was out to make a name for himself and money. He produced huge canvases on which he dribbled and splashed paint with strange titles. These fooled both galleries and buyers but, most of all, himself. He was a well-known name for a brief time but was soon forgotten when some other 'genius' took his place and his métier went out of fashion.

However, there were many young hopefuls who loved to paint and were very talented. Some produced minor masterpieces. One in particular had the gift of depicting moonlit landscapes, but he had to go on painting such scenes if he wanted to sell. This stopped his development. Then there were students who produced semi-abstract pictures made up of unusual materials. Later this became the fashion. One friend went into a moral crisis about whether she should give up painting recognisable scenes, objects and people and produce purely abstract representations. It was a sign of the times when all the skills and knowledge of centuries of painting gave way to so called 'conceptual' images in which a tin can, a stuffed animal or an unmade bed became the symbol of fine art. Those with a visual talent went into films and, later, television to create pictorial masterpieces.

At this point in history, drawing from plaster casts of famous statues and living models was still part of our training. We were taught also to observe everything from different dimensions. One exercise was to draw the busy London street, ignoring the people and traffic but recording the street furniture, such as pillar boxes, lamp-posts and bus stops, as well as the style of roofs, doors and windows. The texture of walls, skylines and smog were drawn, as well as the moods of the day. Until then I had never consciously noticed such things which form the background to the flow of life. My father once asked me, after I had

FIGURE 15—SELF-PORTRAIT
Like many artists, I depicted my reflection. At the age of twenty, one's self-image hovers between vanity and reality. Here is youth full of hope, uncertainty and naïve arrogance. This is due to an innocence as regards the world, in which one was yet to be tested. Most of the students dreamed of their talent being recognised while our older fellows, who had been tried by their war-experience, were very practical, seeking to get a diploma so that they could become art teachers. I, who still lived at home, had no thought of how I would support myself in the future. This shock was yet to come. (Painting by the author).

left the college, what they did teach me. I replied, 'To see what others do not'. This skill was to be vital, not only in observing places but also the people whom I encountered. Face and body language give a great deal away that talk cannot hide and while visiting places much can be discerned by observations the guide books never mention. In a sense it was the Sherlock Holmes approach, as applied to art.

By this time I had learned to read fluently and read all the books I could on art, philosophy and religion. During discussions in the canteen, cafés or people's 'digs' much was learned from others who had quite different backgrounds. 'Digs' were usually a rented room in and around London. They were often in very shabby houses in poor districts, but the conversations were rich in content and a vital part of my education. Many fellow students had been well-educated before coming to art school. There were also the odd characters, such as the aging 'eternal student' type. One, of about forty, was a well-informed and witty man who was somewhat cynical about life. This was a significant encounter as I saw what can happen to disillusioned romantics. To have ideals is fine but they must relate to reality. He was bitter that he was not seen as a great writer, although he had had some literary success. His problem was that although he had a flair for language he had nothing profound to say.

In contrast, my time at home was one of pleasant family life. But this, I realised, put me into a form of sleep, as everything was according to custom and habit. I did not rebel against this as I knew that without a solid base I could become lost, like some students who lived far away from home. Not a few went quite wild and never recovered, some got themselves or others pregnant and had to get married and a job. Drink was a big temptation. I only got drunk once at a student party. When I left to catch the last train to Wycombe and walked up the hill to where I lived I saw the stars, trees and houses swaying to and fro and in and out of focus. As I lay in bed I vowed never to get drunk again. To lose self-control meant the loss of choice. This, I realised later, was a crucial decision in my life. I saw, over the years, many talented people lose their way because of an addiction, be it to drink, sex or the pursuit of a fantasy.

To keep my feet on the ground and a sense of proportion, I took cycle rides to parts of the Chiltern Hills countryside I had never explored as a child. This gave me a frame of reference because the area was full of historic sites. On one of these solitary excursions I learnt an important lesson. On this excursion I found myself in a steep wooded valley where, for fun and to see if there was an echo, I called out, 'I am here'. The voice that came back said the same words but not the way I expected. It had a country accent. I shouted again—but there it was. I sounded like a local yokel. It was a great shock to my ego. From that time on I listened intently to the accents of educated English people and copied them. The noticeable effect was that I was taken more seriously. This was an important fact which I discovered about intellectual life. One day, a little later, my father said to my mother, both of whom had Jewish-London accents, 'Who does he think he is—Lord Oxford?' To which my mother replied, 'Leave the boy alone. I like that he should speak nicely.' In her instinctive way, she understood a law of everyday life in Britain where one's accent, at that time, instantly defined one's status.

One of my cycle trips took me to Hughenden, the country seat of Benjamin Disraeli, the Jewish 19th century Prime Minister, who gave Queen Victoria the Suez Canal and the title Empress of India, besides making her smile. He had become a nominal Christian and married an English lady, and is buried in the churchyard near his great country mansion. When I got there, that summer's day, I saw a gravedigger just finishing a job for a funeral on the morrow. After talking about death, I had the impulse to ask him if I could lie down in the open grave to see what it was like to be there, forever. Assuming me to be mad, he shrugged his shoulders and walked away. I climbed down into the grave and lay there for some minutes, observing the sky and the earth walls of somebody's eternal home. At this thought I shuddered and got out as quickly as I could, thinking that there must be more to death than this prospect. Years later, when my psychic faculty had developed, once while walking round a cemetery I stopped by a recent burial where I saw, lying beneath the soil, a woman waiting and wondering what to do. Her view was that she would be there until the Resurrection. By this time I knew this referred to the time when all humanity would be Self-realised and return to the Absolute. Until that distant event many lives had to be lived. I said nothing to the dead lady as she would not understand the idea of reincarnation, because the Church had declared it heresy. I also doubt if she was aware of being observed by me, as I existed in a dimension other than hers.

8. Exploration

My frontier now expanded beyond High Wycombe as I explored London which was, in fact, my home town. I would spend a day going to different parts of this great cosmopolitan city, which was made up of many villages dating back to Celtic, Roman and Saxon times but now joined up by streets and rail lines. Some of these places still retained their original qualities in a medieval church, house or market place. There were also the abodes of migrants, like Soho, with their Italian, Chinese, Jewish and Irish populations. I sometimes returned to my paternal grandfather's home street, to get a sense of my roots, but it had been bombed and the little house had long disappeared. I had memories of Sabbath candlelight, a circle of family faces and my grandfather's short beard. These were all that were left of a vanished period before the war but they were very potent ones in my memory.

Besides my exploration of the poor districts of London, I wandered through the aristocratic and elegant squares of Mayfair and Kensington as well as Notting Hill and Chelsea where the artists, poets and writers lived. I also visited every museum I knew of and all the important historic sites, besides the many parks, the docks and the Thames shoreline. Here I picked up fossils, fragments of pottery and clay pipe stems. I visited old cemeteries and forgotten buildings like Canonbury tower where, I discovered later, a school of the soul had been in the 16th century. I sat in the Temple Church where the Knights Templar met, visited the Law Courts, the medieval Guildhall and Old Jewry, where my community had lived until they were expelled in 1290. This was a particularly moving experience as it was strangely familiar to me.

All this stimulated my love of history which had begun at primary school. There, our history teacher had graphically described the Romans landing in Britain and their confrontation with the near-naked Celts in blue war-paint. I was so convinced by his detailed account that I asked him, to his delight, if he had gone down to the shore, after the battle, to pick up a Roman sword and a British shield. He introduced me to the art of story-telling which I never forgot. Another historic

FIGURE 16—LANDSCAPE
In the exercise of depicting buildings in their settings, I had to learn about perspective, seeing the scene as a whole and then filling in the details. After this came lighting, colour and texture, followed by imbuing the image with the spirit of the place. In this case, the subject was Greenwich observatory at a particular time of the day. Here I had to catch the rigid qualities of the building and the organic flexibility of the tree. In larger landscapes the foreground, middle ground and distant horizon had to be considered, along with the weather conditions, light and living beings to be depicted. One had to learn how to catch the mood of the subject and then make one's own visual comment about it. This might be, for example, romantic, realistic or symbolic. (Painting by the author).

event that had a great impact on me was told to me by a fellow student at St Martin's School of Art. Her father had been a pupil of Holman Hunt, a well known 19th century painter. While Hunt was working on a portrait of a very old English gentleman, he told the painter how, one night at the theatre in London, the performance was suddenly stopped when the manager came on stage to tell the audience that the people of France had just beheaded their king. This incident went back to 1793. Suddenly I saw that history was about real people. It gave me a perception of Time I had never had before. The Second World War was an event I had witnessed as a boy but had not fully understood, until I talked to people who had participated directly in the fighting. I had seen the London Blitz from afar, had heard bombs falling nearby and collected bits of crashed aircraft; but the reality of war hit me when talking to a British soldier who had gone up to a German he had just shot and vomited at the sight of what he had done. This incident influenced my decision not to serve in the military but do my national service in hospitals.

A deeper understanding of the war came when I went, with a school party, to Paris in 1946. We went by sea and landed in Normandy where I saw from the train the hulks of wrecked tanks and the devastation of towns and countryside. In Paris I was lodged with a Jewish family which had managed to escape the French police and the Gestapo who were rounding up Jews for the death camps. This left a big impression. We in Britain had been blitzed but we remained free. Had we surrendered, I and my family would most certainly have disappeared into the gas chambers. It was from here on that I developed a particular interest in Jewish history. The issue of persecution came out once in conversation with Irish and English friends. The English person could not grasp what it was like to be a subject people. The Irish lady pointed out that England had not been conquered for a thousand years, whereas the Irish and Jews had, up to modern times, no country that was truly their own. It was during this conversation that I recognised that the power of the collective unconscious of a community can blind the view of an individual. The English woman simply could not grasp what we were saying.

Besides the exploration of outer history, there was the inner dimension found in the various religions and philosophies I examined. This line of development came initially from the books I read, beginning with the New Testament which Jews, due to their collective unconscious, tend to avoid. However, I thought it right to examine the

FIGURE 17—COMPANIONS
Many of the students at Art School were of the same age. But being just after the war, some ex-service people returned to complete their educations. These were very valuable colleagues as they had experience of life. Among my contemporaries were many young women who came to study art so as to develop their talent and get a teaching degree, while others saw the college as a kind of finishing school for cultured ladies. The girl here was a friend who eventually married a successful artist. Most students became book and magazine illustrators, fashion or industrial designers. Only a few fulfilled their dream to become a master painter. (Drawing by the author).

text and see what was so powerful about this Tradition that dominated the West. I was struck, first, by how rabbinical it was—and, indeed, Jesus did say he added nothing to the Torah or Teaching. The Gospels were undoubtedly moving and profound but discrepancies between them, despite their claim to be in synoptic agreement, made me wonder which were facts and what had been added after the death of Jesus. I knew by then how people embellish history. Jewish folklore was full of tales of wonder which are highly suspect. An example is the story of the Golem, a humanoid figure created by Rabbi Loew of Prague to protect the Jews. This magical event, in its original form, was performed by another rabbi but it was attributed to Rabbi Loew so as to enhance his reputation as a Kabbalist and magician.

Then there was the problem of Jesus being the Messiah who, it was claimed, saved all who believed in him. The original concept of the Anointed was of a spiritual, political and military leader, like King David, who would rescue the Jewish people and restore them to their homeland. The idea of a Saviour who, by his death, saved only those in the Church did not make sense. Nor did the killing of millions down the centuries in the name of Jesus. Also it seemed very unjust that wicked individuals could avoid Hell, at death, by declaring that they believed Jesus was the Christ. I had heard about the law of karma. All actions had results. How could evil deeds be so easily neutralised? To me faith was not enough. I needed to know the truth about life and death. Here began my search for higher Knowledge.

Buddhism was initially very attractive. It had a purity, integrity and a wisdom about the human condition. To meditate and behave well would clearly bring peace and happiness and, eventually, release from the repeating Wheel of Life and Death. However, I found that many Westerners who practised Buddhism often just wished to avoid the difficulties of the everyday world. Spirituality was very noble but people did have responsibilities with regard to their families and society. To regard life on Earth as unpalatable was to deny the Glory of God's Creation. In addition, according to some Buddhist acquaintances, the individual was dissolved at death. This made the law of karma redundant, which meant an evil person could commit a crime and not be punished while the good person would never be rewarded for their effort. Perhaps the thing that put me off most was the aristocratic English Buddhist who would give money to down-and-outs after a day of shooting in the country, on the basis that this cleared him of deliberately taking the life of dozens of birds. Perhaps I

was ill-informed about Buddhism; even so, it was clearly not my path as I loved the world and its richness.

The *Bhagavad Gita* impressed me deeply with its cosmic dimension that included personal responsibility and an Ultimate Deity. Also, the Vedic metaphysics were particularly fascinating, with their Divine principles, chakras and detailed psychology. The problem here was the complexities of a vast system and myriads of gods. The caste system of India was clearly a political version of the levels of development which maintained the priesthood's superior position and kept the lower orders in their place. Finally, there was the issue, again, that life on Earth was to be escaped from. Yes, there was suffering here but there were also great possibilities to be creative, inventive and wise to what life was really about through discovery and development. I saw Existence as an expression of a Divine plan. Most of humanity's pain came from its own stupidity and ignoring what the Ten Commandments and the Buddha had said about correct conduct, bringing harmony, happiness and prosperity to mankind.

Japanese Zen was a delight to read about. It had the precise focus and practical exercises to reach enlightenment. I loved its concise poems and sayings, but its approach was too stark for me. One could not live a Zen kind of life in London and there were no Zen teachers available immediately after the war. Besides, the image of Japan then was of a cruel regime. I had met too many ex-prisoners of war who hated the Japanese, who had treated them unbelievably badly. To my young mind, words and actions did not match. So, while I admired the ideals of Zen, it was not for me. Years later, in Japan, I learnt that Zen is not about being a samurai, a poet or a monk but becoming an insightful human being.

It did not occur to me to explore my own Jewish esoteric tradition, as I was as prejudiced as much against its orthodox approach as I was

---

FIGURE 18 (Left)—ILLUSTRATION
I went into the course on book design. Here we learnt different techniques to solve a graphic problem. This might be to illustrate a children's book, or design a black and white image within a printed text. Book jackets were a special study as was the craft of lettering. I had a passion for the Middle Ages as shown in this figure of an illuminated manuscript. Unfortunately I did my thesis in this medieval mode and failed my examination, along with the class's least talented student. However, I did learn from one tutor the art of the dramatic image. 'Always take the unconsidered angle', he said. This was excellent training for my eventual occupation in applying an unscholarly view of Kabbalah, by using intuition and imagination as well as evidence. (Gouache by the author).

about the other traditions. It was going to be some time before I realised that there was only one Teaching and that it was universal. However, I had to learn a great deal more about life, and study in depth, before I could discern the same Divine principles behind every Teaching. This meant that I had to penetrate beyond the surface of the Jewish Tradition which obscured the Truth with its rabbinic regulations and tribal customs. At the age of twenty I still had the naïvety and facile arrogance of youth. I had yet to learn a great deal more in order to comprehend the simple Laws of Existence.

9. *Experience*

When my course at St. Martins ended, I was required by law to do two and a half years of national service. Most people went into the military but I chose, as previously said, to serve in hospitals. My first posting was in a mental institution. I had worked in several menial jobs during my college holidays but nothing compared to what I now had to experience. The hospital was a large layout of buildings wired off from the surrounding countryside. Each block was designated for various degrees of mental illness and senile dementia, with a medical unit and administration office at the centre of the complex. It was not a prison but obviously an area clearly segregated from the outside world.

Suddenly I was lifted out of my secure home and open student society into a quite alien world of insanity. I was now washing corpses instead of dishes and paint brushes. While working on the medical ward I witnessed several deaths every week, as the very old or ill came in for treatment or to die. The first person whom I actually saw leave his body was a patient who had no will to live. I was given the task, as an unqualified nurse, just to keep an eye on him. I got permission to draw him in my sketchbook and, as I outlined his features, he was suddenly no longer there. His presence vanished as his face turned to stone. This transition was impossible to catch in a drawing and so, on the opposite page, I wrote down what I observed, felt and thought. This was when I first began to write.

What I experienced, I noted first, was Time. Suddenly history had moved on and the world became different without him being embodied. We are told by scientists that if one bounces a ball on the ground, the planet will react in equal measure but the reaction is so minute that it cannot be felt. However, what I experienced in that moment of death was a shift of levels as the soul left the body and disappeared into the invisible realm. This was a small but cosmic event. Whoever he was, his 'being' was now free from whatever physical ailment killed him. However, was his psyche still saddled with the madness that afflicted him? This and other questions about life and death now preoccupied

FIGURE 19—PATIENT
This is a painting of a schizophrenic in the mental hospital in which I worked during my national service. It was done when I was off duty and the patient was delighted to have his likeness portrayed. Most of the time he was quite normal and helped on the ward. But every so often he would go into a deep depression and would retreat into himself. Here I tried to catch the cross between his suspicion and his curiosity. As a Cockney he had a ready wit but one sensed something odd beneath his smile. However, he was always respectful to the staff who he knew were there to help him. I learnt much about psychopathology at this hospital, not realising at the time how useful this experience would be later. (Painting by the author).

me because I was in a place where one could not avoid such profound puzzles.

This was a very significant event for me to witness for, from that time on, I started to write down what I could not draw. As I recorded such events and made observations in words rather than pictures, I began to consider being a writer. This was a youthful fantasy but it precipitated a process that was eventually to change my life.

In this mental hospital there was certainly plenty of material to write about. While most patients were docile, because they were either sedated by drugs or preoccupied with their inner worlds, there were also many with whom one could converse. One was a high-ranking ex-policeman who would carry on a seemingly normal conversation about the weather while addressing a Judge in an imaginary court. Now, while we all daydream, most so called 'normal' people know the difference between outer and inner realities. This man did not, which is why he had been certified insane. Everyone spends some time thinking about the past and the future but they do manage to relate to the present. Later, I was to learn that this 'normal' sleepwalking syndrome is common for an undisciplined mind. By this is meant that until one is 'conscious of being conscious' the psyche is centred in the ego and operates almost entirely according to instinct and conditioning. This is the vegetable level of humanity.

Here in the asylum I saw people who were at the extreme of the pathological spectrum. For example, there was one patient who had regressed so far that he refused to wear clothes and walked on all four limbs. At the other end was the highly intelligent lawyer who had killed two nurses. He was always neatly dressed and polite in manner. I was warned never to allow him to get between myself and the door when I brought a meal to his cell. Then there was the very small Cockney who declared that he was King George the 118th, who had swum the English Channel backwards and knocked out the reigning world boxing champion. His problem was easy to understand as I had met many would-be celebrities in Soho who believed they were great but unrecognised geniuses. In contrast, some patients were simple souls who liked to sleep all the time. There was one I had to get out of bed every hour during the night to prevent him sleeping in soaking sheets. One night he jumped up and chased me down the ward. I believe we both broke the hundred metres world record on that occasion. This I could understand, but people like the homicidal lawyer were a puzzle, as outwardly he seemed quite normal. I spent many hours pondering

how this could be. This was my early 'hands-on' training in learning how the psyche did and did not work.

There was one patient who was not as insane as he pretended. He had been a luxury liner steward for forty years. This meant that all his basic needs had been met while on board his ship. When he retired he suddenly had to fend for himself and so he decided to act as if he was mad, to get himself into some institution. He would stand in the middle of a London street and shout abuse at everybody until the police came. In the police cell he made no trouble, as he got his regular meals, but started cursing everyone again when they put him out of the station. This happened so many times that the authorities decided to put him in a mental home. Here he made sure that he got a very comfortable room on his own, and a high degree of freedom, in exchange for helping the nursing staff out in their chores. He was very happy in this secure situation. Indeed, he was more sane than some of the staff who were so used to madness that they accepted the hospital culture as the norm and were reluctant to go out into the everyday world, which was not as controlled.

Many nurses were ex-servicemen and women, who quite liked institutional life with its security and social activities, but some of the staff were just one remove from the patients, being neurotic themselves. They were attracted to mental nursing because they felt a certain sympathy with the insane, which made them regard themselves as normal. One nurse, for example, periodically took on a schizoid symptom of freezing in motion, while another never left his room when off duty. Even I, who had a stable home life, began to accept psychotic behaviour as an everyday occurrence. Sudden violence, obstinate silence and verbal abuse were common events to which one had to become accustomed. Out of this came a detachment, similar to that of nurses and surgeons in the operating theatre where the

---

FIGURE 20 (Left)—MOTHER
She was the classic Jewish mother. She had never worked outside home, beyond one week in her father's tailoring business, as her mother said she would be better employed helping at home. The result was that she knew little about the outside world and was innocent, in her way, about life. When she gave birth to my elder brother, it was so painful that she became quite disoriented for a brief time. And yet, she said, in such a strange state she could see the universe so clearly that there was no mystery about it being God's handiwork. When she returned to normal she lost this clarity. Because of this episode, she knew intuitively what my kabbalistic work was about and supported me to the end of her life. (Painting by the author).

instinctive revulsion to blood has to be controlled. This gave rise in me to a degree of objectivity that would be vital in the future.

Later I had to deal with spiritually-oriented people who, to a greater or lesser degree, were insane. By this I mean that they were out of touch with life in general, although they could just about get along. An example was the man who neglected his wife and children because he spent so much time meditating. Then there was the case of the woman who had a profound spiritual vision and believed she was very special, even though she lived the life of an ordinary housewife. When I encountered such situations later in life I realised that I had been well prepared for these aberrations. Indeed, it has been said in a common proverb, 'there are more mad people outside the asylums than inside'. History bears witness to this, both individually and collectively.

I kept my balance by going home on leave. There everything was wonderfully mundane by comparison. Such events as family meals and homely duties like mowing the lawn grounded me. I would usually go out for walks and wander in my beloved fields and woods, where sanity would return to the full. Trees are symbols of friends and one ancient beech tree, which I had befriended as a child, was my refuge for contemplation as I sat in its branches. It is still there to this day, although suffering from old age. I visit it at least once a year, even now, to commiserate about ageing and how the village we knew so many years ago was no longer what it was. Most of the fields are now under brick and concrete, but the memory of that rural sanity is still my earthly anchor.

My other sphere of balance was my London circle of friends. This was made up of would-be artists, writers and intellectuals. We were now in our early twenties and starting out in a world yet to be conquered by our talents. Alas, life confronted us one by one. Most eventually went into teaching or commercial design. I met one old friend of this circle in the street, years later, dressed in a smart business suit. He said, with a mixture of sadness and guilt, 'One cannot make money from pure art'. Then there was one of the beauties of our crowd. She had married a rough diamond of a man. I asked why. She replied, to my surprise, 'I find his crudeness very exciting'. This was very puzzling, as she could have had the best for a husband.

As regards my inner life, study and experience were beginning to come together. I am a slow learner, as all Capricorns are, but with Moon in the Mercurial sign of Gemini I pick up some things very quickly and fit them into a big picture. This manifested in that I decided to be more of a writer than a painter. This was triggered by one of my companions while sitting in a London pub discussing art and literature. She said thoughtfully, after I had described an incident at the hospital, that I should write a book about my experiences. I was very struck by this comment. It was one of those moments when I sensed I was being given a clear message by Providence. From then on I began to be aware of omens, that is, signs that indicate when to refrain from or to go on in a certain direction.

10. Observation

After five months I moved on from the remote mental institution in the country to work in one of London's great teaching hospitals. St. Thomas was founded in the Middle Ages and rebuilt in the 19th century on a site just across the Thames opposite the Houses of Parliament. It was a vast Victorian building with many floors, departments and clinics as well as a number of operating theatres, maintenance workshops and record offices. It also had specialist and general wards, a nurses' home and different dining places for staff and patients. It was a miniature city in its complexity, with every level of its medical and lay society, from cleaners and clerks to consultant medics and administrators.

I was a porter, along with several other young men who had chosen this mode of national service. They included three art students, an actor and one who was going to become a doctor. We were regarded as odd by the other porters but were accepted into their smoke-filled mess room, provided we rarely spoke and knew our place in their social order. My particular leading porter had been in the trenches of the First World War. He would not speak about his experience but, when asked, said enough to convey the horror and madness of that war. I learnt from him much about discipline and service. I was respected by the nurses and doctors, who treated me as an educated person who could be relied on to do certain jobs that required thought or initiative.

This privilege enabled me to have access to almost the whole hospital, except the maternity ward. I saw what went on behind the scenes when the senior staff took off their professional personas. For example, in the operating theatre loose clothing, heat and sweat appeared to stimulate a distinct type of hospital humour and a light-hearted flirting between surgeons and nurses. I also learnt that some doctors only had a limited belief in their treatments. This was summed up by a senior surgeon who said to me, in private, that he had cancer but would not let anyone cut him up. He was going to retire to a country cottage with his favourite books and recordings to die without any fuss.

I witnessed medical mistakes that were covered up and heard nonclinical comments about psychiatric patients under sedation before they were given the electric-shock treatment then in fashion. In one case, a neurotic musician was cured of his anxieties by this treatment but he lost the creative edge of his talent. This and other revelations rid me of the delusion that the medical profession had a solution for every ailment. One doctor admitted to me, 'We can only do our best but, in the end, death must win'. With myself yet to reach my physical prime, this comment was a profound shock. 'Youth' cannot grasp what 'Mortality' means, and I was in the rising tide of life. At that point I was too interested in the St. Thomas' nurses. These girls were mostly from the middle and professional class. This custom went back to Florence Nightingale, who raised the occupation up from untrained working women to the level of highly skilled and respected female professionals who worked alongside the largely male doctors. It was a hospital joke that the girls became St. Thomas' nurses in order to marry socially acceptable husbands, which many indeed did. However, this myth was not always the case. As porters out of the ordinary, I and my artistic colleagues were considered exotic. We were invited to the nurses' home for tea, which annoyed some of our medical student friends. I had to explain to one, who was never allowed to visit his fiancée, that we were a rare and romantic contrast to the sober medics who were commonplace in the hospital. One lovesick nurse had to avoid explaining to the Matron that her work was not up to standard because she was infatuated by a porter. This would have been unacceptable because St. Thomas' girls were expected to behave like ladies. However, several nurses, away from home for the first time, wanted to go wild before they married. Indeed some did, while off duty. I did succeed in kissing one nurse on duty, which fulfilled a fantasy. In her tight uniform, with a slim, belted waist and black stockings, she looked like a beautiful blend of a courtesan and a nun. Irresistible!

Another incident of crossing the established line was when I was invited by one of the young doctors to have coffee in the medics' dining room. As one of the stewards served us, he whispered to me, 'What the hell are you doing here?' This incident took some explaining down in the porters' room. In another case, I asked a surgeon if I could draw him while he was performing an operation. To my delight he consented. I discovered later the reason was to annoy the sister in charge of the operating theatre, who was a snob. Another example of class distinction was a senior nurse who was extremely rude to a

FIGURE 21—OPERATION
This illustration was made in an operating theatre of St. Thomas's hospital in London. While working there I saw every mode of disease and injury, both physical and mental. I learnt much about a different kind of precision, from the application of drugs and surgery to the concise wording of a medical report. I also learnt, in my job as a porter, how to stand in one place until I was given orders. It taught me patience while I observed all that was going on in a life and death situation. In addition I had access to every department, from the medical museum to the laboratories, and a myriad of medical activities around the hospital. The only place I could not enter was the maternity ward. I had to wait many years before I witnessed a birth. (Drawing by the author).

cleaner in a department in which I was serving. I said to the cleaner, 'I thought St. Thomas' nurses were supposed to be ladies'. To my horror, the nurse working behind a screen overheard what I said. And then, to my surprise and delight, she began to behave very respectfully towards her staff. Miss Nightingale's standard of conduct had to be upheld.

The lay hospital workers were, in a way, more remarkable than the medical staff who came from a certain social stratum. For example, there was a man, trained as a chartered accountant, who had decided that sharpening hypodermic needles was more useful than counting money. Then there was the ex-commando who had accidentally shot some children in a hut where he thought Japanese soldiers were hiding. He desperately sought to expiate his guilt by working in the children's clinic. Indeed there were many ordinary and unqualified people who were totally devoted to the hospital and had spent a whole lifetime there in true service.

Seen on a larger scale, there had been a continuous stream of staff passing through the hospital ever since it was built. For me this was impressive and frightening, as some of the long-term employees knew no other life. The outside world was remote and seemed to be a place from where only the sick came to be healed or die. Like all institutions, the structure and regular pattern of its life can imprison. In contrast there were the patients at every stage of life who came and went. The hospital was a microcosm which could be seen in the main corridor. Here half the people were either ill or dying while the rest went about their business. It was my first insight into the concept of the 'passing show of life'.

The hospital generated a peculiar syndrome, in that one believed one had the symptoms of every disease possible. Young nurses, medical students and educated porters all suffered from every malady they encountered. For example, my own chest x-ray used terrifying medical terms I did not understand. It was only after asking a student doctor what these words meant that I learnt none of them were sinister. The report had said that I had a peculiar collar bone. This stirred up a positive fantasy, as I had read that such a phenomenon indicated a certain spirituality. Fortunately I soon realised this was but a symbol.

It was while I was reading the x-ray reports I was delivering to various departments that I learnt about the art of writing. Not one word was ever wasted. They were concise and dense documents that set out the medical situation. Although there was no emotion in these texts, they had a certain poetry about them. From then on I began to formulate

FIGURE 22—ROMANCE
The nurses at St. Thomas' hospital were largely middle-class English girls away from home, or boarding school, for the first time and in the full flush of their hormones. While their uniforms were prim and proper, their youthful figures filled them out in a most provocative way. Not a few were looking for a medical student or young doctor as a prospective husband and ideal father of a future family. However, as an art student—and there were several of us—I was considered, by some nurses, exotic. We were romantic Bohemians with whom a nurse could have fun before any serious relationship came along. One of my early novels was about such a passionate love affair. It was, of course, largely fantasy and was rejected by many publishers, I am glad to say in hindsight. This figure depicts the heroine walking down a London street in a sombre mood as the relationship was not going to end in marriage. This visual idea of that which was not seen is left to the imagination. (Drawing by the author).

a style I would use later in writing about Kabbalah. Meanwhile I made notes of important events, such as patients who were facing a major crisis in their lives. For example, I had learnt to recognise who was going to die when I collected patients from the ward for treatment. The dying had a particular quality in their demeanour and field-force. I noted that this seemed to depend upon how they lived life and viewed death. It was a great privilege to be given such opportunities by Providence, as there was nowhere else I could observe these fatal events in such peaceful circumstance.

In contrast to the enclosed world of St. Thomas's, I lived with an art school friend in one large room in leafy square near Holland Park. This wooded area was once a country estate with a 17th century manor house at its heart. It had been the centre of politics and culture in the 18th century and a place of fashionable soirées in the house's great rooms and gardens. During the war it had been hit by bombs and was now a ruin surrounded by overgrown paths, bushes and trees. It was not then well-known as a public space, which made it a place of peace for me in central London. Years later, when I again came to live in the area of Holland Park, I would walk in the woods while thinking about the next chapter of a book I was working on. It became my sacred ground where I wanted my ashes scattered.

During this period I began to separate myself from my family psychologically, even though I went home at most weekends. This was because the life I lived was very different from the culture into which I had been born. I never spoke of my private life, as it was quite alien to my parents and they would have been very upset because I was not courting a nice Jewish girl instead of liaising with naughty nurses. By this time I was open to any relationship that increased my understanding of women, who were still a mystery to me. I had not yet separated out the difference between the romantic image of youth and beauty from the reality of a girl's individuality. Falling for young goddesses, I realised later, was part of getting to know the power of Nature and the mating game. And at the age of twenty-three such transient relationships were immensely enjoyable, despite the pain of inevitable parting.

11. Intimations

When I completed my national service, I contemplated the years I had spent at St. Thomas's and what I had learnt. I had seen the whole cycle of physical life and death, except birth. Perhaps the most important thing was that I had acquired a certain objectivity. Before, when faced with physical illness or madness, I had been quite squeamish. But now I knew how to control my instinctive feelings when dealing with such disorders, at least in the case of others. As I enjoyed good health and was relatively sane, by normal standards, I had not yet been tested to the extreme. This was yet to come.

Upon returning to ordinary life, I gained a free place at the Royal Academy of Painting as I was still very interested in art. There was still much more to learn about observation, symbolism and imagery. My parents were kind enough to allow me to finish my studies, but I had to live at home. This meant that I lost a degree of freedom but I did not have to worry about paying rent and feeding myself. I think the reason they supported me was that they were very proud of getting me into the Academy school. This meant they had something good to tell about me to the family. At the Academy we had some remarkable teachers who were also successful artists. One had us work for a long period drawing every detail of the human figure, while another would change the model's pose every few minutes, in order to teach us how to catch the fleeting moment. These were important psychological techniques in how to assess long- and short-term situations that were to be applied later in life.

FIGURE 23 (Left)—ACADEMY
This is a view of the Life Drawing studio of the Royal Academy School of Painting. New students were required to do three months just drawing the human body. Such an experience was designed not only to study the external anatomy but develop precision. To contemplate the human image of the Divine was very important as it is a microcosm of the universe. It was also an exercise in patience. Later I was allowed to do creative painting in the main studios. Here were people producing figurative works, while others were experimenting with abstract ideas. It was a time of transition when artistic skill was giving way to conceptual images that were to sweep away conventional painting and sculpture in a new fashion that had little to do with art. (Drawing by the author).

In parallel, I developed my skill in writing. Having not received a literary education, I had no model as regards format. However, this meant I was not confined to this or that mode as set out by classical writers. I wrote in simple English about what I saw, thought and felt. Unfortunately I had no idea about plots so, while my texts were clear and precise observations, they did not fuse together and there was no tension or drama in the first novels I wrote. It was, therefore, not surprising that they were rejected by the publishers. However, one day I happened to come across what was claimed to be the shortest of poems. It was, 'Hired, tired, fired'. Here was the essence of every good story. It set out a situation, a problem and a resolution. Hamlet, for example, is about a man who could not make up his mind. When he finally did, chaos ensued. This is the essence of tragedy. The opposite is when all turns out well after a transforming crisis. This was a formula I had to learn.

I was, at that point, oblivious of this simple plot structure as I was also too preoccupied with philosophical ideas, thoughts and mystical aspects of a story. It took me thirteen novels to find out what was missing. One summer's afternoon, I burnt the lot in a dustbin. One great writer said he had to write a million words to master the art of storytelling. In my case it would take many more. I decided, on looking at the ashes, that fiction was not my métier. This, however, did not put me off writing. I knew my experience would be useful in some way, but in what was not yet clear.

Around this time I began to study magic. This was quite different from philosophy, religion and mysticism. The attraction was the practical application of metaphysical principles and symbolism. The fairy stories of childhood and folklore, with the archetype of the magician and astrologer had, as said, always intrigued me. What secrets did they posses? I decided to explore the occult realm in which rituals and horoscopes might open the door to other realities that I knew were there. I read all I could about the subject but found that those who claimed to be magicians were often deluded. Many were clearly

FIGURE 24 (Left)—STUDY
As I drew the human body I began to perceive the soul that was encased in flesh. While all physiques are based upon the same model, ethnic group, class and character had to be taken into account. The whole of the individual's life is expressed by the body. People might seek to present a certain kind of image but they cannot hide their true nature from the discerning eye. Moods, attitudes and a cultivated manner are exposed to the great artist who perceives what lies beneath whatever persona is worn. (Drawing by the author).

FIGURE 25—CAST
This is a plaster cast of a famous horse that stood in the corridor of the Royal Academy School. The students there were, on the whole, more mature, most having been to other art colleges before. It was here that I joined a small circle of young artists, writers and intelligentsia who would meet in a pub or the home of two comely girls. Here everything was discussed about art, literature, religion and philosophy. We all believed our opinions were valid despite our ignorance of the world, which our generation was going to change. Like all youthful idealists, we saw the old order as being fossilised, like this plaster cast of the Duke of Wellington's horse, atrophied in the past. Each one of us believed we could make a difference in our chosen profession. Such was our youthful naïvety. (Drawing by the author).

weak in life skills and believed they could gain status by magical means. I would meet several such individuals, in the occult circles I encountered, but they put me off by their often grubby appearance, inflated egos and preoccupation with power. No doubt there are great white magicians but I have never met one over all the years of being involved with the esoteric.

My circle of friends, all now in their late twenties, had new people come in from time to time. Some just passed through and were never seen again while others stayed on, at least in my orbit. One man in particular was interesting. He was a young architect who seemed to be unusually self-assured. I was impressed, as most of us were still struggling with what we wanted to do in life. He seemed to know what he was about and spoke about universal principles in a practical way. I used to visit him in his flat, where I met others of my age who had a similar quality of confidence. They would talk about philosophy and psychology but not in an academic way. At first I did not recognise what they were trying to tell me. Later, I realised they were talking about being in a state of psychological sleep. But at that time I was one of millions of such 'sleepwalkers', except for the occasional moment of being 'conscious of being conscious'. This circle of people became my centre of social gravity and I drifted away from my old companions who endlessly argued about whether art was dead and who was the best writer now in fashion.

Meanwhile, my father, recognising I was not going to be a famous artist, said that he had supported me long enough as a student and it was time to face the real world. He was very blunt, I know for my own good. He declared that I had now to pay for my share in the household expenses. I saw my time at the Royal Academy was over. I had to find a job.

My first employment was painting costumes at the Royal Opera House in Covent Garden. This was a totally different kind of experience. It was exactly opposite to the clinical atmosphere of St. Thomas's Hospital and yet it was, in its way, as disciplined. I saw this while observing the complex operation of an opera being put together. Not only was there the problem of designing the many stage settings but also working them into a sequential system, in perfect timing, by ropes, machinery and pure manpower. This all had to synchronise with an ever-changing lighting scheme, the music, singing and dancing. It was a mammoth operation of which the audience was, and should be, quite oblivious. This was a most important lesson for the future in the art of organising when the Kabbalah Society came into being.

FIGURE 26—FATHER

This concrete portrait was initially made in clay from my parents' garden. It was then covered in plaster and sawn in half. After the clay had been removed from the mould, cement was poured in and left to set. I told my father that concrete got increasingly harder over the centuries and it would immortalise him. He was not very impressed because he said it made him look very old, which did not please him. However, years later when I had left home, he painted the head gold to enhance the image. This was the one time that I told my father off. He took it as just, as he was a good man. (Photograph by the author).

I learnt a great deal in the short time I was at the Royal Opera House. Behind the stage there was, as in the hospital, a whole hierarchy of different occupations, from stage hands, carpenters and electricians to the musicians, singers and dancers as well as the principal performers and management. There were also the 'Front of House' people who sold tickets, programmes and served in the bars. In the staff canteen, deep in the bowels of the Opera House, junior ballet dancers ate with us middle-rank artisans. It was quite an experience to see these exquisite creatures in their costumes smoking, laughing and squabbling like a bunch of schoolgirls. On stage they appeared to inhabit another, ethereal, world but in the canteen they were all too human. Another fantasy was blown away.

My next job was not so exotic. Through a friend at the Opera House, I went to work for a company that built stage sets for the West End theatres. My first task was to paint a fake cuckoo clock, which struck me as a great come-down from being a fine art student at the Royal Academy. However, my colleagues in the studio were either unemployable artists, resting actors or out of work theatre designers. Most were relatively young people, like myself, who still hoped for a great future in their chosen field. All saw their work in the 'prop' making department as at least a job in which their skills were useful. All were waiting for the opportunity to leave, if they could get a breakthrough in their creative sphere.

One of the chief scene painters was a German aristocrat. He had been a successful portrait artist until the Nazis took over. He had seen Hitler up close, too, and soon realised that the man was a psychopath. He decided to get out of Germany before the war as he foresaw what must inevitably happen. To listen to his accounts of British and German high society, where he met people I had read about in the newspapers, was most informative as it was first-hand. This was a person who had been close to the seat of power and seen it for what it was. He had deep insight into the motivation of those who seek high position; and yet here he was, dressed in paint-covered overalls, modestly working with people he normally never would have encountered socially. He was, indeed, a true noble who left a deep impression on me and countered all the negative propaganda about the Germans during the recent war. Here was a remarkable individual who stood out against the insanity of the Nazi regime. This took great integrity and courage.

Meeting such people was very important. In High Wycombe there had been a highly cultured man, who lived at the end of our road, who took a small group of young people, including myself, to Italy in 1950. He showed us the sights of Florence and Sienna in a way no book or film could do. He made the Renaissance come alive, especially Leonardo da Vinci who was a hero of mine. I learnt on that trip that most of what is seen as Great Art is more about skill than profound vision. Only people like Leonardo had any real depth in their imagery because he went deep beyond the surface of things. Most of what we saw in Italy were decorative offerings dedicated to some patron's vanity, while many sacred pictures were propaganda supporting the Church rather than Christ's Teaching. This journey to Italy gave me a sense of discrimination. This was ironical because here I was making fake trees, armour and thrones for the theatre. However, at least everyone knew the stage settings were an illusion and accepted them as such, while many religions presented symbolism as the reality. I could now see the reason behind the commandment not to make graven images, because they could become idols. This realisation was vital in preparation for encountering the esoteric teaching that lay behind many religious objects.

12. Initiation

I was with the theatre workshop for around three years. During this time I learnt many practical and psychological skills. I could make all manner of objects, such as armour made of felt stiffened with glue, which looked like hammered steel, and crowns that glittered with rubies made of red boiled sweets. But, more importantly, I learnt to improvise and invent, making use of whatever material, or even junk, we had available to get a desired effect. This exercise in thinking 'outside the box' of the ordinary proved to be a great psychological asset in dealing with certain problems in the future.

As a group, we worked as an intelligent and efficient team, building the sets and props for many shows, such as the very successful musical 'My Fair Lady' and the Royal Ballet. However, there was a striking difference between us and the carpenters. Although they were skilful at constructing scenery, their trees looked like children's cardboard cut-outs whereas the prop department produced, out of plywood, wire and ragged felt hardened by glue, oak trees that looked like the real thing. This was an interesting lesson. It required more than high technical skill to produce such quality. It needed imagination and the ability to apply new approaches to old solutions. This meant discarding fixed attitudes and being open to innovation. These lessons I applied to my study of the esoteric.

Each day, while travelling on the train to the studio, I worked on my new 'Great English Novel'. I thought I would have a go at this one last time. This epic actually had a plot. I also laboured on it in the local library, after a quick lunch. By now I did not have the time, energy or space to do any painting of my own. Indeed, I had concluded not only that my pictures were not good enough but also out of fashion, as abstract art now dominated the London gallery scene. I therefore decided to concentrate on writing. Unfortunately, while the story now had the classic dramatic format, I was still more interested in the interior processes of the characters than their actions. This might have gone down well at the high-point of the reflective novel, but the cinema had taken over from fiction in that it instantly portrayed

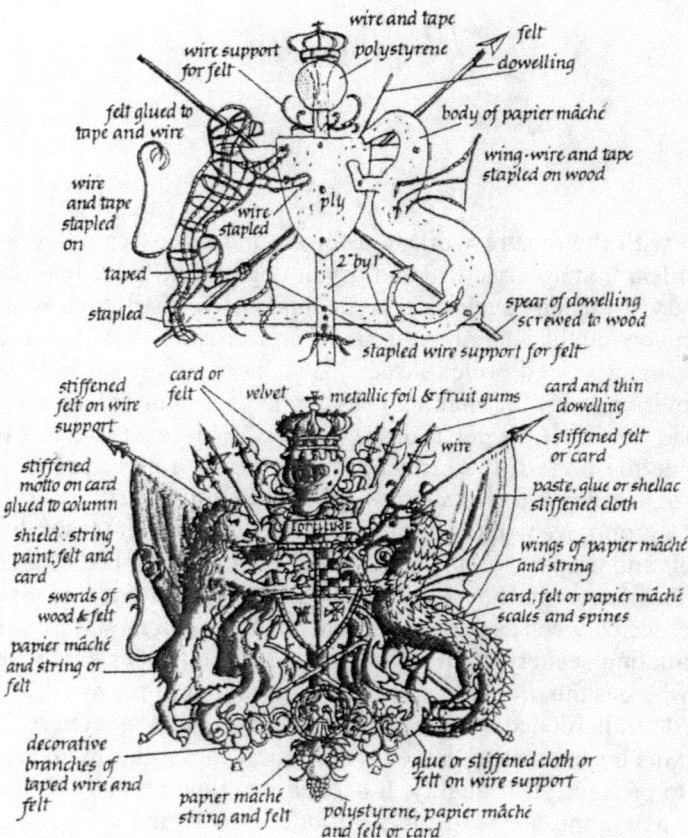

Figure 72

FIGURE 27—PROPS

I produced a book called Stage Properties and How to Make Them. *This was the first volume I ever had published. It was the result of having worked in a theatre workshop where sets for stage productions were built. This was the first job I had after leaving the Royal Academy. The first task I was given there was to paint a wooden cuckoo clock. It was a long way from a master art work but there I learnt many new skills, especially how to turn newspaper, soaked in glue, into almost any object. In this figure I used shredded string stiffened with glue and stuck onto the Lion's head made of wire, while the dragon scales were made up of felt and the crown studded with fruit-gum 'jewels'. The end product could then be painted to look like a metal, wood or stone. On stage and well lit, one would have to look closely to see what this coat of arms was really made of. As a craft, it taught me to be resourceful and inventive, using anything to hand to be converted into whatever was needed which, in the theatre, could be anything from a tree to a telescope.* (Author's illustration for *Stage Properties*).

the mood of the protagonists and no novel could compete with this. Moreover, publishing was now an industry more concerned with the popular market. There was no place for a spiritual story that could be made into a film. Even so I plodded on with my masterpiece, knowing deep down that it would never be published. Such was my delusion—but it did keep me writing and learning the craft.

During this period I wanted to know the architect and his circle better because they seemed to have access to some form of esoteric knowledge. In the discussions about astrology, philosophy and mysticism, he spoke with such clarity and authority that I would often visit him so as to question him closely about all manner of subjects. His response always had a measured order, as if he had some solid frame of reference. One evening, when his girlfriend was present, she said with a knowing look: 'Perhaps we shall tell him about the School'. He nodded, but said that first I ought to read a book called *In Search of the Miraculous* by P.D. Ouspensky. The name rang a bell but I could not recall where and when I had heard it.

As soon as I could I bought a copy from Watkins, which was considered the best esoteric bookshop in London, if not in the world. In this treasure house in a side court off Charing Cross Road, every available volume on the occult as well as books on Oriental and Western mysticism could be found. I had spent many hours in there and yet I had not picked up on Ouspensky before. Now I began to read his book whenever I had time, as I sensed it was an important brick in my spiritual education.

Peter Ouspensky was an early 20th century Russian writer and metaphysician who had travelled far and wide over Europe, the Middle and Far East examining various esoteric traditions. He had written other books on various related subjects, including a novel on reincarnation about re-living the same life over and over again. However, in *In Search of the Miraculous* he described how, in Russia, he eventually met a remarkable man who belonged to a group which had travelled even more widely than he and encountered, somewhere in Central Asia, a Shangri La type of monastery. Here people of every nationality worked, as equals, within a school of the soul. This man was a Greek Armenian who spoke bad Russian but undoubtedly had a genuine body of esoteric knowledge. It was a system which had no obvious cultural roots or religious affiliation, and yet it was clearly concerned with objective and cosmic laws and the potential of an evolving human being.

FIGURE 28—EXAMPLE
This armillary sphere was made from wire and papier mache, with a golf ball as the Earth. The original design was usually made of brass and was used to teach students of astronomy and astrology. It is based upon what can be seen from the Earth and was the first scientific scheme of relativity. I added the angel, for decoration, and painted the Sun and Moon and the Zodiacal signs to enhance the blue and gold colouring. The base was filled with old nuts and bolts to give it weight and stability. This object was made around the time I became seriously interested in astrology. Below is a book called The Secret Teachings of All Ages *which was to have a great influence upon me with its succinct text and important esoteric engravings. The picture on the wall is an early self-portrait while the swinging sphere is a painted rubber ball, representing the Earth, on a thread hung from the ceiling.* (Photograph by the author).

I was stunned by what I read. This is what I had been looking for. The book had no hidden religious agenda but it set out to awaken the readers to the fact they were psychologically asleep. The notion that most of one's time was spent daydreaming was not unfamiliar. I had had an insight of this phenomenon when once seated on the steps of the National Gallery, above Trafalgar Square. I saw a Buddhist monk making his way through the crowd during the rush hour. He was clearly alert as he moved among thousands of sleepwalkers. Had I not been 'awake' at that moment, I would have missed this insight. Such was the power of that experience and Ouspensky's book that I was determined to find out at what 'School' the architect's girlfriend had hinted.

When I enquired about the School, he replied that he was not permitted to tell me of it until I asked. I then went one evening, as directed by him, to an introductory lecture at a place in central London where Sir Isaac Newton had once lived. This, I thought at the time, was an interesting omen. Before the lecture, while waiting in an anteroom, I saw a man of great presence; and yet there was something about him that made me shiver. I took this to be an instinctive response to his charisma. A few minutes later I was seated, with about forty other people, awaiting the evening to begin when the lecturer stepped up to the rostrum. It was this man. I was immediately entranced by his eloquence as he explained how most humans drift throughout their lives and never awaken to the possibilities of their development and fulfilment. This notion was not new but he obviously knew what his own destiny was about and spoke with a profound understanding. Here was what I took to be a 'master' who had a genuine and modern version of the Teaching.

When it came to questions, there were people who either objected to the idea that people were 'asleep' or wished to show off their knowledge of esoteric matters. Those he dealt with skilfully, by asking how much they could remember of that day, yesterday or even of much of their life. Most admitted not a lot, when it came to it. This did not silence them but the rest of us got the message as they rambled on justifying their delusion that they were 'awake' when it was clear they were not. This episode impressed me and I decided to take the first course. I later learned that the lecturer was the Head of the School.

I could not sleep that night. This was the Teaching for me and this 'master' soon became my esoteric father figure. While I worked at the theatre studio and on my book, my mind went over and over what I was now learning about what was called 'the System'. I quite forgot my initial impression of the Head of the School. I bought and studied all Ouspensky's books and committed myself wholly to the 'Work' as it was known. Here I learnt about the esoteric anatomy of the psyche, which made more sense than Freud, Jung and all the other psychologists who had no comprehensive understanding of the mind as they worked on observable evidence and came to speculative conclusions. Freud was impressive but he focused primarily on the instinctive part of the psyche while Jung, although seeing deeper into the mind and even into the mystical dimension, was too vague and diffuse in his expositions. In contrast, 'the System' set out the basic structure and dynamics of the mind and the seven degrees of consciousness within it. These levels were related to the macrocosm of the universe and its objective laws. Neither Freud nor Jung had discerned the essential metaphysics of Existence. Indeed, Jung had said, in private, that he was not a mystic, while Freud suggested that God was perhaps just a 'father figure' projection.

Each week we were given an exercise in self-observation. We were required to be 'awake' as often as we could. It was horrific to discover that one was indeed daydreaming most of the time and that our lives were run by conditioned habits and instincts. Most of the time one was preoccupied with the past or the future. The present was rarely there, except occasionally when it required attention. This was a serious revelation which demanded not just conscious effort but a long term commitment to work at. Here began an ordered progression, as against a random encounter with spiritual disciplines.

I was to remain a member of the School for many years. Here I became part of a goodly company of people who shared the same values. This meant that my old circle of friends became less important, as it had been only circumstance that had brought us together. These connections eventually faded. Now the School became the centre of my life. There I had found companions, some of whom I sensed were people I had known in previous lifetimes. At last I had made a connection with a real soul-group.

13. *Changes*

During the time I had been with the theatre studio I had managed to save a thousand pounds. This was possible because I lived at home and what I paid there was minimal. While the situation was very convenient, it meant that I was not as independent as I had been when doing my national service. I greatly missed my freedom. In Jewish families then, it was customary not to leave home until one got married, as my brother had done. As I had no lady in mind to marry, I could be doomed to continue living at home. This I did not relish as I was expected to be at home every night. I loved my parents, who had been very good to me, but I needed a space and time to call my own. My small room, which my house-proud mother kept immaculate, was no longer the right place for me to develop. What was more, my mother began to rely on me emotionally as my father and she no longer got on well.

When a girlfriend offered me the option of her one-roomed flat at a very cheap rent, in a poor but central area of London, because she was moving to a larger place, I knew Providence was giving me a signal. My father was philosophical at my leaving home, because he had been a rebel in his youth, but my Cancerian mother said, 'You belong to me'. I replied, 'No. You gave me a body but not my soul'. She responded, 'How can you leave me alone with him?', meaning my father. I said it was not my rôle to be a substitute husband. However, I made a deal with her. I would telephone her at 6:30 pm every Friday and come home periodically, which she accepted. This I did, to the day she died.

My new home was very small but I could do what I liked with it, because the landlord never came as long as I paid the rent. I could stay out all night without feeling guilt and have anyone I liked visit me. With a thousand pounds in the bank I could live well on the simplest of foods. Around this time I was beginning to weary of the theatre workshop. The novelty of working for the theatre had lost its glamour, as it had become a routine. Moreover, sometimes there were very long hours and occasionally we worked all night to meet a deadline. There

FIGURE 29—WORKSHOP
This is an illustration for a book on how a play is conceived, written and produced. Having participated in many productions during my time at the theatre workshop, I decided to write a documentary novel based on my experience. I added to my own knowledge by interviewing people at every level of the operation. The book begins with the author's initial idea and works through the process to the first-night performance. The book was written about what I knew and was quite different from the romantic and philosophical novels. The book, The Play Begins, *took time to find a publisher but it did eventually get printed, which was a great encouragement as I had a large file of rejection slips for my early masterpieces, which I later burnt in one afternoon.* (Drawing by the author).

were also periods when there was no work until the next production. I took these unpaid days off to spend time in the local library working on my Great English Novel. One day, I decided to take a break to see an actor and a member of the School who sometimes helped us in the workshop. I found him sitting in the sunshine under a tree in his garden, drinking tea and reading Plato.

This sight hit me like a revelation. This was how I wanted to live. Such a situation would give me time to contemplate, to write without urgency and do what I wanted to do, when I liked. This was the moment when I must act or remain trapped for life as a wage-slave in a job that now bored me. I had no academic qualification, so I could not teach in the education system. Most of my old art circle friends were now doing this but, I noted, many of them had given up painting, because teaching used up their creative energy, and some now had families to support. I was still free and on the young side of thirty.

The moment to move came by the hand of Providence. A gap opened up when a show had just been put on the road and the workshop had little for us to do. I requested the head of the prop department to ask the boss if I could take off two weeks to write. The boss had been an artist. However, he had turned to the theatre as he could not sell his work. Because he had a talent for organisation, he got several commissions to build stage sets. He became a very astute businessman but had no time to paint. When my team leader explained why I wanted time off, he replied, 'If he really wants to be a writer, why is he working here?' I took his wry comment as a strong hint. I left the workshop, on the basis that I would come and help him out if they needed an extra pair of hands—which in fact they never did.

To support my decision my parents, to their great credit, gave me a small allowance, so that 'I would not starve', as my mother said. With this small security and my own money, I believed I would find out if I could be a writer. This seemed a long way off, as I had by now a very large number of rejection slips. These events occurred around the time I was also studying the principles of magic. One day, I thought I would try a practical experiment. I did an invocation of Mercury over my Great English Novel, now finished, after drawing the symbol of the god on the parcel containing it. I then went down to the Post Office, where there was a big queue, and so I prepared for a long wait. To my surprise, the person at the counter rapidly whisked through all the customers in front of me. Suddenly I was at the counter and the parcel on its way. As I walked home, I thought, 'Magic really works'. I had

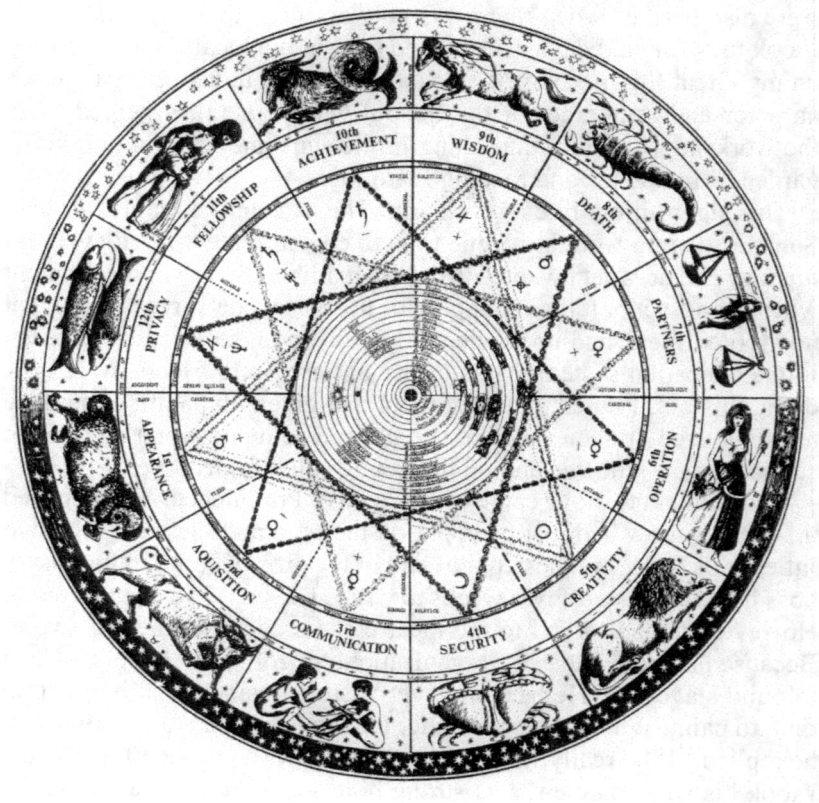

FIGURE 30—ZODIAC
*This design is a synthesis of astrological principles. It was drawn for our study group in the form of a book-sized card and a large poster. The latter was pasted onto a board and hung on a wall. The celestial bodies, made of movable disks, were stuck on to it. Besides the Zodiac and mundane Houses, the four intersecting triangles represent the four elements and how they relate to the various signs. Also shown are the active and passive rôles of the planets ruling each sign and their strong or weak positions in the Zodiac. In the central circle are the planetary gods, metals and human ages associated with the Sun, Moon and planets. This depiction proved a useful tool for teaching and contemplation of the esoteric view of the Solar system. (*Cosmic Clock* by the author).*

never known such efficiency in that Post Office. However, Heaven's lesson was that I got the typescript back by return post. I had never had such a quick rejection. I knew that Mercury was the god of speed, publishers and writers, but this was ridiculous!

In another experiment with magic I evoked the archetype of Venus, because I was without a sweetheart at that point in time. One evening, while walking alone in a wooded part of the Thames, I saw the planet Venus in the twilight sky. 'Well, I can only ask', I thought. I called upon the love goddess for help and I sensed a distinct response which I took to be my imagination. However, within a short while I got involved with a very sensuous and athletic girl who came and went, like a summer storm. The lesson here was that magic works but, if one displaces the normal order of the universe by a magical act, it will react but not in the way one may have intended. In my reflection on this episode, I recalled the story of an occult group during the war. They invoked Mars to help in the war effort. That night their lodge was hit by a German bomb. They had not specified which side was to be supported.

Astrology was a different matter. This was about the effect of the cosmos on human life. While I was doing some work at the School, where a garden was being laid out according to an esoteric design, one of the people I was working with looked up at the sky and observed that two planets were conjoining at that moment. I was intrigued by this observation for, while I had read much about astrology, I had never met a practising astrologer. When he gave me a brief account of my character according to my birth chart, I was very impressed. We became friends. After a time he offered to teach the basics of astrology to a small independent group which was joined by several people from the School.

In a short time we became a tight-knit outfit under discipline, studying astrology in the light of the System. For example, we examined the different functions of the mind in terms of the planets. This was done by observing our psychological processes when stimulated by celestial conditions. Thus the effect of Mars transiting one's own Sun sign was closely observed as an impact upon the essence of one's psychology. We also learnt about the cosmic archetypes by bringing in poems, pictures or any object that evoked a particular zodiacal sign or planet. Over months we integrated these astrological symbols with personal observations that gave an insight into the astral realm with which the human psyche resonated.

For my personal studies, I drew horoscopes of friends, family and historic figures. I collected dozens of charts of current, well-known people and anyone who gave me their time, date and place of birth. At a certain point I became convinced that astrology was not a spurious fantasy but an ancient and medieval version of psychology. It matched well with what I had learnt about cosmic metaphysics at the School, with the added attraction of being extremely useful in understanding one's inner nature and that of others. During this period I came across references to an 11th century Spanish rabbi called Ibn Ezra who was an astrologer, Neo-Platonist and Kabbalist. I did not realise at the time this was an omen for what was to come.

14. Providence

In astrology there is a cycle known as the Saturn return. This means that the planet comes back to the same position that it occupied at the moment of one's birth. It occurs around the age of thirty and its character is like the grinding hardness needed to polish a metal plate. It is a time when one's youthful delusions are challenged and the reality of adulthood becomes apparent. If one acknowledges the truth of one's situation, then it is possible to learn from this difficult time and move on with an understanding of what one's fate might be about.

This occurred to me during my first Saturn return. Being in the 1st House of my birth chart, Saturn affected my relation to the immediate everyday world. In my case, it was concerned with the basics of survival, at a mundane level, in that there was no returning to my parents' home. That would have been defeat. I was in debt for the first time, having used up my savings. What was more, I was without a sweetheart for emotional support and so I had to face the situation alone.

Over this period I learnt much about loneliness, after being in a close family. I also felt very guilty at having not been so thrifty. I refused to get a job, as that would have meant another defeat which would have made me lose the freedom I had tasted. The idea of going back into the chain gang of the theatre workshop was appalling. I was not qualified to teach, having failed my exam because I presented my diploma thesis in the form of a medieval manuscript, which is not what a conventional board of State Examiners wanted. However, at the lowest point of this dire situation, an event occurred that changed my whole outlook. I was sitting on top of a number 52 bus, outside a particular London underground station, when a quiet voice said to me, 'Have I ever let you down?' It was my own voice but it was not me who spoke these words. I looked around but there was no-one else on that top deck of the bus. Suddenly a great sense of relief came over me and, while I was still concerned about my circumstances, I knew I no longer had to worry. Providence would take care of me, if I acted correctly. The Presence that had descended upon me filled my whole being and then it was gone.

FIGURE 31—I CHING
This is the Chinese version of Divine metaphysics. The eight trigrams around the central symbol of Yin and Yang are the equivalent to the kabbalistic concept of the three pillars on the Tree and their various levels. The black and white dots represent the active and passive poles within their opposites. This system fascinated me with its precision and comprehensive cohesion, not unlike the integrated metaphysics of Jacob's Ladder. The source was said to come from the Chinese equivalent to Enoch. Like the Tree, the I Ching is too elegant and complex to have been invented by the ordinary mind. It must have been discovered by a combination of revelation and reason. (Drawing by the author).

I had been brought up to believe in God. The order of the Universe indicated a Creator but the possibility of being personally addressed was almost unbelievable. Mystics of every tradition spoke of such events but they were great saints, sages and prophets. Why should I be of any concern to the Absolute? And yet, if the Deity was all knowing, why not? Many others had had such an experience. The Bible was full of such incidents. Was I deluding myself? Only time would tell, I concluded, as the bus moved on from that timeless and indelible moment.

Indeed, things did begin to change. I now had to respond to what Providence put in my way. A small teaching job was offered to me by an acquaintance who could not take an art class in a secondary school on a Saturday morning. As it needed no qualification, I thought this had to be the hand of Heaven. This was confirmed, years later, by a young woman who had been in my class. While I had walked up and down the studio, talking about life to children just about to take their first serious academic examination, she reported I said that the 'real world' lay beyond the school gates. This remark had a very deep impact on her mind and relieved her of much anxiety as she realised the examination was not that important. Suddenly there was a wider perspective by which to live. Little did she know I had been actually talking to myself about handling the great examination of life.

Providence and its workings fascinated me from then on. I began to study the I Ching, a Chinese oracle that operates on the principle that the universe runs according to a distinct order. The key is to see when and when not to act. With the I Ching's system of sixty-four sets of laws, defined by a graphic mode of solid and broken horizontal lines, it was possible to be shown the anatomy of the situation by throwing three coins while posing a question. When casting the coins, strict attention was vital so as to tune in to the state of the cosmos in relation to oneself. The psyche is a very sensitive instrument, like a barometer that can resonate with the moment. Every ancient culture has an oracle. The usual form is a seemingly random action that generates a symbolic pattern. This can then be interpreted by a set of rules that have been compiled by observation of results over time. A parallel is the pointer of a barometer that gives the air pressure which indicates the state of the weather. The I Ching does the same but in relation to a situation.

Over time I became very impressed by the accuracy of the I Ching in its descriptions of a given situation and its recommendations on how

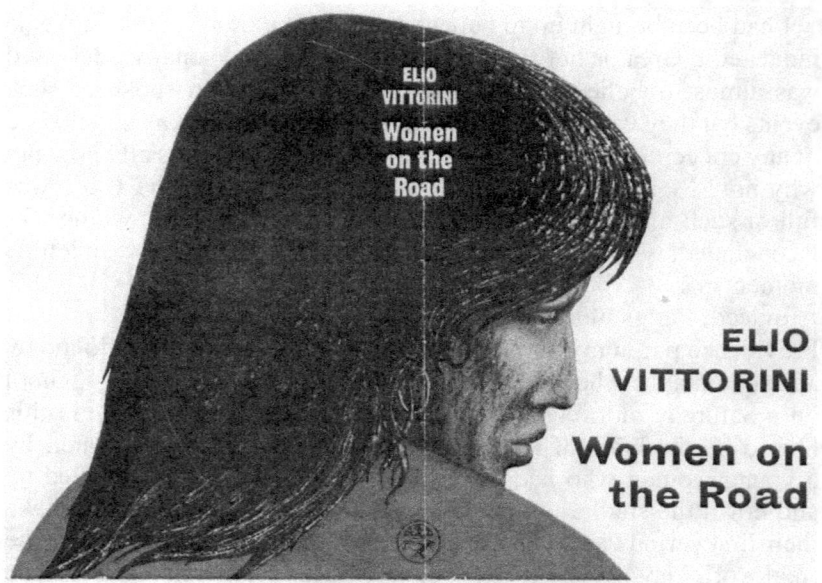

FIGURE 32—BOOK JACKET
For a time I earned my living by designing covers and illustrations for new publications. These varied from novels, as shown here, to children's books and works from the Rudolf Steiner School. In a conversation with one art editor, he said my work was good, but he would not remember me when it came to giving out work, because I was not a specialist. He could only recall the work of those who were very good at children or animals, for example. This advice, and the belief I could write better books than most I had to illustrate, made me decide to concentrate on being a writer rather than a graphic designer. This shift was a step closer to my fate. (Cover design by the author).

to respond to it. The texts were the result of many centuries of analysis, which even the great philosopher Confucius respected. As a device for dealing with personal problems or asking profound questions, it was most helpful. I spent much time, late at night, conversing with the oracle which was like talking to a very old Chinese rabbi. I have been prevented, more than once, from acting before the time was appropriate and encouraged when the moment was right. I came to regard the I Ching as a close friend and counsellor.

My other major advisor was the Head of the School whom I got to know well over the years. He, I believe, saw my potential as a writer who could be useful in spreading the Teaching. He said to me, at one interview in his study after I had told him about my publisher rejects, 'Write about what you know'. This advice was a major turning point. All my novels, as noted, were a mixture of fiction and philosophy, a deadly combination, too metaphysical for the general reader and too facile for any serious scholarly publisher. 'What did I know about well?' I asked myself. The immediate answer was how to make theatrical props. After my conversation with the Head I decided to produce a good textbook on prop-making.

I sat down in my little flat and, over a few weeks, I did a series of drawings on how to make thrones, crowns, flowers, wigs, candlesticks and a dozen other objects out of wire, papier-maché and felt. On a facing page I wrote a brief account of how to construct each prop. This text was cast in the style of a curt x-ray report. I sent the manuscript and illustrations off to a publisher and, to my surprise and delight, they wanted to do it. This book went into several editions and sold over many years in different countries. Thus encouraged, I then wrote a documentary novel about how a stage play is conceived and written and how it progresses through an ordered sequence of production. This involved all manner of people, from the producer, director and actors to the designer of sets, lighting experts and everyone else, down to the prop-makers. It was called *The Play Begins*. It, too, found a publisher because I was writing about something I knew about from direct experience. This, I now knew, was the only thing that gave authenticity to a book of any worth.

Out of these books came a job teaching prop-making at the Royal Academy of Dramatic Art, which helped to pay the rent. There I learnt much about the psychology of animal-level people who wanted to be the star, on or off stage. For most people it was the glamour of fame and fortune which celebrity promised. But there were also people who had a genuine love of the theatre. These stood out above the others as distinct individuals. Many of these, I noted over the years, did indeed become masters in the profession because of the quality and maturity of their psyche. This was seen in their deeper understanding of drama as a reflection of life. As for the rest, many talented students quit the profession when they did not attain instant fame upon leaving the Academy. In one case a very gifted young man became a public toilet attendant before committing suicide. This was the shadow side of an inflated ego. Others, like my art school circle, became teachers or worked in advertising and the media.

During this period I designed book-jackets as a source of income. This was a hazardous business for a freelance because while one might put a great amount of work into a design, it could be rejected by an art director who would pay little for the effort put in. It was while I was working on the jacket of a successful novelist's new book that I saw why my novels would never be published. One had to write either a true masterpiece or fashionable rubbish. My books fell in between. It was a terrible but truthful realisation. However, I had proved that I could write a good textbook. I now began to think what else I could do using this skill of explaining a subject in clear terms. All of a sudden it was obvious. I could write about astrology. However, this meant a great deal more study and, more importantly, the practice of interpreting birth charts before I could write on the subject.

15. Crisis

In 1962 there was a conjunction of the Sun, Moon and five planets in Aquarius. This constellation, in the sign of political revolution, was seen by astrologers and some of the world's esoteric community as potentially very dangerous. The cold war between the Western powers and the Soviet Union was now reaching a point when everyone feared a nuclear Armageddon. Indeed, with a four-minute warning for London, people wondered if they would survive such a holocaust, as the government's preparations were clearly no real protection against an atomic rocket attack.

There was a palpable atmosphere of fear at this time, as memories of the Blitz were still close. Even people far from any target centre felt threatened, if not by the initial blast then by the deadly cloud that would spread worldwide. In reaction to this, a Guru came out of India to teach a simple technique of meditation. While people were told that it would benefit them personally, the real reason was to neutralise the negative field-force that had surrounded the Earth since the Second World War. Millions had died in that conflict and many were still suffering from its effects. The notion that this astrological configuration might trigger a third global conflict was a distinct possibility.

When the School recognised what the Guru was really about, it began to support him with its disciplined organisation of several thousand members. The great Royal Albert Hall in London was hired so that the public could hear the message that meditation was of great benefit, not only to individuals but also to the community. One proof was that the crime rate went down in cities where meditation centres were set up. No mention was made about the offsetting of a global war, as this would have increased the tension. Meditation centres for initiation were founded all over the world, especially after a famous musical pop group became disciples of the Guru.

The conjunction in February came and went without incident and the media made much of the non-event which, some had predicted, was going to be the extinction of civilisation. The people who had left their homes for remote places of safety were seen as fools. Meanwhile,

FIGURE 33—CRISIS
The year of 1962 was a time when humanity was very close to self-destruction as America and Russia confronted each other over Cuba. The astrological configuration of that time, as can be seen, was one of both concentration and potential explosion. In this figure Kennedy and Khrushchev, each sitting on a hydrogen bomb, have their fingers on the button. Fortunately, it is said by some, disaster was averted due to a worldwide campaign of meditation to neutralise the expected cosmic and political tension. Such was the possibility of war that many people fled to remote places or decided where they wished to die, if the missiles came. One man and woman I knew decided they would make love when Armageddon came. (Redrawn from a cartoon of the time with the Zodiac added by the author).

the meditation campaign began to fade as the potential crisis seemed to have passed. In the School the enthusiasm for the operation started to wane. Its members felt depressed that such a major conscious effort had brought about no obvious positive effect on the world. A number of people now began to question the aim of the School. The Head had turned it into a highly efficient organisation that had become almost militant. The spirit of the early days had gone and the School had become, as one member said, too much like the army. The Head's response was that tight discipline was needed. The result was the building of a hierarchy of those who agreed with him. Here began the start of a struggle for the soul of the School.

Later that same year, the two major world powers of the time and the two nations with the greatest populations were on the verge of war. The Soviet Union had set up secret rocket sites on Cuba from which they could easily attack the United States. The Americans, upon discovering this threat, set up a blockade of ships and were prepared to invade the island. This brought about a serious confrontation between the two superpowers which was only an itchy trigger finger away from Armageddon.

Meanwhile, China and India were fighting fiercely over a disputed frontier in the Himalayas. Both of these countries were ready to call up millions of men to defend what was seen as their territory. Meanwhile, the world watched with horror and deep fear as to the outcome.

Fortunately, all sides realised in time that a war would mean total mutual destruction. Each one backed down into an armed truce. Suddenly the cloud of fear lifted as everyone was relieved that the end of humanity was not going to happen. Perhaps the Guru and the School's effort had tipped the balance. After 1962 the world seemed a different place, where fun took the place of fear.

From that time on the School underwent a major change. Perhaps its purpose of coming into existence was just to be in place to organise the worldwide meditation campaign to help offset a Third World War, and now its job was done. Slowly it became increasingly rigid, with those who supported the Head of the School being given increasing powers. They were not always the best of people, as they toed what became a party line of strict rules and controls with watchers in every group who wrote reports on potential dissidents. An incident convinced me that all was not well when someone said he was going abroad. He was told he had to have permission from the School. This horrified me. From then on I became a dissident. When I was offered the chance to be a

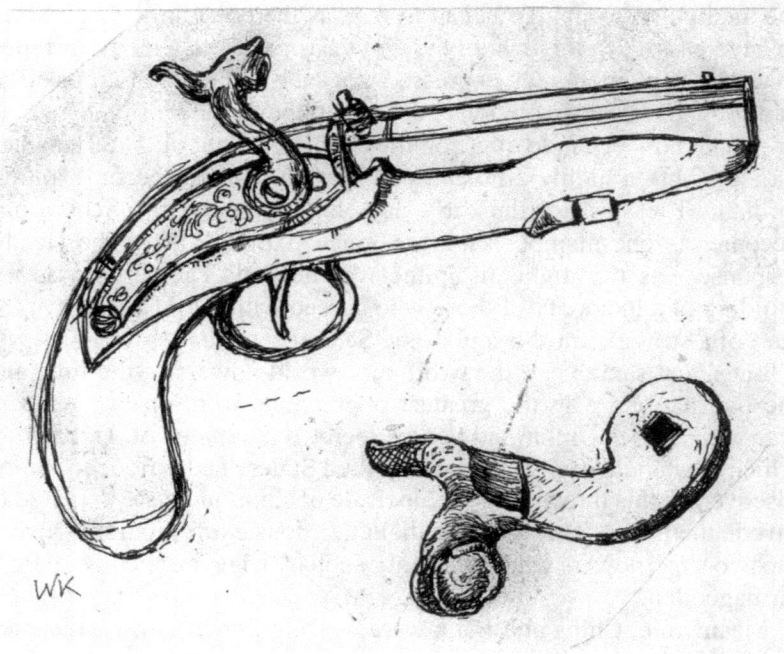

FIGURE 34—WEAPONS
This old pistol was part of a collection I had. Having lived through the war I was familiar with the military. This may also be due to having Mars in Virgo, which made me admire the precision of weapons. The other reason may have been that I had a dim memory of being attacked, in some former life in Russia, by Cossacks who destroyed the Jewish quarter of our town. By the time the full extent of the Nazi Holocaust was known I gave up my pacifist view for the Israeli motto, 'Never Again'. Besides this pistol I had a samurai sword, which is the epitome of Mars in Virgo as great care goes into its making. (Drawing by the author).

tutor, I saw this as a seductive bribe and not in the spirit of the Work. This was a warning of the first order.

Some of the senior and founder members of the School drew the Head's attention to what was happening. However, he thought it necessary to have a solid structure so as to maintain discipline in what was now a very large organisation. This made sense for a commercial company or political party but not an esoteric school. Early on he had been a parliamentary candidate but had failed to become a Member of Parliament, which his father had been. His motivation now appeared to manifest in creating an organisation not unlike an Italian Renaissance court in which he was the princely Head with an elite circle of devoted people. The School now had, in London and in the country, several great houses which were taken care of by students who also contributed to the cost. Here artists, musicians and various study groups performed and practised like at the court of the Medici.

Indeed, someone actually remarked that the Head looked like Lorenzo de Medici. As if to confirm this observation, the Head applied Machiavellian methods to control his critics by isolating them in a single group. This nullified their influence, although whichever tutor they were given had a hard time maintaining the party line. Those of us who realised what was happening tried to keep the original aim of 'Good Company' alive, but this became increasingly difficult. 'The School comes first', we were told. When I heard that some people were actually being ordered to live in communes I realised the School was in crisis. A policy now emerged, justified by a limited version of the Teaching, which was used as a psychological pressure to contain the situation. One idea was the belief that people would become lost souls without the School. The Church had had a similar approach when it came into power as the official religion in the Roman Empire. Several senior people left the School. These were strongly individuated characters whom I much admired for their integrity. This troubled me greatly.

Because I had a personal connection with the Head, I occasionally went to see him in his barristers' Chambers. As he was my father figure, initially I could not believe what was happening. Those close to him were good people who now seemed to be mesmerised by his projected power of authority. Only his personal secretary, a remarkable woman who worked for him every day, knew him as he really was. Gradually she, having been deeply devoted to the School and the man, became increasingly disenchanted. She suddenly left, which shocked many.

Then the Head's own wife left him, which shook the School even more. My moment of truth came while talking to him in his study. Suddenly it was as if my inner eye was opened. He, I perceived, had been taken over by something. There was no doubt that he believed that the way in which he was acting was for the good of the School. At that moment I recalled the darkness that hovered about him at our first encounter. It was still there but much stronger. I owed much to this remarkable man and the School but I could neither be an unquestioning follower, nor be a member of a well-meaning but rapidly crystallising entity. The 'Work' was about freeing people, not binding them into being some kind of clones. Many religious orders of the past had gone this way, such as the orthodox Jews who dressed and thought alike. The next phase, I thought, might be declaring any dissident a heretic and excommunicating them. The Head was a Scot, with a strict background. I saw that this cultural factor was his unconscious model. I had fought the battle against my Jewish conditioning and was not prepared to lose the freedom of being an individual. I decided to leave the School.

Several hundred people also left the School around this time. Many were so disillusioned that they turned away from the 'Work'. Some became trapped in a limbo of knowing too much, which meant they could not go back into everyday life and sleepwalking again. One man I knew became quite cynical. He spent the rest of his life playing with puzzles to avoid facing his emptiness. After I had left, a very disturbed woman came to me saying how she was split between loyalty to the School and her lover. I asked her what she wanted. She shook her head and said, 'I don't know'. The next day she killed herself.

I had connections, through my old architect friend, with the original Ouspensky Society, so I applied to join it. This was a much smaller organisation which had among their members a more cultured level of people. Not a few had held high rank in the arts and business. The Head of the Society, as it was called, was a doctor who had been very close to Ouspensky and had carried on the 'Work' after his teacher died. The discipline here was gentle but quite firm. Joining the Society was a 'God sent' opportunity in a dark hour of spiritual need.

16. Discovery

Having found several part-time teaching jobs, I could now move back to Holland Park in Kensington. I saw it as my natural London habitat, because I had good memories of my first sojourn there. It was an area where trees and gardens were abundant so that it was like being half in the town and half in the country. With the then Bohemian Notting Hill district nearby, it was the perfect place for me in a small flat in a Victorian house, overlooking a pleasant road and a communal garden. I was to live here for nearly twenty years. This stable and delightful environment allowed me to develop without undue disruption.

There were a small number of us from the School who joined the Society. Here we were integrated into the 'Work' again. Added to this were new modes of practice, such as the Gurdjieff Movements in which the choreography acted out the laws of Existence, in the great hall of the Society's building. This was a ritualistic discipline that demanded great body-mind control when several ranks of people moved through a different sequence of changing posture that represented, for example, the cosmic octave. The precise gestures were designed to awaken various levels within the psyche, as one had to be consciously alert at every moment. There was also the Whirling Dervish ceremony, brought in by a Sufi from Turkey, and of course a number of weekly study and practice groups designed to extend the mind and work in the everyday world.

The Sufi ceremony was the result of one of the members of the Society going to the city of Konya in Turkey, where the poet and mystic Rumi had founded a Sufi order in the Middle Ages. This ritual had been practised there ever since then. In it the Dervish spins on the ball of one foot with arms outstretched, one hand palm up, the other down. The symbolism was that the 'Turner' turned upon the axis of his inner self, so that the world was seen as the 'passing show' while one hand received Grace and the other imparted it. Each Turner moved with the others, in a circling motion like the Solar system, while the Sheik, or master, stood still on a rug observing every motion. He represented the Tradition while another senior member moved among

the Turners as the all-watching Presence of the Absolute. The format was composed of four sessions of about fifteen minutes. The phases symbolised a rising up from the mineral world, through the vegetable and animal levels to the human. At a certain point each participant cast off their outer garment to reveal the inner self. Just to watch such a ceremony had a profound effect. It symbolised our situation in the outer and inner cosmic and personal process.

Such activities as cleaning the Society building were not seen as chores but exercises in self-observation. This was in contrast to the School, in which they were viewed as a service. The difference was that people were allowed and encouraged to be individuals. One of the voluntary duties I took on was to be a night watchman every so often in the Society building. In this rôle there was nothing to do except read the books in a wonderful library, full of esoteric works, and check each room from time to time. One night I sat in what had been Ouspensky's study. This was very moving, as he had been an inspiration to me as a writer and a man. During my hour there, I picked up the psychic residue of a very rare individual whose integrity had made him seek his own path. He had left Gurdjieff because he did not agree with his teacher's severe working methods. I felt great kinship in this, as I had just parted from my teacher who did not, alas, practise what he taught.

One of the people who left the School with me was the friend who instructed our small study group in the art of astrology. His training had been based upon the Occult, Magic, the Tarot and Kabbalah. This was a composite approach, dating back to the Renaissance. As such it was not a unified system but it did open the door to the Higher Knowledge through symbolism. Having mastered astrology, he proposed to instruct those who were interested in a private study group on Kabbalah.

At first I was resistant because of my prejudice against any form of orthodox religion, especially my own. I believed the façade of rituals and customs of Synagogue and Church hid the Teaching. For example,

---

FIGURE 35 (Left)—FRIEND
This statue tucked into a niche in the Dutch Garden of Holland Park was an important companion when working on my books. He reminded me of Marco Polo, the Italian medieval traveller who visited China. In a way I was on a similar journey of exploration of an ancient culture. In my case it was Kabbalah. As I wandered about the woodlands of Holland Park I was refreshed by Nature. The bomb-ruined house had once been a country mansion, far from London. Now it was surrounded by streets but it still retained a rural feeling which reminded me of my boyhood. I still visit him from time to time. (Gouache by the author).

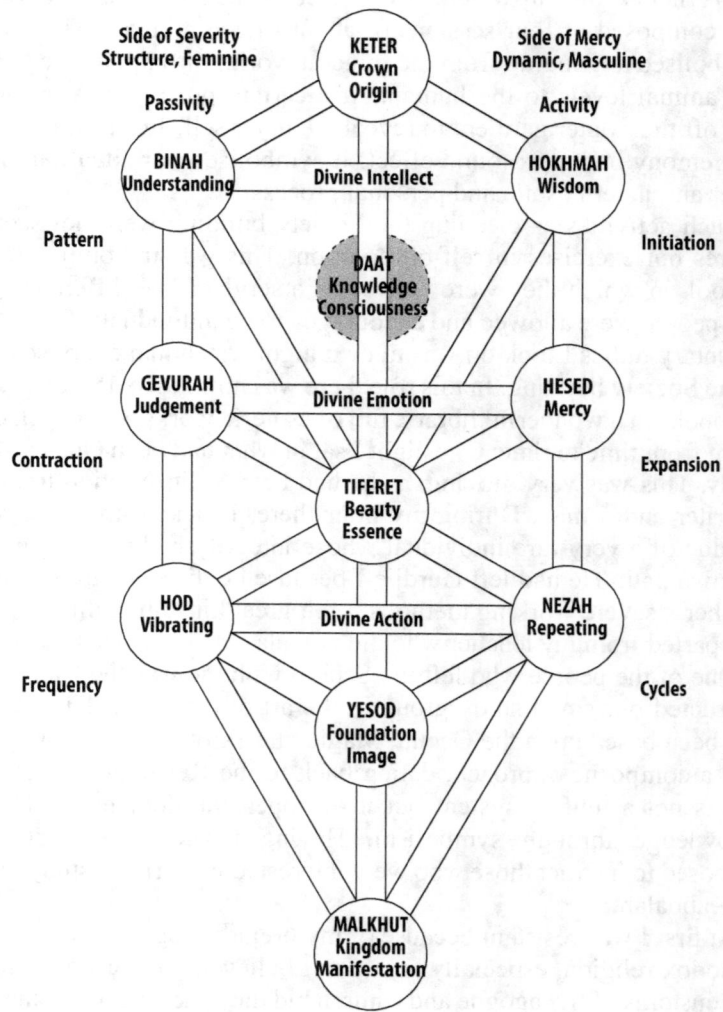

FIGURE 36—TREE OF LIFE
In this diagram the Hebrew names of the sefirot are set out with their symbolic meanings and the metaphysical principles they represent. Above are the definitions for the pillars, while below come the levels within the Divine scheme. Everything in Existence is based upon this model. The paths reveal the relationship between the sefirot while the triads define the functions of the system. In the Tree of the psyche, the left and right pillars represent structure and dynamic while the central column indicates levels of consciousness. As a metaphysical tool this kabbalistic mandala has few equals. (Modern version of the Tree).

the 613 regulations, that some rabbis claimed we must obey, struck me as excessive. The original Ten Commandments covered more or less everything. The rest were just rules which the rabbis still argued about. However Kabbalah, the esoteric aspect of Judaism, did attract me as it had things in common with the 'System'. This I could see in its key diagram, the sefirotic Tree of Life. Our 'Instructor', as I will call him, knew the subject from an occult viewpoint but this did not put me off as I sensed I was coming home to my own tradition.

About ten of us met in a private house over a period of time. The reason for such discretion was that Kabbalah was not considered respectable because of its association with Magic. As all of us had been under the 'Work' discipline, there was no danger of any Faustian deviation. Magicians like Aleister Crowley had given Kabbalah a bad name by ruining several people and themselves in their distorted use of its principles. I had met, some years before, one of Crowley's students who said that Crowley was a genius until he became inflated and believed he could break universal laws without fear of consequence. Crowley died in old age, a burnt-out wreck of a man in the rented room of a boarding house, wondering, and I quote him saying, 'What it was all about'. He had fallen for the Lucific temptation of power.

The first thing we examined was the kabbalistic Tree of Life. As our Instructor explained, the structure and dynamics of this diagram, the mystery of the ten prime numbers, or sefirot, and the twenty-two Hebrew letters slowly began to make sense. Here, too, was the Law of the Octave, the seven levels of consciousness, as well as the focal points of Essence and Personality which I later related to the Self and Ego of modern psychology. The left and right sefirot clearly related to the six psychological functions of Gurdjieff's scheme of the psyche while the doctrine of the three forces, or the Yin, Yang and Tao principles, became apparent in the triads made by the paths between the sefirot. Gradually this kabbalistic mandala became the focus of my interest, not only because it made sense but in that it was more than familiar to me.

This was a revelation. I now experienced that awe and excitement I had felt when I first encountered the 'System'. This is what I had been unconsciously searching for all my life. Why had I never found a book on Kabbalah that set out the metaphysics of the Tree so plainly? Why had the rabbis obscured what was a wonderfully precise version of the Teaching? They wrote great tomes about the Torah but never explained what it was. Could it be that they did not understand its simplicity? Maybe, as one critic said, 'The Tree diagram is too simple to be believable'. Later, one rabbi actually asked me if Kabbalah was a genuine mystical tradition. I was even more shocked when a tutor in a rabbinic college declared he did not believe in anything beyond what was in the Talmud, the rabbinic commentaries on the Bible. Both rabbis were very learned but saw Kabbalah as no more than a medieval body of superstition. I knew, because of my training and knowledge of the psyche and metaphysics, that I had now encountered the original Teaching that lay behind the Old Testament. The conclusive proof was the seven-branched candlestick in the Tabernacle. This was clearly a symbolic version of the Tree of Life with its ten nodal points, twenty-two decorations, left and right arms and central pillar.

The Tree was the perfect tool for explaining how the macrocosm of the Universe and the microcosm of man worked and related to each other. Suddenly everything came together. I began to read as many books on Kabbalah as I could find in English. These included the classic texts such as the *Zohar*, the *Bahir* and the *Sefer Yezirah*. The original editions were beyond me as my Hebrew and Aramaic were too elementary. This, however, was a blessing in disguise as I did not get caught up in the obscurities that had been accreted to the subject over the centuries. Besides this, most of the learned works on Kabbalah were written by scholars who could not tell the difference between levels of fantasy and mystical experience, real events and symbolism.

As I picked up the principles and workings of the Tree so rapidly, my Instructor remarked that he had never known anyone absorb so much information so quickly. I replied, 'I am not learning. I am remembering'. I experienced the sense of having learnt about Kabbalah before in a previous life. It all came back to me very vividly, but in modern terms. My Instructor told me that his teacher had said to him 'We need a writer to present the Tradition for the current generation'. I knew, deep down, that these words and instructions were meant for me. And so I set out to explain the Tree of Life diagram for the intelligent lay person in my first book on Kabbalah. I now knew this was my text-book literary métier.

17. Relationships

I based the first book on Kabbalah on my Stage Properties text-book format. I applied the Tree diagram to different topics, such as the planetary gods, government and religion, after outlining the dynamics of the sefirot and paths. Also included were chapters on the triads and the octave, as well as what are known as the four Worlds within the single Tree. Years later, in a revised edition, I was to add a more detailed description of the psyche and the Tree and show how Jacob's Ladder of four Trees was integrated in an extended form that represented all the levels of Existence.

The *Tree of Life*, as it was initially called, was designed for the intelligent lay reader. I knew it would be of no interest to scholars, because I decided not to encumber the text with cross-references. Besides, the work was original in that I applied Kabbalah to a modern situation. I knew that the rabbis would not approve of this approach, as it was not traditional, so I did not seek to placate the conventional view. With this intention I included the study of the Tree and economics and the process of a love affair, based on the Law of Octaves and the Tree. This metaphysical angle I hoped would make the book stand on its own merit.

After having had the typescript checked by my Instructor, I sent it off to the first publisher. In the case of this type of book, there were about five publishers who specialised in the esoteric in English at that time. Most were interested either in the Occult or scholarly readership. As I had had so many rejection slips with other books, I was quite philosophical. So it came as a great surprise to learn that the first publisher to which I sent the manuscript decided to print it. I learnt about this in a strange way, which indicated that Providence had a hand in the process. I was at a friend's birthday party where I was introduced to the editor of the publisher to which I had sent the book. When he heard my name, he said, 'By the way, have you had my letter?' I shook my head. He then told me he had decided to recommend my book to his board of directors. Here began a whole new phase in my life.

FIGURE 37—ANIMA
This was an image of my ideal of beauty before I fell in love with a lady who resembled it. Like the great lost loves of many people's lives, there was more than a little fantasy conjured up by the notion of a soul mate. Alas, real relationships are not about passion but everyday life. For a love affair to be transformed into a marriage where the couple share identical aims and complement each other is very rare. Such unions are the result of much interior psychological work as well as spiritual maturity. Unfortunately both the lady and I proved to be short on both accounts. It was, however, an important lesson as regards projection. (Drawing by the author).

I used my Hebrew name on the cover, because I knew that my English one would carry little weight with any Jew interested in Kabbalah. The fact that I was a Levite would give the book a certain gravitas and I had the cultural background to give the book an authenticity. My Instructor, who was Welsh although married to an Israeli, agreed. This was a turning point in our relationship. Although I accepted him as my Instructor, I regarded him as a peer in age and knowledge. We had had the same training at the School and the Society. I did not regard him as my 'Teacher' in the conventional sense. In any educational system, one is taught by experts in different fields, such as art, mathematics or history. Only rarely does one come across a 'master', by which I mean a person who not only knows their subject but has a wide view of universal principles. My friend had that potential, for he was an original thinker, but he had certain limitations, as I did. His gift was to see things in an unusual way. An example was when we were talking about a big bank robbery. His comment was that the loot would be quickly spent and support many people in the crooks' community. This was an angle none of us had thought about. While it was an immoral action it would indeed be, as the proverb says, 'An ill wind that blew nobody any good' in the grand scheme of life.

While I was in his Kabbalah study group, I fell deeply in love with a fellow member. We had known each other since we were at art school. Her marriage had failed and I felt very sad that such a beautiful, intelligent and sensitive young woman, with four children, should be without a man. While these thoughts and feelings were all very noble, it was the power of what Jung called the Anima that attracted me. She dressed in Victorian-style clothes that made her look like a sensitive but stoic heroine from a classic 19th century novel. With her long braided hair, aquiline nose and exquisite eyes, her image resonated with the three planets I had in Virgo in my House of partnership. She was a Sun Virgo with Moon in Scorpio, while her Jupiter was exactly conjunct my Sun. It was a fatal combination. As I, too, was alone at the time, the inevitable was bound to happen.

We conducted a discreet and passionate love affair in my small flat. This intimate space was a perfect place for a delusion, for both, as we lived very different lives. It suited us both initially, as it fulfilled a deep need for companionship without any real responsibility. 'Falling in love' is exactly what it says. One is immersed in a mixture of very strong instinctive desires and a psychological obsession with the other person that does not match everyday reality. As my birth chart also

FIGURE 38—HIPPIES
I was in my thirties when this free and easy popular culture took hold of the youth of the 1960s. Many, I believe, were people who had been killed in the war and were reborn in the baby boom just after. Upon reaching puberty they sought to have the fun they had missed in their last life. While most just wished to enjoy themselves, others sought to find out what life was really about. Psychedelic drugs offered an insight into the invisible realm but the cost was high. The more prudent and intelligent sought out alternative mystical traditions because the church and synagogue had become social and political entities. Kabbalah, like Zen and Sufism, was one of several options. (Drawing by the author).

had my descending Node in the House of partners, it meant it would eventually be a difficult relationship. However, I enjoyed the situation until I began to visit her home. She had separated from her husband and her four children accepted me, as I was an old friend of the family. One even asked me to be her new father. On the practical level, I had to cycle several miles to be with her at weekends. However, after some time a moment came when I was weary of this journey through every kind of weather and wanted to make the relationship normal, giving up my flat and moving over to her house, with the view to marriage. She hesitated at the offer as it meant a complete rearrangement of the space she had carefully created for her family. I gave her three months to consider the proposition but she could not make up her mind. I then retired from the situation for another three months, which was very painful. On the last day she came to see me to say she did not believe it would work.

I was devastated but I could understand that she did not wish her territory to be invaded by my visitors or the group that met each week in my flat. However, at the age of now forty I could not accept the idea of cycling back and forth across London for the rest of my life and still be living the rest of the week alone. Her long-considered decision revealed that her love was not that deep. I heard later, from a mutual friend, that one reason why she turned down my proposition was that I put God and my work before her. At that moment my 'Anima' projection faded. Although I still had great love for her, I needed someone who would share the kabbalistic way of life I knew I had to live. This kind of relationship can only happen by Providence. Besides this, our relationship was illicit and I had to pay my karma for getting involved, even though she had split from her husband because of his *affaires*.

By this time I ran a group in my flat. As a result of the publication of the *Tree of Life* I attracted the attention of a Western Sufi School, headed by a Turkish aristocrat who lived in London. He wanted to create an organisation where various esoteric traditions could meet. I was invited, along with Christian and Zoroastrian teachers, to give lectures on our Traditions. His school was based on a remote farm and was in full flower during the 'Hippy' period when young people were exploring the occult, psychedelic drugs and every spiritual cult. The aim of the Turkish master was to provide a place where genuine esoteric lines could point to a solid path of development. This greatly appealed to me, as it also meant that I could work alongside the

Muslim Tradition then at odds with the Jews over Israel. Out of this could come some mutual respect.

The main line of teaching at the farm was that of Ibn Arabi, a medieval Moslem poet, mystic and philosopher. He had lived in Spain at a time when Jews, Moslems and Christians got on well and shared the Hellenic philosophic ideal coming in from the School of Translators in Baghdad. The farm set out to recreate a similar situation in our time. I would sit and listen to a Sufi concept of 'Reality', watch a Zoroastrian fire ceremony and listen to a talk on Christian theology. My contribution was to talk about Kabbalah.

One result was that a number of people came to study Kabbalah with me. At first they came one by one, until I realised it would be simpler to have them all on the same night as my other students. Sometimes there would be, perhaps, twenty or more people crammed into my flat which seemed to expand magically to accommodate them all. It was a perfect balance for me, an introvert 12th House Capricornian Sun with a highly sociable Geminian Moon in the 5th House of the teacher. During the sessions I was stretched by many questions which drew upon all I had learnt. But there was another aspect; answers sometimes came I know not from where. Perhaps, I thought, I had been a rabbi in a past life and simply recalled what I knew then. But there was more to it than this. I was hearing a voiceless voice from deep within which was not my own.

One of the people who came to take me to the Sufi farm for a weekend course was the daughter of a missionary in Africa. She recognised the Teaching of Kabbalah when she saw my study with its Tree of Life diagrams. We became close friends, but never lovers, as we were more like esoteric brother and sister. Years later she taught Kabbalah in Nigeria and South Africa as well as in America and Britain. She was one of several people who clearly belonged to the same soul-group as myself. These companions I met on my travels. What was surprising was that the recognition, as with my 'Sister', was instant and mutual. Here began the preparation for the Kabbalah Society. However, it would take years before it became a School of the Soul.

18. Visions

While the romantic breakup was going on, I kept myself steady by centring on the Tiferet, the Self, the pivot of the Tree within my psyche. This was possible because of the discipline I had taken on in the School and the Society. With the determination to write another kabbalistic text, I buried myself in research and writing. I read all the translations of kabbalistic works then available. These were now being published as there was a rising interest in the esoteric at that time and Jewish scholars were digging out old texts that had been almost forgotten.

As I had a non-sectarian esoteric education, I saw the texts in a relatively objective way. I had also been taught to meditate using an Indian sacred word as a focus of consciousness. This did not make sense, as I had no personal or collective associations with Indian culture. I decided therefore, upon committing myself to Kabbalah, to use the Hebrew Divine Name EHEYEH-ASHER-EHEYEH, I AM THAT I AM. This had a potent freshness and a profound effect, in that I had to realise WHO I was addressing. To utter inwardly, 'I AM', then, 'THAT' and then, 'I AM', and perceive the personal self reflecting upon the absolute SELF, was awesome. Moreover, to see the word THAT representing Existence was to recognise that both I AMs were the same, as God beheld God in the Mirror of Existence.

One result of this exercise occurred when I was sitting on top of a bus in central London, during the rush hour. Suddenly I saw the tens of thousands of faces in the street as the microcosmic visages of the Divine. Although they were 'sleep-walking' as they daydreamed about the past or the future, they were nevertheless the organs of perception of the Holy One. This was a powerful recognition that each person had a spark of the Godhead within them, even though it was, as yet, unrealised.

Another exercise practised, as an extension of my interest in astrology, was to spend time looking up at the Heavens on any particularly clear night when I could see the Moon and planets against the Zodiacal constellations, with or without a telescope. Over the

FIGURE 39—WORK
This wall hanging shows the Kabbalist below on Earth with the mineral, plant and animal kingdoms together with the works of man. Above is the Moon, Sun and the Solar system, in the form of the Tree of Life, within the dome of the stars. Over this hovers the angelic world with Great Michael presiding over the celestial hosts. Beyond this are the archangels with Metatron, the transfigured Enoch, at the juncture point between the World of the Spirit and the Divine Realm represented by the Holy Name YHVH. It was painted on a white window blind and is now used as a motif of the Kabbalah Society. (Drawing by the author).

years I became sensitive to the music of these celestial beings, which Kabbalah regarded as angels. Sometimes, if I was in a particularly balanced state, I could actually pick up resonances of each planet which had a distinct quality. Mars, for example, was like a sharp trumpet, Venus a soft guitar while Jupiter sounded like a full orchestra, in contrast to Saturn's deep cello note. These observations clearly related to the effect they had on the psyche in the same way that certain songs, melodies and symphonies set our feet tapping, put us in a particular mood or make us rise up to the spirit. These experiences, over many years, taught me something no book on astrology could convey.

Then there was the contemplation of inner space. This meant total internal silence. Some Kabbalists used the technique of turning the Hebrew letters over and over in the mind in order to occupy the ego while the Self entered a state of deep quiet. Sometimes, in such a quiescent state, the door of Daat, the non-sefirah of direct Knowledge, would open up and I would perceive the Divine Light, if only as a faint glimmer. During such moments I felt in a direct contact with the Godhead, who is not as remote as most people believe. There is a Jewish joke that sets this in context. A devout rabbi had prayed for forty years hoping to enter into a dialogue with God, like Moses, but without any response. One day he became desperate and cried out, this time with genuine concern, 'Lord, why art Thou so silent?' After a moment, a very quiet voice said deep inside him, 'It is because you are so boring'.

Another approach to entering the higher Worlds is to go 'up' the Tree, stage by stage, through the seven levels of consciousness on the central column. This enables the psyche to shift its centre of gravity slowly but surely into a state where the mind is at maximum receptivity. At this point it is in contact with the central sefirah of Creation and the lowest sefirah of the Divine Tree. Here it is possible to receive an insight into where the three higher Worlds meet. To hold this position, if only for a moment, is to enter the world of the mystic.

Most prayers are either petitions for something or praise for what has been received. Meditation is about coming via devotion into the Divine Light. Contemplation, in contrast, applies the deeper intellect. In this method questions are asked which may or may not be answered, depending on how real they are or whether they are relevant to a situation. Some people seek higher Knowledge that they cannot possibly understand or make good use of. The wisest thing to ask is to enquire what one needs to know at that point in one's life. A direct

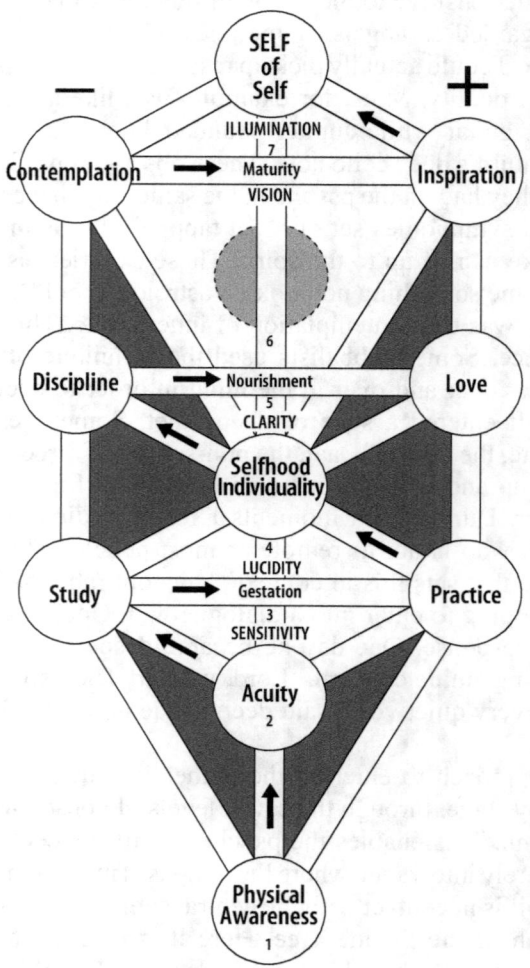

FIGURE 40—LEVELS

This Tree sets out the seven levels of perception possible under the discipline of a school of the soul. Everyone has illuminated moments but only those trained in an esoteric method can choose to reach the upper levels by an act of conscious will. The four lowest levels are concerned with ordinary life. In contrast the level of clarity relates to the soul while that of vision gives access to the World of the Spirit. Such a transpersonal dimension leads, eventually, to illumination and enlightenment. This diagram was a model for those practising Kabbalah, irrespective of their religious background. This approach was the hallmark of the Toledano Tradition, where tolerance and acceptance of the Universal Truth was the aim. (Tree illustration from a Halevi book).

answer may come in a symbol, word or image but it is more likely to manifest in an unusual external event that indicates what needs to be done—or not done.

An example of this was when I asked about the kabbalistic classic, the *Zohar*. I quote from my notebook. The response came in a flash of vision:

"I was shown the image of a great ruined palace. It had once been a magnificent edifice with grand halls, arches and windows filled with fine works of art. Surrounding it were the remnants of beautiful gardens, terraces and pools, all now overgrown. However, there were the paths cut through the encroaching wilderness which gave access to certain chambers, that contained fragments of what had been a high culture which had existed long ago. And then I saw, coming down from the sky, an immense vortex of lights which focused upon the heart of the ruined palace. This penetrated the solid fabric of the building, making it look like it was composed of glass. An ethereal light then filled the halls and chambers, revealing apparitions of people who still haunted the place. After this came the rumble of thunder and flashes of lightning, that touched particular sections of the structure indicating a symbolic or metaphysical feature, such as the seven-branched candlestick."

The message of this vision was to explore the text and discover within the ruins the kabbalistic body of knowledge embedded beneath the obscuring rubble. I had to be like an archaeologist working through the rubbish to find the jewel of an idea, a hidden meaning or a buried symbol. It was my task, I had been given to understand, to put together my findings into a coherent system suitable for the time. This vision was a profound confirmation.

Such events did not always occur in the quiet solitude of my study, but in the midst of everyday action. Once, when I was in old Jerusalem, with my hands and head against the Wailing Wall in a state of contemplation, I picked up the echo of millions of people who had prayed there over the centuries. Then suddenly, the substance of the wall became transparent and, for a moment, I was gazing into Eternity. It was too much. I stepped back, so as to regain my time and place in this world, but I was left with the knowledge that the Temple Mount was indeed the anchor of the Heavenly Jerusalem high above. In the Holy Land such experiences are not unusual.

A similar incident occurred at Mount Carmel, where Elijah's cave is situated. I had been there earlier that day but, because there were so many people present, I could not tune into the field-force of the Prophet's home. I returned later that evening after the visitors had gone. I thought I was alone but, as I came up to the cave, I saw a figure seated by the entrance. It was a rough-looking man dressed in an old army coat with a leather belt about his waist. He was staring out to sea with the most clear and bright blue eyes I have ever seen, as if he were looking beyond the horizon. As I had worked in a mental hospital, I had seen this dissociated look before, only this time it was different. I went onto the alert. According to Jewish folklore Elijah can take on all sort of forms, including beggars. This was no vagrant. He had strange dignity and power despite his odd mode of dress. I asked, in my limited Hebrew, if he spoke English. He shook his head without turning. I suddenly had the strong feeling that I should retreat. If this was a manifestation of Elijah such a glimpse was sufficient. I made my way rapidly down Mount Carmel to Haifa and everyday life. If this was not Elijah himself, then whoever the man was, he was certainly someone of a very high order.

I had a similar but lesser experience on a London underground train. I noticed a Middle Eastern man of about fifty amid the rush hour crowd in the carriage. While they were all daydreaming he was more than just alert. There was a radiance about him I have only rarely seen. We had a brief eye contact of mutual acknowledgement before he got off the train, leaving me sad that we did not speak. There was a rumour at that time that Maitreya, or the Axis of the Age, lived in the East End of London and so I wonder to this day whether I saw the current Messiah or just a remarkable individual. It is said that one cannot see beyond one's level. So I may never know the answer.

19. Journeys

Over the decades my exploration of the outer world extended increasingly. I began to travel around Britain. These journeys were often a mutual culture shock as I was as strange to the denizens of distant parts of the kingdom as they were to me. In a trip to Wales, a local shopkeeper heard my London accent and concluded that I must be English. His conversation was loaded with an unconscious resentment. This was a thousand years of Celtic anger against the Anglo-Saxons who had stolen the best land from their ancestors. However, when I said I was Jewish, the atmosphere instantly changed; 'Oh', said the shopkeeper, 'One of the Children of Israel. You must come to our chapel. It would be great honour to have someone from the Bible there.' Many such moments deepened my understanding of collective psychology and history and these gave me great insights into human evolution.

When I visited Italy in my youth I was initially impressed by its glamour. As a Leonine nation, artistic creativity is abundant. But I also observed, upon later reflection, the corruption that still haunts the country, in which style is more important than substance as seen in its politics and the Mafia. This is the shadow side of the Sun that rules Leo. This was an important perception of the collective unconscious which I bore in mind whenever I went abroad. One can read the history of a people but it is usually written by patriots who cannot see the dark side of their community. Germany is a prime example, because the destructive and cruel aspect of its Scorpionic nature was seen in the Second World War. When I recently went there to lecture, I saw that the guilt has been repressed by the older generation by not speaking of their part in the disaster. In the group of young people I taught were several women who clearly had male souls. I perceived that they had been killed during the war and chose to be reincarnated as women so as never to be called to fight again. Their interest in Kabbalah was perhaps to do with what they had done to the Jews. It may have been guilt that made them invite me or a genuine search for spiritual knowledge. One German lady in particular caught my attention. She

FIGURE 41—TOLEDO
When I was about ten years old, I saw a picture of this medieval Spanish city in an encyclopaedia. It electrified me although it was not until ten years later, when I visited it, that I realised I had been there before in another life. This city was the centre of a cultural revolution in the Middle Ages, in that individuals from the three Abrahamic faiths met on equal terms to discuss philosophy and mysticism. Here discussions took place in private homes, taverns and the royal court where Arabic and Hebrew translations of Hellenic texts were rendered into Castilian and then Latin. Toledo, at that time, was the spiritual capital of the West. (Toledo, 19th century print).

was about thirty and had no legs, either by accident or she had been born without them. While teaching a very attentive group, largely of women, I saw for a flash this girl as a German soldier blown up by a landmine, as a result of which both legs were lost. This was a shock and insight into a country that had lost its moment of greatness by seeking revenge for losing the First World War. This refined and intelligent young woman, and her generation, paid the price.

I had much to think about in my relationship with Spain which had always had a fascination as my ancestors' homeland. As I wandered around the streets of Toledo, Cordoba and Seville I was reminded of long-forgotten memories in the synagogues that were still there. Particularly in the Maria Blanca in the Jewish quarter of Toledo, ghosts of the medieval congregation still hovered around, despite the fact that the Jews had left the city five hundred years before. These individuals appeared to have chosen not to move on and were trapped in a time bubble. I was able to discern this because by now my psychic organ of perception was beginning to operate upon command and not just spontaneously. Especially when abroad, the unfamiliarity of the environment often stimulates this level of perception. As I grew older I was able to shift my consciousness, at least to the psychic level, at will.

An example of this was a visit to the battlefield of Waterloo where I managed to track down the place where Napoleon viewed the confrontation from a low hill, marked by a clump of wild trees and bushes. As I stood there on a spring day, with sunshine and a gentle wind playing across a seemingly peaceful landscape, I became aware of the distant sound of cannons, the frightened neighing of horses, war cries and shouts of wounded combatants. Close by, I heard the jingle of bridles of horses pawing the ground. I then picked up a faint impression of a group of uniformed officers. It was like a dim action replay of that terrible event in which tens of thousands died on one day. Later I saw, in a local museum, the death mask of Napoleon. It was beautiful, intelligent but quite cold and cruel. It is the best example I know of a Lucific face. He had said, after an earlier battle in which thousands were killed, 'What is that to a man like me?' I shuddered as I turned away from this possessed countenance. To have a psychic capacity is not always pleasant, as one responds to whatever subtle field-force or mental projection one encounters.

To develop a psychic ability one has to be able to make the screen of the ordinary mind blank and focus sharply upon a target. This may

be a place, person or symbol. Then one has to wait for the psyche to respond. Spontaneous images then come, or phrases or words. The art is to be able to interpret them accurately. In Kabbalah we have the Tree mandala and this contains all the archetypes needed for unravelling such symbolism.

Over time, I devised guided meditations based upon kabbalistic principles by which one could examine the current state of one's own mind or that of others. This is done by using an imaginary structure, called *The House of the Psyche*. Here the Tree of Life is transformed into a building. The basement, kitchen and utility room where gas, water and electricity are found, represent the bodily process while the front door and entrance hall symbolise the ego. An office, workshop and lounge represent the functions of thinking, action and feeling, with the garden and house-pet standing in for the vegetable and animal levels of instinct. The social area, on the first floor, is seen as the working part of the lower mind while the soul, symbolised by a bedroom or private study, is where one's most personal life is lived. At the top of the house is a sanctuary, the spiritual aspect of the psyche.

The people who inhabit this House of the Psyche are sub-personalities, that is, conscious or unconscious aspects of the mind. These are based upon sefirotic archetypes, such as Gevurah being a soldier, representing emotional discipline, or a wise old grandfather Hokhmah who inspires. A beautiful Nezahian young woman archetype tells much about one's impulses, while the efficiency of the Hodian secretary denotes the clarity of one's thought. One can discern, by this method, how the various functions of the mind relate. For example, the Binah grandmother-figure of Understanding may be blind while the butler and house-keeper, who represent the male and female side of the ego, may be lazy or over-active.

This exercise is very useful in detecting an imbalance. However,

---

FIGURE 42 (Left)—CULTURE
While painting this picture of a chapel at Harrow on the Hill, the home of one of England's famous public schools, several students who came from the British ruling caste came up to me and made interesting comments. They were clearly well informed about art and very bright. At the time I was very struck by their distinctive character, in which a conservative outlook was matched to an adventurous flair. It was this combination that had built the British Empire. Their polite speech hid a martial streak which, when provoked, was backed by a stoic endurance. Hitler and Napoleon had misjudged the English, to their cost. Even though I had not one drop of English blood, I felt very grateful to be able to write in this precise, poetic and international language. (Painting by the author).

it is only applicable for that hour or day. A psychological crisis could be represented by a fire in the bedroom. At other times the house may appear to be in better order. The Tiferet of the House is the Self which may or may not be in charge as the master or mistress of this symbol of the psyche.

Another exercise composed at this time was an imaginary pilgrimage to the Heavenly Jerusalem. This type of inner journey was practised by early Kabbalists. It is only carried out under special conditions in which one will not be disturbed, led by someone who can take participants into the higher Worlds and then bring them safely back down again. In such an ascent one leaves, in the imagination, one's home and passes through a familiar area into a forest. From here on various places, symbolising levels of the mind, are traversed. One is the town of Yesod which reveals the state of the ego. Later a sea is crossed in the ship of one's soul, during a storm, which illustrates how one handles a major crisis. On the far shore one disembarks in the Port of Paradise and climbs up the Holy Mountain while viewing Hell, Paradise and the lower part of Heaven. Here one enters the home of one's Maggid or spiritual teacher who takes one up to the Heavenly Jerusalem. There one may ask three questions about one's life in the Sanctuary of the Temple. One is then brought slowly down and back home. A compact disc was made of this and *The House of the Psyche* some years later as the recorded meditations proved very useful to people without a group in remote parts of the world.

20. Books

I began to work on *Adam and the Kabbalistic Tree* with the aim of setting out the four Worlds of Action, Formation, Creation and Emanation in terms of the body, psyche, spirit and Divine elements in a human being. I now knew enough of the metaphysics of Jacob's Ladder and the interaction of different levels of reality to make an attempt. This perception, combined with a modern understanding of physiology and psychology, enabled me to build a precise picture of how the mechanical, chemical and electronic systems related to the lower levels of the mind. It required much research and I talked at great length with physicians and psychologists as well as reading all I could. One of the sources of information were children's and school books, which gave the principles of various systems. From such generalities I moved on to detailed accounts in more advanced volumes, until I had enough information to begin writing.

Here is where my Gemini Moon came into its own. This Mercurial sign loves facts and is quick to pick them up. With Mars in Virgo, I could get straight to the essence of a mass of data and define it in simple terms. My Sun in Capricorn oversaw the whole operation, with its talent for organisation. One day I actually thanked my 'lucky stars' for being given such a birth chart. Without its particular configuration of Sun, Moon and planets I could not have made a coherent analysis and exposition of the 'Adam' project. This gave me food for thought and reinforced the notion that the moment of birth and fate are not random but carefully considered prior to incarnation.

The deeper aspects of the psyche required a different order of effort. Fortunately, having been trained in esoteric psychology and explored the mind, through meditation, contemplation and various other interior exercises, I was able to view the psyche's structure and dynamic in terms of kabbalistic metaphysics. This was quite a different approach from modern psychology which has no precise agreed model. There are the Jungian and Freudian theories and several others, each with a particular emphasis. One believes that an amorphous collective intelligence influences the mental processes, while another concludes

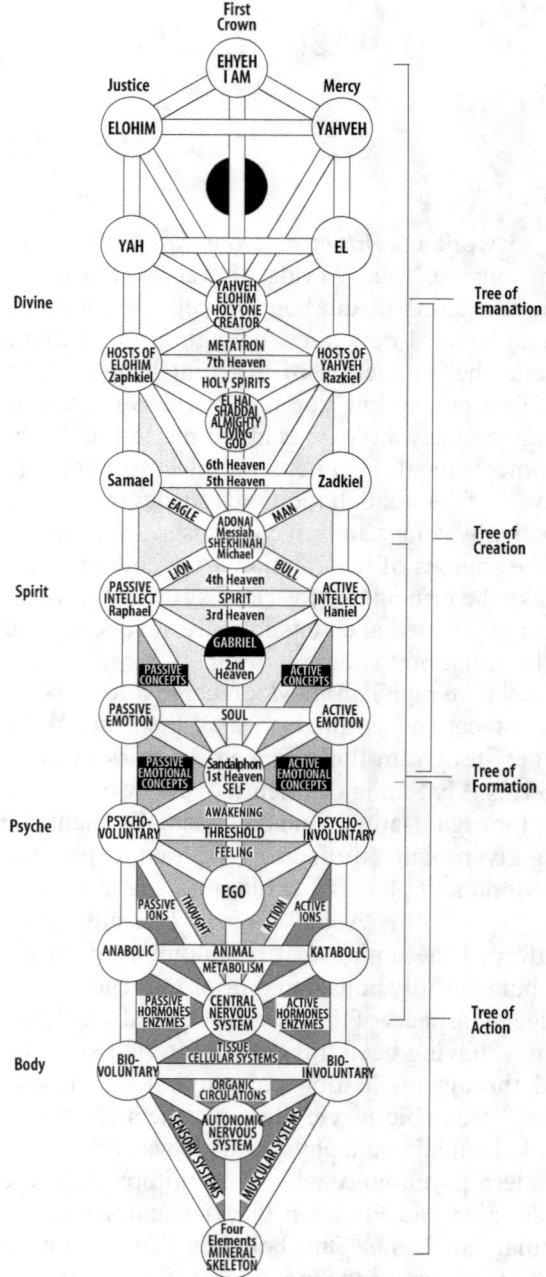

it is instinct, while yet another subscribes to social conditioning or just body chemistry.

Astrology, the ancient and medieval psychological system, is not as unscientific as most people believe. It is based upon thousands of years of observation. The astronomer Edmond Halley believed it to be just superstition. Sir Isaac Newton chastised him by saying that either Halley had a great knowledge of astrology or spoke from total ignorance. We have this situation today when the popular and corrupt form of astrology is mistaken for the genuine study. However, what is not generally known is that some serious scientists sense there is much to be learnt from this ancient art. I myself was once asked to meet a Nobel Prize winner in order to explain the principles of the subject. He required me not to mention his name as it might damage his reputation. He was fascinated with the idea of cosmic influences affecting human behaviour and saw how it could work through the principle of resonance, even as a mobile phone does from a remote signal.

Consciousness was a major factor in the Adam book as it was the key to the level of an individual. Thus someone whose focus was primarily on their body was usually a vegetable type of person. They were generally not interested in anything beyond comfort, food and sex. Those who had their conscious centre of gravity in their ego-Moon could be either in the vegetable mode or moving towards the animal stage of development. At this level the motivation is competition, in order to be the dominant male or female in the pack or whatever company they keep. Those people, centred upon the Sun or Self, could be advanced animal people or true individuals. The place of the Self, according to Kabbalah, is where the three lower Worlds meet within the psyche. Here arises the choice to be a master of the physical level, like a great sportsman or warrior, or an individuated human being. This higher level is someone who is primarily concerned with inner development. The ideal in Kabbalah is to co-ordinate and integrate all three levels so as to be useful in the evolution of humanity.

FIGURE 43 (Left)—JACOB'S LADDER
Here is the rediscovered 'extended' Tree of the four Worlds, with its central axis of a fifth 'Great' Tree, hinted at in old texts as the mode of '50 Gates'. It was my task to fill it out with ancient, medieval and modern concepts and symbolism. This was possible after studying the folk stories in the Talmud and various classic kabbalistic texts. Thus I was able to put the angels and archangels in their traditional places, together with the Seven Heavens and the Divine Realm with its Holy Names. The two lowest Trees were set out in modern terms of the body and psyche. (Chain of Being).

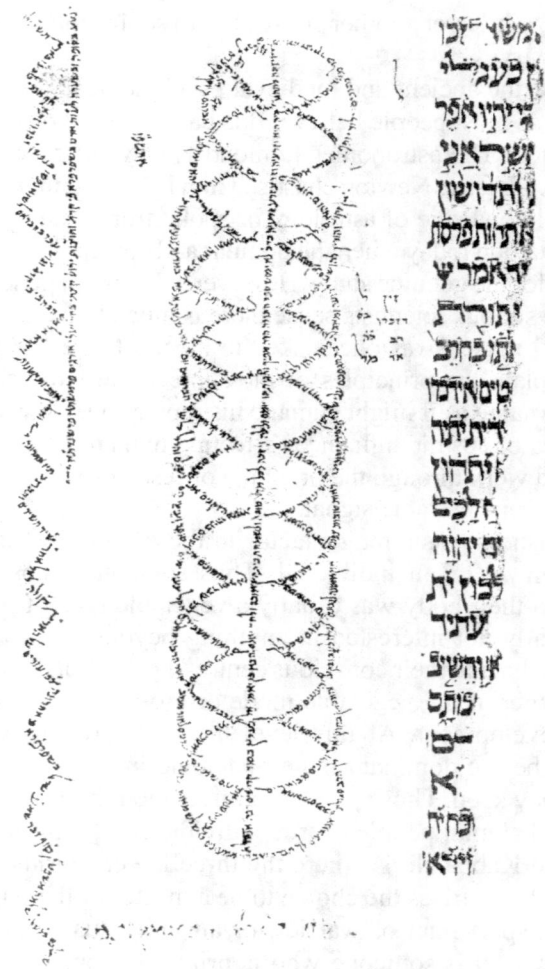

FIGURE 44—EVIDENCE
This image, made up of Hebrew verses from the Bible, comes from a 15th century manuscript from Yemen. With its eleven circles, it is clearly a version of Jacob's Ladder but without the paths. It was confirming evidence for the metaphysical model spoken of, in symbolic terms, in some kabbalistic texts. In the Zohar the interpenetrating Worlds are described in terms of the brain inside the skull, or a nut inside the shell, and so on down through the Worlds. This discovery was a great relief, as it backed the interlocked Ladder as against the generally misunderstood view that the Worlds were joined by the bottom and top of their Trees. This view did not explain how they interacted, whereas the overlaying and underlying upper and lower Trees did. (Medieval manuscript from the British Museum).

Adam and the Kabbalistic Tree set out to explain the evolution of the soul by gaining access to the transpersonal level of the spirit and making contact with the Divine at the top of Jacob's Ladder of Trees. This was a massive literary operation but the years of writing semi-philosophical fiction gave me a way of presenting concepts in everyday situations. Take, for example, the fashions in dress and music that express the collective mood of a generation. In contrast is the way of a remarkable individual who might choose a modest lifestyle in order to follow his star.

Jacob's Ladder is the kabbalistic version of the Chain of Being or interacting Worlds, well known to the ancient and medieval mystics and philosophers. In the *Zohar*, the Ladder is spoken of symbolically as one reality inside another, like a nut within its shell, which in turn is inside another nut and shell. In the extended diagram of interlocked Trees, the lower 'face' of a higher Tree overlaps the upper 'face' of the next Tree below or World down, and so on. However, this metaphysical diagram was never openly revealed in the public domain, although it was hinted at in many kabbalistic texts. The nearest reference I have seen is a document from Yemen in the late 15th century, as seen in a figure for this chapter. In this, a chain of eleven interlocked circles clearly define Jacob's Ladder but without the sefirot or paths. This meant that the original scheme of what was called the Great Tree, running down the centre, was not shown. The *Kav*, or middle column line of Divine presence that permeates Existence, makes up what is seen as the fifth 'Great Tree'. Together with the forty sefirot of the four Trees they make the Fifty Gates spoken of in some texts. The eleventh, mysterious non-sefirah, Daat or Knowledge, representing direct experience, adds the eleventh circle of the Yemeni Ladder which is composed of Biblical verses.

Jacob's Ladder was rediscovered by my Instructor and another member of our circle. The latter brought him the reproduction of a modern painting of kabbalistic Trees, set inside one another. The idea, that within each sefirah there is a little Tree and within that another and so on until there were ten, is well known but not in terms of a Ladder. The painting had several Trees telescoped inside one another, but in no obvious order. My colleagues then saw that if this image could be pulled out, like a telescope, it might make more sense. They redrew the model in terms of the four Worlds and suddenly Jacob's Ladder was there with the Great Tree on the central column. When the Kabbalah group was shown this scheme, we were stunned. It explained many of the obscure texts in kabbalistic literature where a 'Ladder of Ascent' is mentioned.

I took this 'Extended Tree' and used it as the basis for the Adam book. There were many discussions about physical and psychological terms to be used that would make the 'Ladder' intelligible to the modern reader. My job was to put the scheme together in a coherent way. When this long labour of love was finished, I sent the book off to my publisher. He was a highly educated and wise Jew, who saw straight away that *Adam* could contribute to a deeper modern understanding of the Tradition. This was in the 1970s, when many books on the esoteric were being published to meet the need of those who were interested in such matters. *Adam and the Kabbalistic Tree* was accepted, to my delight, as it meant I did not have to go through the grim routine of finding another publisher.

The *Tree of Life* had received some attention from book reviewers and had prepared the ground for *Adam*. When it came out, it got some very sympathetic support which established me as a writer on Kabbalah. From then on I had no problem with publishers, especially when my books went, over time, into fourteen different languages. Years later I learnt from one rabbi that *Adam* was a very important contribution to his development, while an eminent scholar said my books were an inspiration. Perhaps the most moving compliment was from a man who came up to me after a lecture in America with a battered copy of *Adam* in his hand. He said it had saved his sanity as it gave him something spiritual but solid when he was in danger of going mad.

An important event happened to a retired American scientist and businessman when travelling the world, seeking he knew not what. While flying over the Atlantic he came across the Jacob's Ladder diagram in the *Adam* book he had bought to read on the plane. This gave him a key to understanding things that modern science could not explain. As a Jew, it also resonated deeply in his soul. He sought me out when I was in New York. He became, in time, the organiser of the Kabbalah Society's visits to the Holy Land, Spain and several other countries where we ran courses, besides setting up a conference in the Ashmolean Museum in Oxford. My books also became part of other people's experiences. One was found on a houseboat in Kashmir, another was stolen from a Moscow hotel room during the time such literature was forbidden in Russia. In the Czech Republic, then under communist rule, *A Kabbalistic Universe* was translated and published in secret. Indeed, the publisher would have been arrested if someone sympathetic in the police station had not warned him that his house was about to be raided. In another case my book almost fell on a Mexican woman's head in a bookshop. She took this as a sign that she should read it. As a result I was invited to Mexico, where she founded one of the earliest groups of the Kabbalah Society and created a kabbalistic garden. It seemed that a long gestation was now bringing about a fruition.

21. Psychism

My mother telephoned me one Friday morning. This was unusual, as I usually rang her on Friday evening. She spoke about some money being hidden at the back of the garden in case of fire, war, or any disaster. I thought that this was very odd. This was after I had told her my news which, as my brother had observed, was usually a great deal about nothing. I had learnt to keep my personal life private because she would only complain about my lack of wife, family and a real home. On the following Monday I had a sense of something impending; but what I could not tell. At 1pm I felt a cold shiver pass through me as I listened to the radio news. Then the phone rang and I heard my father's stressed voice say, 'Come home! Your mother has just died of a heart attack'.

On the way to my parents' house, many images of her passed through my mind. She was a great woman and mother who had supported me when I wanted to be a writer, after reading one of my typescripts. She must have seen some talent, despite the books being an unsound mixture of metaphysics and idealistic love. These thoughts gave way to facing the death of someone I loved and knew well. I had seen many dead people during my time working in hospital but they were strangers. Then I had taken on the cool persona that medical staff adopted to control instinctive feelings in the presence of death. But this was going to be different.

When my father took me up to their bedroom, where her body lay, my first impression was how small it was. In life she had always been

---

FIGURE 45 (Left)—INSPIRATION
The expression 'bolt from the blue' is not just a poetic metaphor. Such moments are just like a lightning strike from the sky. I recall one such experience during the war when all was blacked out. Then a whole landscape was illuminated for a second during a thunderstorm. Similar interior phenomena occurred to me while working with Kabbalah. One example was when I came across the Hebrew word Kav *which, in Kabbalah, is the 'Line' that stretches from the top to the bottom of the central column of Jacob's Ladder. This is the axis of consciousness, that is, the vehicle by which the Divine can observe and intervene at every level of Existence.* (Illustration for an unpublished novel by the author).

bursting with energy. Now there was nothing but a shrivelled corpse with little or no resemblance to her ebullient personality. At that point, my brother and an uncle came into the room. For a moment we were silent, contemplating the reality of her abrupt departure. I then noticed a most beautiful aroma pervading the room and spoke of it, to which my uncle said he could also smell it. My brother could pick up nothing. I was surprised because the fragrance was so potent.

When they had gone, I sat in my old bedroom to meditate. I then remembered that my uncle was a natural psychic. Indeed, he had conducted a séance for my parents in which my father's dead father came and said, 'Be happy while you may'. This had greatly upset my parents and they never asked my uncle to demonstrate his psychic ability again. In fact, later he gave up the practice, as some lost soul tried to take possession of his body. My aunt had banished this German speaking *Dibbuk*, a kabbalistic term for such souls in limbo, by putting her arms around my uncle and screaming at the spirit to depart. My uncle, however, clearly still retained his psychic faculty.

While I was recalling this incident I heard my mother's voice, quite distinctly, say, 'All I want is that you should marry a nice Jewish girl'. To which I automatically replied, 'Stop nagging me'. Then came a surprisingly mundane request from her. Would I put a certain chair in the lounge back in its proper place and sweep the front path of leaves, so that all would be in order for the funeral? I knew my Cancerian mother was extremely house-proud but this was extraordinary. I said I would carry out her orders. I put the chair back into its place and swept the path. My uncle then told me, just before the funeral, that my mother had spoken to him and wanted a certain chair put back in position and the front path swept of leaves, as she did not want the family to think she was a slapdash housewife. I replied I had already carried out her order. There is no doubt the dead have the ability to communicate and this was a conclusive proof to me.

This episode also revealed that people do not change much after

---

FIGURE 46 (Left)—SYMBOLISM
A great hero set on a high pedestal is an archetypal symbol. Over the years I came to understand the power of such classic images. With the aid of the Tree of Life diagram many dreams, visions and expressions of the practical, psychological and spiritual realms could be interpreted. Here Admiral Lord Nelson's column could be replaced by a figure of the Buddha, who could be positioned at the Crown of the Tree which represents the Divine Man. Likewise, the dream about a monster could represent the shadow side of Yesod, the ego, while the halo of a great sage could symbolise the light of Tiferet. (Drawing by the author).

death. Indeed, it appeared to take the deceased a while to realise she was actually dead. Immediately after the funeral, when the house was full of people taking refreshments, I went into a back room to be alone and reflect upon what was going on while the family and friends grieved and consoled each other. In that moment of intense solitude I felt the strong presence of my mother. I said, to test out that it was not just my imagination, that she should make her presence known to me in some manifest way. After a few moments, I suddenly began to go very cold. I then observed energy being drawn from my body, as a faint figure started to emerge before my eyes. I became alarmed and said, 'Enough'. The process stopped and faded as the freezing sensation receded. I learned, later in my studies, that she had drawn upon my vital field-force in order to become visible. This is possible within three days of death. Her etheric body, that held the physical body and psyche together, had not yet dissolved and could therefore draw upon my etheric vehicle.

From that time on I knew I had a psychic faculty. Whether it was a latent talent or developed by the interior work I had done, I did not know. What I had learnt, in that moment, was how to switch on to a more subtle frequency of my psyche and perceive a realm not accessible to the senses. This was borne out when I once visited Stonehenge. Here I saw the figure of a Druid priest in full regalia standing just outside the circle when I tuned in to the charged atmosphere of the area. A similar event occurred in Turkey when I was in the market area of the ancient ruined city of Ephesus. As I switched levels I saw all the buildings as they once were, filled with people, animals and stalls. I could also hear all the sounds of the period and even detect the smells. I concluded, on reflection, that I had picked up on a psychic hologram left by tens of thousands of market days. This phenomenon was like an electronic recording but within a subtle field-force that permeates places where either dramatic events have occurred or, like ancient Ephesus, where the site is saturated with the residue of centuries of human activity.

The metaphysics of psychic phenomena are quite reasonable, if one accepts that there is more to the physical world than the four states of matter. Indeed, science tells us that beyond the subatomic, there is no substance. We are, in reality, but a 'standing wave'. By this is meant that our bodies are but an ever-changing pattern of form that alters every moment, giving rise to the phenomenon of ageing. Again, science states that if all the atoms that make up our body were to be compressed together, it would occupy less space than a full stop.

Our physicality is an illusion. What holds the body together is a fine and complex field-force which is dispersed at death. The psyche is composed of an even more subtle field-force which retains its essential nature even after the body dies, as I witnessed by my mother's distinct identity. The worldwide experience of ghosts and apparitions confirms this notion. Indeed the departed appear to be very much alive but in another dimension, which Kabbalah divides into different Worlds containing the levels of Hell, Paradise and Heaven.

My mother's death had drawn my attention to a psychic faculty which was to become very useful. At first, I applied it to the practice of astrology. While doing a birth chart, with the person in front of me, I could discern another order of insight. While this could be put down to accumulated experience, my insights opened up a different dimension. In one case, as I was explaining the astrological pattern of a man's fate, I became aware of the presence of a figure of a warrior in full armour. The client was of Iranian origin and the figure behind him was clearly an ancient Persian. This apparition, I realised, was the man's guide who spoke to me in words I could not hear but clearly understood. I passed on to the client what I was being told because the guide, it seemed, found it difficult to communicate with his charge. What I transmitted shook the man. This incident changed his life. He gave up his lucrative profession of accountancy and became, in time, an eminent teacher of the Zoroastrian tradition. He is now a major spiritual and political leader among the Parsees, restating in the face of modernism what their tradition stands for.

Another example was a telephone call from a young man, who said he was the Maitreya. This is the equivalent of the Messiah. I had been warned about him calling upon me and was most curious to see someone who claimed to be such an illustrious being. As I had worked in a mental hospital, I was used to people with such delusions and so I said, 'Come and have tea'. The man appeared to be in his early twenties, dressed in a tweed jacket and grey flannel trousers and wearing an old school tie. He was the perfect young English gentleman, except he had no shoes or socks on. It was clear he was deluded, in a genteel way, and quite harmless. However, what caught my inner eye as we sat and talked were the various misty figures standing around him. One was a woman weeping and a bearded man shaking his head. There were also three hooded figures on his left, dressed in blue woollen cloaks but with no faces.

I asked the boy who these apparitions were? He did not know they were there, until I began to describe them in detail. The woman was recognisably his mother. I surmised that she might be what is called an 'astral projection'. This phenomenon is not unknown between closely related people. She may have been deeply worried about him and hovered, psychically, over him. The other figure, he told me, must be his spiritual teacher. Obviously the teacher was concerned about the young man's state of mind. I realised then that I had been given the task to 'earth' the boy and dispel his delusion. I began by asking him the question how he supported himself financially. He had money in the bank, he said. 'And when it runs out?' I asked. He replied he did not know. 'And then what?' I asked. 'I do not know', he muttered. I then asked him who were the three hooded figures with no faces? He shook his head and asked me who I thought they might be. The words 'Beware of wolves in sheep's clothing' came out of my mouth quite spontaneously. This pricked the mental bubble he was in and he came suddenly to himself. He left me in a very sober state. I learnt later that he had been classified as a mild psychotic with delusions of grandeur. Because he was extremely well read in the Hindu spiritual classics, he had set out to impress his fellow students that he was very special. Unfortunately he had got caught up in living out his fantasy of being the Maitreya. When he phoned me some weeks later he sounded more sane but still a loner.

This psychic faculty, however, could be a burden. I would sometimes wake up at night with someone's image or name in a vivid dream. Later I would discover the person had been in trouble and had turned to me as their teacher or father figure for support. Some even came later, physically, to talk about their problem. In the daytime I would often know who was about to telephone me. Initially I was troubled by this phenomenon but eventually I became philosophical about it as it seemed to be part of the job.

22. Poetry

Like many young people I wrote poems. The first ones were inevitably about love. They were usually about the games played by both parties upon first acquaintance and the processes of courtship, including the delicious madness of falling in love and the creation of delightful fantasies. Then came the struggle as to who would be dominant in a relationship. Such an issue usually manifested in a quarrel over a trifle. Later came poems about the dawning of reality as regards marriage that involved family, friends and the everyday world that usually marred the romance and led to a parting.

However, as one of my teachers observed, such vivid love poems are usually written by people less than twenty-two years old who, as yet, have no idea how difficult real relationships are, let alone marriage. It is therefore no great surprise that I burned all these romantic verses along with my early novels, after the end of an intense love affair with a goddess who wanted a beautiful home, children and a comfortable life. Later she got what she desired, but at a price.

Having been half-cured of my naïvety in still believing that there was someone in the future for me, I turned to metaphysical verse. This was stimulated by the esoteric ideas of the School and the Society. At first they were short and sparse poems which came more from the head than the heart. The first is from a personal viewpoint:

EGO
What impostor binds me closer
To the myth of my persona
What fool seeks to steal time away
And delay, my perceiving and receiving
One moment of Peace, and release
From the ego's delusion
So I might have an illumination

The second is from a transpersonal angle:

TIME

The mayfly lives its brief hour
The willow tree its yearly flower
A nation has its century
Humanity moments of Eternity
Life on Earth will be gone
When the Sun ceases to shine
While the Milky Way will fade
When the Universe comes to an end
Only the Absolute will remain
When all else is gone

I then decided to bring in a more emotional factor. This would be enhanced by graphic and evocative images. Death is one of the most emotive themes, after love, and so I decided to put together a small book with appropriate illustrations to complement the verse. I had made several drawings of old tombs and so I began to search out a sequence of edifices that would include ecclesiastical buildings which asked questions about death but also offered a solution in esoteric terms so that the poems would not be a morbid exposition.

Having written the poems to match the pictures, I drew the lettering in the style of that inscribed on old tombs, to give a sense of those who had long passed away. Some of the graves and buildings are based upon actual sites while others come from the imagination. Here will be seen medieval brasses, the carving of John Donne, the poet, wrapped in his shroud, and a doorway from Highgate's famous cemetery together with the ascending pillar of Westminster Abbey's Chapter House, a carving of the Resurrection and a sundial on the side of a country church. All tell, I hope, the story of everyone's fear and hope in life after death.

The little book was never published and so I include it here as an important part of my development.

Time's Lock is Broken

A Meditation Upon the Mystery of Death and Rebirth

Warren Kenton

Does time
Twist a spindle
Spread out a mantle
Of skeins that bind
Hold the entwined
In locks of lives

Is this juncture
Common feature
Of our nature
Slim spectrum
Of other dimensions
Or dim apparition
Of further illusions

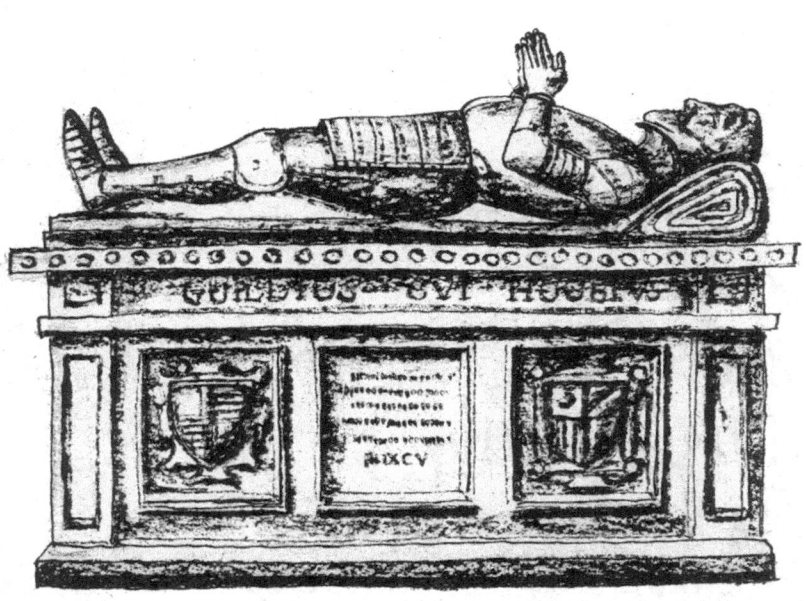

King
His throne
Over ruled
Majesty and precedence
Dissolved
Takes his turn
To don the crown
Marks his time
Then sets it down

Time's Lock is Broken

Lord
His rank
Resolved in dying
House and crest
Cease their meaning
Wig and worship
Wilt away
At the ending
Of the roundelay

Merchant
Family pivot
Toiling balance
Of trading equilibrium
Leaves at the graveside
For the living to reclaim
Profits of fortune
Destined to return

Peasant
Serves each season
Labours all his day
With no question
Sleeps through his time
Plods the familiar way
Towards the waiting tomb

What means
This shedding
Of lives
Generation
Of leaves
Continuum
Life spanned
Momentum
Discharged at death
Returned to earth

Where
Go
I
Enshrouded individual
Enclouded unsubstantial
Shade of soul
Bound between
Heaven and Hell

Where
Leads Hades gate
Does the doorway
Seal finality
Cul-de-sac
Of Eternity

Does Time
Only turn
The crisp sepulchre
Into weathered stone
Is reclaiment Nature
Mere cover
To rain blurred sculpture

Does memory
With the rememberer die
Or only underlie
Last season's
Fallen leaves

What dream ecstasy
Nightmare phantasy
Moves behind the
lowered lids
What unfurling of weaves
Unwinding of lives
Comes in the severing
Of the threads

Books
Silent speakers
Words
Mute makers
Of inward question
Open our eyes
With interpretation
Unstop our ears
In revelation

Teachers
Keepers of Keys
Masters
Guiders of Ways
Give us now
Instruction
That we may know
Your Freedom

Angels
Watchers of the night
Gods
Movers of men's fortune
Infuse in our thought
Direction
Help in our heart
With preparation

Allay the dreads
Stories of terrible deeds
Tales of horrible imagery
Invented by man's imaginary
Knowledge of turning time

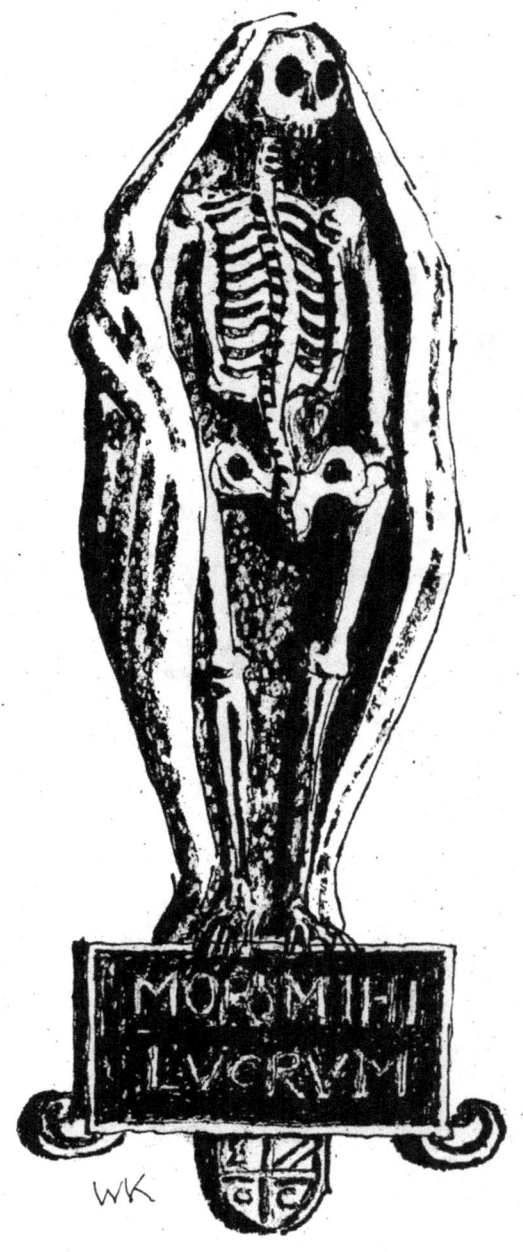

Dissolve
Dreams of false paradises
Dispel
Illusions of sweet mirages
Gardens of delight
Conjured by the mind
Offered in deceit
Blind unto the blind

Reveal
How long
Must the sleepers
Slumber
Is it endless
Or a season's
To and fro
Is it boundless
Or a moment's
Here and now

Explain
The confluence of Time
How
In being born
We forget
What we have known
Where
In being gone
We return
 To what will come

Speak
Speak
For mortal mind
To comprehend
Speak
Speak
For mortal heart
To understand

Knock
It shall open
Gate
Straight
To the heart
Of Heaven

The Way
Is approached
Entered upon
Centered upon
The door
Is breached

Become Still

Awaken

The Needle's Eye
Is pierced
The Soul
Is upward thrust

Up
Up
Leaping
The vaults of Heaven
Reaching towards
The place of Haven
Concentric Creation
Ordered expansion
Returning involution
Completion
Perfection

Time's lock
Is broken

The Dead
Are reborn
Bursting the body's tomb
Breaking Nature's dream
On being inward drawn

Soul
Its seed
In earth sown
Begins to grow
Fructify and bloom
Again.

23. Resistance

The next book, *The Way of Kabbalah*, was intended to bring the reader in touch with the Biblical origins of the Tradition. It began with Abraham's initiation by Melchizedek who, Jewish legend says, was a manifestation of Enoch, the first self-realised human being. The history then went on to explain that there was an inner and outer aspect of Judaism. For example, the seven-branched candlestick in the Tabernacle of Moses and the Temple of Solomon was not just a decoration but a symbol of the Tree of Life and the four Worlds. The book then set out, as in all my works, the basic metaphysics of Kabbalah, so that the reader had a theoretical framework of what was to follow.

Then came an outline of Creation, as seen by Kabbalah, and a brief account of the body and psyche according to ancient, medieval and modern perceptions. The early part of the Old Testament was then examined, from an esoteric viewpoint, in order to reveal that characters symbolised principles. For example, Jacob and Esau represent the higher and lower elements of human nature. This led into the esoteric aspects of the Old Testament in which the stories illustrate the hidden Way buried in the text, when seen from a kabbalistic perspective.

From here on, group and individual work was examined through the three working methods of literal, allegorical and metaphysical approaches, also known as the Ways of Action, Devotion and Contemplation. The importance of will, will-lessness, wilfulness and willingness was then presented, as well as methods by which to access the lesser and greater states of consciousness. Then came a study of the soul and its function within the psyche. The act of *Kavanah*, or conscious attention, in the practices was explained with regard to everyday life, prayer and deep thought. The book concluded with an account of an ascent of Jacob's Ladder up to the seven Heavens, as defined by the Tree diagram, in traditional terms and a modern interpretation.

The material used for this book came from various sources. Much of it was from the kabbalistic classics but re-worded in contemporary

FIGURE 47—INSTITUTIONS
Most religions begin as schools of the soul. Over time, when the founders have gone, the organisation is often taken over by people more interested in power and position than the Teaching. They do this by adding to the Master's sayings regulations that must be obeyed, sometimes on pain of death or, worse, damnation. All other traditions are considered false and mystics are usually regarded as heretics while senior clergy are turned into saints. Here the Pope wears the Crown of the three higher Worlds and is dressed in the robes of wealth and prestige. (Drawing of a Pope's tomb by the author).

language. This was the result of talking to scholars, rabbis and Kabbalists. However, my encounters with Jewish orthodoxy in Europe, the USA and Israel were not always easy. At one meeting, a Hasidic rabbi asked me why I was not wearing a hat. I replied that I was wearing a Keter, or Crown, meaning that each one of us is a living Tree. He was not amused by this response but could not argue with it, because I said that, according to the Talmud or rabbinic opinion, the wearing of a head-cover is not a law but a custom. Then there was the confrontation with a very zealous American rabbi, who came to tea at my flat to convert me but refused to drink or eat anything I offered. This was discourteous by any standards. He asked me whether I fulfilled the 613 commandments. These were rules that certain rabbis had extracted from the Biblical texts. I said, before I answered, 'How many of these laws do you fulfil?' He became flustered and replied, not as many as he would like. I responded by saying that he, therefore, had no right to question me. I then asked him, which did he worship, God or the Tradition? He was silent when I suggested that he had made an idol of the latter. He was very thoughtful but did not come back with a counter-argument, which was impressive. Or perhaps he thought I was a hopeless case. He left almost immediately.

My karma for this incident came in a severe review of *The Way of Kabbalah* by an eminent British rabbi in a Jewish journal. He tore my work to shreds, picking on details, such as how to transliterate Hebrew words into English. His view was that my book was 'New Age', then in fashion, and had little or nothing to do with the Jewish Tradition. I wrote back to him, via the editor of the journal, that he should look at the evolution of Kabbalah. I pointed out that, for example, astrology was used in the classic *Book of Formation* and that Ibn Gabirol's Neo-Platonic view had been incorporated into the Tradition, as had been many other gentile esoteric ideas. These were seen as alien by some medieval rabbis. I also observed that when any innovation was introduced there was always initial resistance. When the great Jewish philosopher Maimonides published his philosophical *Guide to the Perplexed* it had been burnt, and yet now his ideas were included in the orthodox prayer book. The editor declined to publish my letter and I received no response from the rabbi.

However, a year or so later, it is interesting to note that the British rabbi was severely criticised by the ultra-orthodox rabbinate because he stated that the Five Books of Moses were not written by God but by people inspired by the Divine. Such was the fierce debate over

his view that the synagogue he led split off from the mainstream and started a new line within the British Jewish community. I experienced a great pleasure when I was invited to give a lecture at the rabbinic college where he taught. He had told the students, before the event, that he strongly disapproved of my books. Later I was told, by one student, that several of them had gone out and bought them. They were amazed by my explanation of how the Menorah, the seven-branched candlestick, was the symbolic origin of the Tree of Life diagram with its ten nodal points, twenty-two decorations, three columns and levels of the four Worlds. This they had never seen as my critic, while a brilliant scholar, was not a Kabbalist. He went fastidiously by the book, that is, a second or third-hand view of someone else's direct cognition.

Organised religion, in any form, was to be a recurring problem. There was no way of convincing people who 'believed' or only trusted an 'authority'. This word means, 'by what is written'. In reality the only true source of Kabbalah is through personal experience and insight, but this is considered too subjective by the academics who cannot tell the difference between a quote, a learned opinion and a genuine vision. Many scholars mix levels, confusing speculation with superstition, delusion and vision. This problem was demonstrated in a conversation with a famous Israeli academic who said, in a humorous moment, that scholars made a good living from lunatics like me. I retorted, in a similar sharp humour, that scholars were like sports writers; they knew all the angles of a game but had never been on the field. He was very annoyed at this comment as it was his Achilles' Heel. I sent him one of my new books later but he never replied, not even out of courtesy. This was sad. I had invited him to our group, to experience the modern version of the Living Tradition, but he declined as he said this would spoil his objectivity. This revealed just how

---

FIGURE 48 (Left)—REVELATION
A revelation does not have to be on the scale of Moses on Mount Sinai. It can be just a moment. One man I knew saw all of Existence, for ten silent seconds, in a tavern where he saw the Wheel of Life and Death. Others may experience such events on a smaller scale but in a steady stream of flashes over a week, while yet others may receive such an illumination in a dream. In the case of Moses it was almost overwhelming. Such a revelation is of quite a different order to those of reflection. It can change the course of history. In this figure the Children of Israel, who symbolise the habit-ridden body and mind, are about to begin the journey of development to the Land of the Spirit after they receive Moses' awesome revelation. (Print from Rev.T. Bankes's Bible, 19th century).

subjective he was.

To me, being a Jew means to be conscious of the Holy One as often as one can and marvel at Creation and the workings of Providence. The Ten Commandments cover all the rules of correct conduct, while Kabbalah clearly is a way of Life. This is different from general Jewish culture, in that most people have no idea what lies behind their customs. The Passover, for example, is not just a celebration about the historic event of leaving the slavery of Egypt and crossing the Desert to the Holy Land. It is symbolic of one's personal inner evolution from being subject to instinct and freeing oneself from psychological conditioning in order to attain access to the spiritual and Divine realms. This theme and process was discussed in detail in the book *Kabbalah and Exodus*. I hoped that perhaps some rabbis might take up some of its psychological and esoteric ideas. Years later this began to happen as one or two rabbis, who were open to innovation, began to incorporate kabbalistic concepts into their teaching and even their sermons.

It is interesting to note, in hindsight, that I knew unconsciously what had to be done. Anyone who has written anything truly meaningful will have experienced the strong flow of inspiration that comes through the ordinary mind and hand onto the paper. At this point in my life I began to remember the conversation with the three 'Beings' prior to my birth, which I had almost forgotten. This, I realised now, was necessary in order to learn how to live on Earth and be familiar with the current culture, so as to be able to communicate. As I did my research into the medieval and ancient texts, now in English, there were many things I did not understand because the references were peculiar to a remote time and place, such as the ways of a camel. It was only when I came across a passage that spoke of universals, or direct experience, that things made sense. No doubt some scholars in the distant future might have the same difficulty with my books when they read about 'pop stars'. This led me to reflect upon what I might have written in the past and whether it would be possible to recognise such texts.

I did have a strange feeling when I came across a particular book which I suspect I might have written in a previous incarnation. In this case, the author's character was very similar to mine. However, what he wrote about was very embarrassing because, if it was me, I clearly did not know the subject as well as I do now. He had, for example, a very scholarly understanding of astrology but he lacked insight based upon personal observation. It was like coming across a very old diary, with its youthful conclusions, based upon theory rather than practice. If it was me I had now some eight hundred years of experience behind me and knew a little more about the subject. As an experiment I followed the trail of this particular medieval Kabbalist between two English towns I knew he had visited. As I walked through the relatively unchanged sections of the terrain, there were places and names that were strangely familiar. I therefore concluded I might, I repeat, I might, have been this person. In one place, as I stood looking at the site of the old medieval Jewry, I knew I had been there before, but in which century I could not be sure. What I did know was that we had indeed trodden a very similar path.

24. Parallels

Since becoming directly involved in esoteric work some fifty years ago, I have made a point of studying other schools of the soul. Contacts were made providentially, by encountering individuals, or formally by being invited by people who had read my books. I began to see that this two-way operation was part of a Divine scheme to get the world's esoteric community together and work as a unit, in the light of the Global Village emerging since the end of the Second World War.

As I became acquainted with various traditions I observed that each had what might be classified as preparatory schools. These were a kind of spiritual kindergarten in which an outline of their version of the Teaching was studied and simple exercises were done. As such, these sometimes public operations were vital so that the person on the street of everyday life had access to the Teaching. Some people, perhaps, had heard or read about Sufism, Buddhism or Zen but never came across individuals who actually practised this or that discipline. Times had changed. Many oriental schools were now to be found in the West. Two examples were the Tibetan monastery in Scotland and the Zen groups in the United States.

The second level of the schools was for those who were committed, to a degree, but not yet on the Path. Such people can attend a school for years but not really get involved. They will go on courses, even joining specific classes but, when it comes to it, they put their personal interests first. An example of this is the person who practises yoga for health and beauty reasons. Then there are those who attend initially with a zealous passion but leave when they do not get to be enlightened within a month. These people usually go off to find another school where the same pattern occurs. For example, a lady I met in New York said, upon meeting me again, 'What are you into now, having studied Kabbalah?' One school of the soul defines such people as spiritual tramps who climb a little way up the Ladder and then decide to try another tradition when the 'Work' becomes too demanding. This becomes a pattern.

The third level, I noted, were those who had chosen a specific way of working on their souls but were primarily concerned with psychology or wished to solve some personal problem. Nothing wrong with this, but they were not interested in the transpersonal realms of the spirit or the Divine. A school that contains all levels is very rare. It is either the result of decades of work or is inspired by a genuine mystical leader. One of the difficulties here is that a school may appear to be led by a spiritual master who may be no more than a brilliant charlatan. I have come across several of these false teachers over the years. An example of this was the man who had read all the books on the Occult and impressed his largely gullible followers with obscure ideas and elaborate ceremonies in which he was the focus of attention. He required absolute obedience from every student so that they might benefit from his being the agent by which they might enter the higher Worlds. The signal that all was not well was that he demanded financial support, as he could not hold down a regular job.

Another instance was the Indian businessman who entranced his Western followers with his knowledge of the Vedic tradition. He seduced the prettiest woman in his congregation and got her husband to give him a portion of their income. When I met him he offered to initiate me, but I declined. In both of these cases their careers, as gurus, came to an abrupt end. In the case of the magician, he killed someone in a street accident because he was not looking where he was going. This was a literal metaphor. The Hindu was eventually found by the husband in bed with the wife, which totally destroyed his credibility. The followers of both were left in a terrible limbo, some never to trust any spiritual teacher again.

A contrast was the Native American medicine man I met in Canada. He was dressed up in blue jeans and lived with his family in a motor caravan on a Red Indian reservation. When shown the Tree of Life diagram he smiled in recognition and said, 'Ours is in a circular form'. A similar encounter occurred in Japan where I was shown the sacred object seen in the illustrated figure in this chapter. In a long conversation with a Shinto scholar we found many similarities in our metaphysics and even in some words like *Rishi* and *Roshi* which mean, in Japanese and Hebrew, the head of a school. There is some historic evidence of Jewish traders in Japan. The Japanese are masters of refining others' ideas, as they did with Buddhism and Western technology.

Over the years I visited various Jewish schools in Britain, the United States and Israel. These varied from the conventional modes of ritual, prayer and learned debate to the New Age mixture of Kabbalah

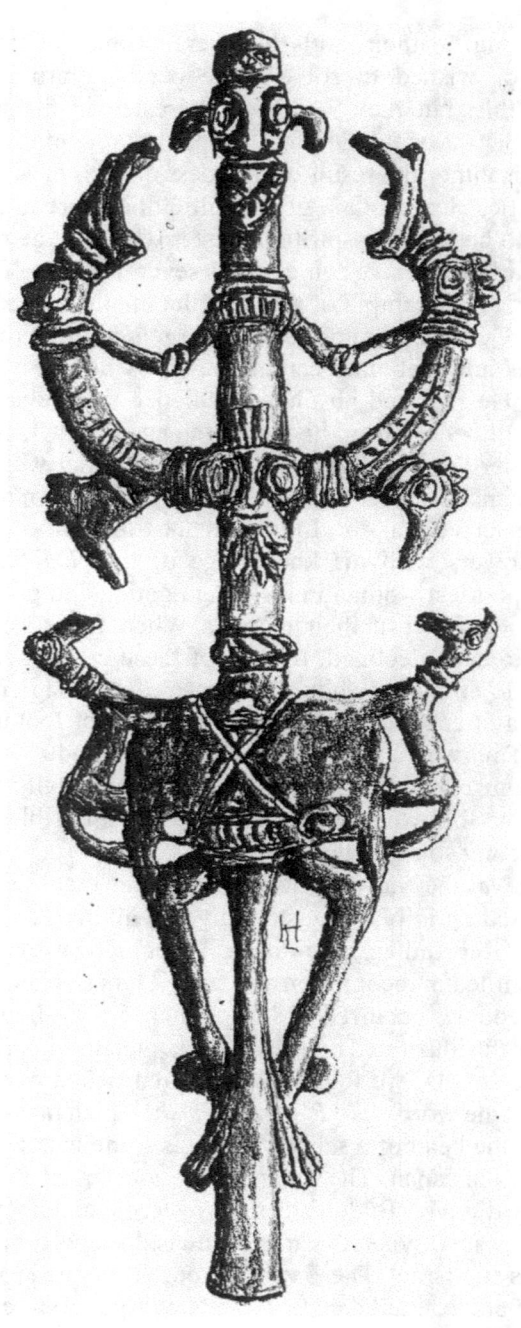

and whatever 'ism' was then in fashion. When in New York, I went to see the 'Rebbe', the leader of an Hassidic line. He was a university-educated man who had to take on the rôle of leader via marriage as the original bloodline of men had died out. Many of his followers believed he was the current Messiah. While observing him during an afternoon session of prayer, I saw a highly developed soul in a very difficult rôle of preserving a spiritual tradition which had been brought over from Europe. His and the other men's mode of dress and manner belonged to 18th century Poland. This meant that he could not change anything about the old form for it had become too rigid over time. He was doing his best but I perceived a deep weariness in him, as his devotees projected upon him the rôle of messianic leader. His only way out was to die and, even then, people went to his tomb to pray for his intercession.

Schools die, like people, when their work is done. There are the shells of many once-important esoteric organisations littering the centuries. In one case I encountered the image of the long-dead founder on the walls of a decaying building. This structure had once had thousands of students but now it had only a few devotees. Its time had come and gone. Another example was a Masonic Lodge. It was beautiful in its symbolic layout, banners and symbols, but there were no young people present at the session I attended, possibly because it had become a kind of esoteric senior citizens' social club. There is nothing wrong with this, as personal relationships within such a mutual support group are vital, but without a real 'Master' Mason the beautiful ceremonies were empty of any inner content. I gather now that there are those who seek to revive the tradition with an input of kabbalistic knowledge cast in Masonic terms.

Several schools I came across did have that inner light. One was a Sufi group that would chant the Name of God, conscious of Whom they were speaking. This generated a most powerful atmosphere in which one felt the Holy Presence. The same occurred when I witnessed

---

FIGURE 49 (Left)—ZOROASTRIANISM
This is the ancient Iranian version of the Tree. As can be seen, the basic metaphysics of Existence are the same in any genuine tradition. Here the central column and the side pillars are clearly defined in the symmetrical arms; so, too, are the levels. In this case the symbols of various creatures represent higher Worlds according to the Persian culture. Among the North American Indians, the totem pole with its carved figures, wings and eagle's head symbolises their version of Jacob's Ladder. Unfortunately such knowledge is hidden beneath the surface of religious superstition. (Zoroastrian sacred object, drawing by author).

a Shinto ceremony. While walking back through the precincts of the temple, I noticed a monk observing our kabbalistic party very closely as we were seemingly, by our demeanour, not just ordinary tourists. I caught his eye and he nodded in a silent fraternal greeting that crossed the cultural barrier. A similar event happened in Israel. I was talking with an old Moroccan Kabbalist who could not believe that someone in Western dress could know anything about Kabbalah. He opened his eyes wide when I made some observation about his son's psychological disposition. He said that I must be a Kabbalist, if I could so accurately discern the nature of the soul of someone I had just met. According to the *Zohar*, which he avidly studied, the reading of faces was a kabbalistic art. Suddenly I was accepted as a colleague. He then confided to me that he could not understand much of the *Zohar*'s peculiar Aramaic but he loved to chant the text. He was a prime example of the Way of Devotion.

One of the very old schools I visited in Jerusalem was the Bet El. This was famous for its tolerance. There is a traditional joke, 'Where two Jews are debating there will be three opinions'. At the Bet El people from different sects, who normally avoided each other, could meet. The spirit of openness was still there, as I saw secular Jews studying alongside orthodox scholars. I had a similar feeling of openness when visiting St. Catherine's Greek Orthodox monastery at the foot of Mount Sinai. This community had been there for over a millennium. While talking with the head monk, another came up and saw my book *Kabbalah and Exodus*, which I had just given to the library, on his desk. As the junior monk stretched out his hand to take a look at it, his senior gently whisked it out of reach. It was a touching action that revealed that discipline could be applied with humour and love. This is the hallmark of a living school of the soul.

While in the Middle East I also encountered the Druze, a small

---

FIGURE 50 (Left)—SHINTOISM
In remote Japan, this version of the Tree of Life represents the three pillars and the four levels of Existence. The decorations mark out the three central sefirot, plus that of Daat. Sometimes a dark mirror is part of the design to represent the veil before the Divine, symbolised here by the top plate. Although Shinto ceremonies relate to the Earth and the Sky gods, this object demonstrates that there is an esoteric aspect to the Tradition. This I discovered in conversation with an eminent Shinto scholar who instantly recognised the Tree and Ladder scrolls I showed him. It was also interesting to note that the head of a Japanese school of the soul is called a Rishi. *This is phonetically very close to the Jewish title of a Master.* (Drawing by author).

independent sect. They had things in common with Kabbalah, in that they shared certain esoteric ideas. I believe that they are one of the few ancient schools that was not swamped by Christianity and Islam. There were many such groups in the area in the Roman period, ranging from the Gnostics who really 'knew the Field', as some call direct mystical experience, to the Neo-Platonists, the last school of the soul of the classical epoch. This Platonic line had a profound influence upon early Christianity and, later, medieval Kabbalah. Today it is not so much philosophy as science that is being absorbed by esoteric schools. Even the Dalai Lama recognises this fact. The same is true for Kabbalah.

These journeys and meetings enriched my understanding of the way the Teaching is matched to different cultures and times. I perceived how my experience might be useful to a kabbalistic line that had become obscured by the accretion of centuries. An incident illustrates the point. Once, while in Jerusalem, I was invited to see a key rabbi. During a very polite conversation I saw three faint figures, in rabbinic garb, shaking their heads, standing behind this great scholar. I asked him who they were. He was unaware of their presence. He then asked me to tell him why they were present at our meeting. I communicated their words, 'You are not fulfilling your mission'. The rabbi lowered his head and said, 'They are right'. He then admitted he had become too concerned with his books and not people. This was an extraordinarily honest admission, as he found community politics very difficult. Only a great rabbi could exhibit such modesty and integrity.

25. *Cosmos*

Ever since I was a boy I have been fascinated by telescopes and microscopes. The reason is that they can see beyond what the naked eye can. This stems from a great desire in me to know more about the Universe. My first efforts were to improve the performance of a pair of old opera glasses, by taking them apart and putting the lenses in a tube of cardboard with other lenses I had collected. Needless to say, such combinations worked not by any calculation by but luck. My first sight of the mountains of the Moon was an early cosmic experience. The same was true of my first microscope which opened up a world of minute animals whom I could observe without them being aware of me. I thought, in my boyish way, that this must be how God sees us while we are unaware of being watched. I realised later that this was close to the truth.

When I became an adult, at least in physical form, I built a telescope, out of lenses and a prism from a broken camera, which could magnify up to 120 times. This enabled me to see the slow but steady Saturn. This was a very powerful experience because it is my ruling planet and revealed much about my Capricornian nature. The feeling of raw power, when pointed at Mars and Jupiter, was likewise awesome but each in quite a different way. These observations made astrology real as the planetary symbols of a birth chart came to life. From then on I could pick up the resonance of these angelic beings when looking up the positions of the planets in an ephemeris. To experience directly how each of these celestial bodies influences the psyche was a revelation. For example, the heaviness of life when Saturn is in an unfavourable position is quite discernible, if one is sensitive to cosmic weather. This must have been how the astrologers of old plotted the effect of each planet in each zodiacal sign and mundane House over many centuries. Most people do not realise that a human being is the finest scientific instrument on Earth.

In relation to this concept I built a 'psychic' telescope. This was part of my exploration of magic. It was made up of an antique silver salt-cellar with a silver coin at the bottom. When held it looked like a 'fairy'

FIGURE 51—TELESCOPES
These instruments were a practical manifestation of my desire to see beyond the eye's normal capacity. There is a great difference between reading about astronomy and having a direct experience of space and the celestial bodies through a telescope. In a recent trip to the United States I was able to visit the Lowell observatory in Arizona, where Pluto was first seen. With Lowell's high altitude and usually clear skies I saw Mars and Saturn, through its huge telescope, with awesome clarity. Before going to the observatory that night, cloud covered the sky and I feared we would miss the opportunity of a lifetime. I put in a petition to Heaven. Just before we arrived the sky suddenly cleared, much to the surprise of the scientists present. Coincidence? (Galileo, drawing by author).

monocular. The theory it was based upon was that such a symbolic object might work. Silver is the metal of the Moon and imagination. Like a 'seer' with a crystal ball, the viewer is actually the instrument. Those devices, however, help to focus attention on the target. The psychic faculty of the mind, not being distracted by anything outside, can then open up the interior eye and produce a sight, sound or image, perhaps for a moment, that represents what is being aimed at. Later I learnt that one does not need such a physical device. It is possible to pick up on an individual, for example, by focusing intently upon their name. Then the psyche will produce an image in a literal but more often in a symbolic form. The art is to interpret what is seen.

These experiments led to the examination of clairaudience and clairvoyance, in which it is possible to perceive events at a distance. This technique is known to shamans and sorcerers worldwide. In the *Bhagavad Gita* a seer describes a far-away battle and reports the conversation between Arjuna and Krishna in great detail. In the Bible, the prophet Elijah is said to have had this ability, in that he knew what was being said in an enemy king's private chamber. I came to understand that the psychic capacity was not that different from a cell phone or television. The mind can pick up very subtle emissions given off by all living beings and turn them into an intelligible image or sound, like a television. This is because the psyche is like a pool of water that responds to any incoming frequencies. The key is to tune in to a particular channel by giving it a cipher associated with a particular person, place or situation.

All these enquiries led me, with the study of astrology and Kabbalah, to produce a picture book called *As Above So Below*. It was composed of photographs from deep space, beginning with the galactic world and then coming down through the stellar constellations and star clusters to the Sun, planets and Moon. The next sequence was made up of the very first pictures of the Earth from space, with ever closer pictures of the continents, countries and cities, concluding with a shot of Stonehenge from the air in which one could just make out people. My text was not scientific but esoteric, viewing the cosmos as a living organism. It was a photographic version of Jacob's Ladder. To my delight it was published and received some good reviews.

Out of this exercise came the idea of describing Existence in both kabbalistic and scientific terms. The result was *A Kabbalistic Universe*. The book starts by asking, 'How can one describe the indescribable?' and then seeks to bring spiritual metaphysics and material science

FIGURE 52—POSTER
The London Transport authority commissioned artists to produce posters for the Underground. These designs were meant to promote different features of the capital. I chose Greenwich Observatory, where the meridian line between the eastern and western hemispheres is to be found. I did several versions, ranging from a straightforward depiction of the old observatory to this more symbolic image. The accepted one was printed and displayed in many stations. I hoped my parents could be proud of me. They were. Indeed, one of my aunts pointed out to passengers that this was her nephew's work. At last I was almost respectable in my family's eyes. (Artwork by author).

together as a complement to each other. After dealing with the origin of the invisible realms of Creation and Formation, emerging out of the Divine, which had come from 'No-thing-ness', the physical theory of the 'Big Bang' is examined. While this initial burst of radiation had been detected by science, it could not explain where it came from, or why it came into being, which Kabbalah did.

The Hindu tradition depicts Existence being like a flower unfolding and blossoming. This expansion is seen by current scientists as unending. However, by the very laws that Newton had discovered, there has to be a reaction, once the impetus is spent, and the process goes into reverse. Like a withering bloom, the universe must reach its limit and begin to implode. It must then return to its single point of origin and disappear into 'No-thing-ness' again. The evidence that there is 'nothing' beyond the sub-atomic particles is a great mystery to science but not to Kabbalah, which sees EN SOF or NO-THING-NESS as the basis of Existence. This area lies in the realm of metaphysics which science does not explore and is a problem its method cannot resolve.

The biblical account of Creation, seen kabbalistically, presents the Seven Days in terms of cosmic epochs. However, what is not mentioned in the text is what came prior to Day One. This knowledge was part of the oral tradition, as it was believed that undeveloped people, or Children of Israel, would not be able to comprehend such an abstract concept. In Kabbalah the primal realm of Emanation is symbolised by the Tree of the sefirot and the humanoid figure known as the *Kavod* or Glory of God. This image took on the form of the Divine Name YHVH, when written in vertical mode. This is depicted by my calligraphy of the Holy Name, seen in Figure 87. The Tree and this Divine Adam represent, metaphysically and symbolically, the Divine World of Emanation. The Absolute is beyond Existence.

The rest of *A Kabbalistic Universe* was concerned with man, the microcosmic image of the Divine realm, because within a human being are all the Worlds. These are contained in the body, psyche and spirit with the Divine dimension as a spark of consciousness deep within each person. The destiny of humans is to 'Aid God to behold God'. We are the Divine organ of perception, potentially at every level. It is said that when all humanity reaches full Self-realisation, then what is called the Resurrection occurs, as all the human sparks return to their original place in Adam Kadmon. In that moment, tradition says, when the Divine portrait is complete, the eyes of the Divine Adam will open in recognition of being a vast reflection of I AM. Then, as I AM THAT I AM closes the cycle, all the Worlds and their inhabitants will return to 'NO-THING-NESS' again. The writing of this book was a powerful learning process with ideas coming into my mind from somewhere other then myself. This I know now for certain.

A Kabbalistic Universe was recognised by theosophists and Hindu scholars as having great similarities to their esoteric systems. This is not surprising, as all the great mystics have come to the same conclusion about the ground-bed of reality. What surprised some Christian readers was that the Kabbalah clearly underlay the Church's angelic and cosmic theology. This had been denied for centuries. It was good to see this fact reinstated. It could serve as common ground in a reconciliation between Jews and Christians. Indeed, many Christians in our group became aware of what lay behind their mystical tradition.

Around this time I was commissioned to write a short text for two picture books, one on astrology and the other on Kabbalah. They were part of a whole series on the esoteric. This was a period in which those interested in going beyond conventional religion became a target market for some enterprising publishers. From here on came a stream of books on magic, Sufism, Zen and many other esoteric topics. Gone was the time when one had to hunt in the corner of an old bookshop to find a volume on such matters. Suddenly, a whole shelf of reprints of good and bad books on the esoteric could be found, under the heading 'Self-development', along with others on psychology and healing. Then came new authors, like myself, who had their versions of various Teachings. Many were serious works but some were simply cashing in on the fashion. However, in the larger picture, even these facile books sowed seeds that were to bear fruit decades later. Providence works at every level.

26. Group

My small flat in leafy Lansdowne Road, Holland Park, was a conversion made out of the grand saloon room of a large Victorian home. It had high ceilings and large windows and was divided into a main room, a small kitchen and bathroom. The white walls were hung with Tree of Life and Jacob's Ladder diagrams, an enlarged image of Robert Fludd's 17th century engraving of the kabbalistic Worlds, and a poster version of my Cosmic Clock Zodiac design. This was used to plot the current positions of the planets by moving little wooden symbols around the board. There was also my favourite engraving of a seeker heavily robed, carrying his staff of knowledge and breaking out of the physical universe to see the celestial wheels that govern Existence.

Besides these icons of contemplation were many small pictures, diagrams and sacred objects that were meant to provoke thought. In addition there was a bed, a chest of drawers with a large telescope on it, three 19th century black ladder-back chairs and a scrubbed medieval style garden table, on which I worked at my books and ate my meals. Against the wall were two bookcases full of esoterica, and a papier-mâché figure of the Tarot Magus with his hat of Eternity, as well as a terrestrial globe and a celestial armillary sphere I had made. The general impression of the room, visitors said, was a cross of an Alchemist's cell and a Kabbalist's study.

Living here with me was a small brindled cat called Hymie, who kept me company. I learnt a great deal about the animal soul from her. She was entirely governed by impulse, curiosity and the need to defend her territory. I was just tolerated as I fed her. When the tom cats came to court her she would sit by the window, like a beautiful courtesan, while being admired and lusted after from the branches of the blackthorn tree just outside. She was a wonderful companion and I enjoyed her company, even though she lived her own social life as I did mine.

She did, however, once contribute to the group that met in the flat, by taking the floor when we were discussing the nature of the vegetable and animal souls. She sat for five minutes by a potted plant,

FIGURE 53—CAT
I drew this plaster cast of a panther as an exercise at the Academy School of Painting. It is a skinned version, to demonstrate the animal's muscle system. My beloved cat Hymie was not quite as ferocious, except when she went out to hunt. To her credit, she did sometimes bring her prey home as a gesture towards the rent. However, her lively presence, company and entertaining ways were payment enough. She taught me to cultivate my senses and instinctive perception as well as how to relax. This was vital, as I suffered from severe migraine from time to time until I learnt to control the creative impulse and keep it within a time regime. For this I was very grateful to my feline companion. (Drawing by author).

preening herself in a moment of glory as the centre of attention. To her credit, she did come to most of the meetings that took place every Thursday evening and would often sit on the lap of someone who, she sensed, liked cats. She undoubtedly had an instinctive psychic capacity and would often react to my moods. Of additional interest, she would sometimes respond to the psychic projections of people not present in the flat. This often occurred when the group did the exercise of remembering each other at certain times of the day in the setting of the flat.

Another beloved companion of this period was my old bicycle. It was painted red and black with white stripes so it could be seen at night. The stripes were also to put off thieves who might have problems selling such a conspicuous machine. This metallic being and I had numerous adventures exploring out-of-the-way places and shared romantic episodes. Two memories of our friendship stand out. One was cycling through a blizzard and the other was crossing a London park in the early hours of the morning looking up at the stars after a visit to a sweetheart. Our twenty-five years together kept me fit, cycling being the perfect complement to the sedentary occupation of writer.

By now, the group fluctuated between ten and twenty-five people. Somehow the room miraculously expanded to accommodate people sitting on the bed, table, chest of drawers and floor. The group was composed of students from the Architectural Association, where I taught part-time, people who had been sent by the Sufi teacher to learn about Kabbalah, others from the local Art school and some students, from both London and Oxford Universities. These last individuals were particularly keen to learn about the metaphysics of the Tree of Life as it explained the sacred texts they were studying. For example, the angelic hierarchy described in early kabbalistic works had no clear system of order, until placed upon Jacob's Ladder. Here the names of the Archangels of the World of the Spirit clearly related to the three pillars and various levels. This was a revelation to one brilliant Oxford man who had originally come to demonstrate his knowledge of Judaism.

Angelology was one of many topics examined, which could range through psychology to the pattern of history and life after death as well as the levels of Hell, Purgatory, lower and upper Paradise and the seven Heavens. The idea of reincarnation was discussed, but this was a problem for those studying Islam, as this tradition had no obvious

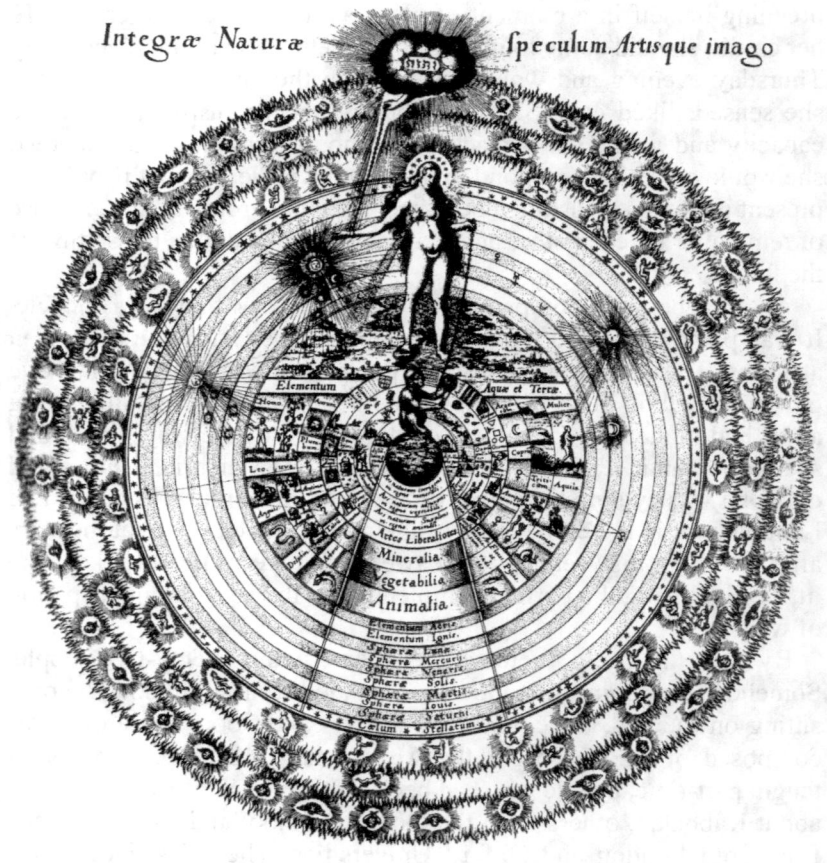

FIGURE 54—MIRROR
When I first saw this engraving at seventeen it made a deep impression on me, even though I had no real idea, then, what it depicted. It was only later that I discovered that it was a kabbalistic mandala designed by a 17th century English mystic, Robert Fludd. Its title, **Speculum,** *is crucial, as it reflects the concept of 'God beholding God' in the Mirror of Existence. Below the Hebrew Name of the Deity is the female principle of the Shekhinah, or Divine Presence, that governs the universes below. At its centre is the physical World. Here the various grades of the animal, vegetable and elemental levels are defined while the monkey-mind of the physical brain tries to understand the World. The chains represent the laws that hold all in place. A large version of this image has always been on my wall wherever I have lived.* (Engraving of Existence based upon a Rosicrucian view, Robert Fludd).

reference to the notion of transmigration of souls through different bodies over time. However, one verse in the Koran did state that, 'Allah generates beings and sends them back over and over again, until they return to Him'. This was not enough to convince the Sufis present, even though the Dervishes spoke of passing through the various stages of being, a stone, plant and animal, before becoming human. However, it was argued by some present that this was an analogue of human development and not a literal process. In time those who were committed to this view left to follow their own line. Over the years many people came and went, while a devoted core remained at the heart of the group.

As regards levels, the group could be loosely divided into those who were just curious and left after a while, those who wanted to learn about the Tradition but not practise its disciplines, and those who were committed to the Path. This last group might be Jewish, Christian or non-sectarian, as there was no exclusion of anyone who wanted to learn about Kabbalah. Indeed, as noted, we had a Zoroastrian who returned to India and taught a Parsee version of Kabbalah, without mentioning where he got such a clear understanding of what Zoroastrianism was really about. The Buddhists who came saw parallels with their line but they too left as did those who wanted to study magic, spend an interesting evening or find a mate. Out of this came the joke idea of a kabbalistic Marriage Bureau, but this proved a dismal failure as people in the 'Work' are very choosy.

The core of committed people gradually raised the level of the group by operating at an increasingly subtle level. One visitor picked up that there was obviously an 'inner circle'. I replied that this was composed of whoever was 'awake' during a meeting. He did not grasp what I meant and believed I was being coy in order to hide who was on the 'inside'. Occasionally we had people who were extremely well read and would quote from texts often in the middle of a discussion they could not understand in order to get attention. As a result, I made it a rule that only personal experience could be spoken about. This usually made such people leave after one evening.

There was also a problem when one very bright member of the group began to challenge what I was doing. He clearly believed he had mastered Kabbalah to such a degree that he could speak with authority. Recognising his need and to avoid a confrontation I asked him to start a 'beginners group' on his own. He was delighted as he had got the respect he thought he deserved. However, a month or so later, some of the people I had sent to him phoned me to complain that they were not being taught about Kabbalah but his opinions about all manner of esoteric subjects.

When these students eventually left him and his group dissolved, he asked to return to the main group. I consented, and for a while all went well, but then I heard from various people that he was still criticising my working method. By this time I had been involved in the Work for over a decade and had witnessed such a phenomenon. He was a classic case of what is called the 'star student syndrome'. In a large school of many groups, he would have been given yet another group, hoping he would have learnt his lesson, but in our situation this was not possible. I pondered for a while what to do and concluded I was dealing with something more subtle than a human foible.

In Kabbalah there is a term the 'Opposition'. By this is meant anything that opposes development. It can come in many forms. It may be a seemingly quite sincere objection by a person who believes they know more, or is just envious. This allows the shadow in them to justify their opposition. The Inquisition is a prime example of this negative process, resulting in the execution of so-called heretics for their own good. In this case I was faced with both personal and general issues. I had to either confront the problem, or hope it would go away. The young man concerned, however, had crossed a 'line' when he tried to undermine years of my work. I invited him to tea and said, in my most English diplomatic manner, what I had heard about his criticism. He went as white as a sheet when he realised people had reported his disparaging comments. He left my flat somewhat shaken and went to the other side of the world to avoid facing what some saw as his treachery. The tragedy was that he was essentially a good man who had failed the 'Lucific' test that such talented people must face. He later recovered and became someone who regained his integrity in an important court case in which he stood against the greed of a commercial company. He had learnt his lesson.

One morning, after a particularly good group the night before, while meditating upon the autumn leaves outside my window and how the 'Life' principle must wane, wither and die, a quiet silent voice spoke to me. It said, 'All I require of you is that you should teach Kabbalah'. I was awestruck, as I knew exactly Who had spoken. This short but profound moment confirmed what I was to do with the rest of my life. Suddenly all the training, my cultural background and personal experience fused together. Kabbalah was to be my Path.

27. Practice

The next book was *The Work of the Kabbalist*. The revised edition has been re-titled *The Kabbalist at Work* because the *Way* and the *World of Kabbalah* might be seen as the same to a casual book browser. It starts with the notion that the Holy Name 'I AM THAT I AM', given to Moses on Mount Sinai, is not just a Divine title but a statement of intention. That is the 'going forth' of the 'Word' and its reflection in the Mirror of Existence, symbolised in the conjunction 'THAT'. Here is the origin of the notion of God's will to behold God.

After the general explanation of Jacob's Ladder, the text moves on to the microcosm of humanity describing how an individual can develop out of the vegetable and animal levels of mankind to become fully human. This requires training to understand what is involved. A body of esoteric knowledge, in itself, is not enough. There has to be a regime of practice. This means that the person has to seek and find a genuine school of the soul which is under the direction of a trustworthy teacher.

Practical work does not just mean physical rituals but psychological exercises and the development of the soul. If these elements are not in place, then all that is learnt becomes a kind of esoteric academic operation. One of the exercises is, as we have seen, the 'Art of Active Imagination'. This enables the individual to penetrate beyond the ordinary mind and enter the World of forms and symbols, a technique that can be conjoined with physical exercises. For example the body, with the arms up and outstretched, is the Tree. The positions of the sefirot start with Keter as the Crown, Binah and Hokhmah as the two sides of the brain, with the throat, eyes, ears and mouth at Daat. The heart and lungs are aligned with Hesed and Gevurah with the solar plexus at Tiferet and Yesod at the crotch. Hod, Yesod and Malkhut represent the lower part of the body. Then there is the approach of contemplation, in which one reflects upon the Tree after addressing it with a question. The answer then comes from within as this kabbalistic mandala triggers a response from deep within the mind.

There is also the art of interpreting the images that arise during a

FIGURE 55—MERKABAH
This Hebrew word means Chariot. *It is used in the Bible as a symbol of the World of Formation, which carries the Throne of Heaven and the Divine Adam Kadmon. The term 'Merkabah Riders' was applied to Jewish mystics who went on an inner journey deep into themselves and then rose up into the higher Worlds. Here the prophet Ezekiel views Existence in an archetypal form that became the model for Kabbalists. Unfortunately this led to much confusion, as uninformed people did not realise that its symbolism was not meant to be taken literally. For example, the wheels represent cosmic cycles while the Throne is the metaphysical basis of Heaven, and the Fiery Man the archetype of the Divine, in the form of a human being, the perfect image of God. (Ezekiel's Vision,* Bear's Bible, *16th century).*

guided inner journey. One meditation used is a visit to an imaginary Temple School on the top of a Holy Mountain. During the stay there, one spends the first day in the school of Action, the next in the school of Contemplation, followed by a day in the school of Devotion. In each of these departments an instructor gives a mark according to one's performance. They then take one a stage further in each of these working modes. The last day is spent in the upper chambers of the Temple School, where one is examined as regards all the things one has done well or badly. Then the inner teacher, the symbol of the Self, goes through the journal of one's life. Together with the teacher one formulates three important and relevant questions. These may be about the past, present and future, or some issue that has yet to be resolved. The teacher then takes one out of the Court Chamber of the soul, up to the Chamber of the Spirit in the Dome of the Temple School. Here one is lifted up, by invisible hands, into the Holy of Holies in the Crown of the Dome to enter into the Divine Presence. There one can ask the questions and hopefully receive answers.

Upon descending and being taken by one's teacher back down to the Chamber of the Soul, a discussion takes place regarding the answers received. Here, perhaps, an important decision is made. During this conversation one may get to know who one really is or discover that the teacher is not the Self but a discarnate Maggid, who keeps an eye on one, like a guardian angel. This exercise, like all others, is loaded with symbolism and meaning, as are the dreams one has each night during the visit to the Temple School. On the last day, one gathers with others of the group in the Great Courtyard of Yesod to await the dawn, before returning home. As people depart, the doorkeeper gives each one a present. What is it and what does it signify? Many are given a key, which suggests that an inner door to one's development can now be opened. This exercise is now on a CD and can be used as a periodic assessment of one's development.

This and other exercises were formulated when I was invited by a charitable trust to run weekend workshops in a London College. The large college classroom meant we had the space to perform, for example, the 'Ritual of Chairs'. In this, eleven seats were set out in the form of the Tree with the chair at Daat, the non-sefirah of Knowledge, facing all the others. This was to enable the person sitting on it to look back at the path they had travelled up the Tree. With a group of perhaps forty all moved, on command, chair by chair from the base of Malkhut the Kingdom up the Tree to the Throne of the Crown. This was a very

FIGURE 56—FAVOURITE
This image is my most loved of prints. It shows the mystic, well protected by his heavy coat and carrying the Staff of Knowledge which enables him to leave the physical World and enter the cosmic realm. Anyone who has experienced these higher Worlds becomes aware of very powerful forces that can sweep one away, if the discipline and knowledge of an esoteric tradition is not securely in place. The minds and brains of many psychedelic drug users have been blasted to such a degree that they never recover. The Path is no easy ride. It needs a solid and earthly connection, a stable psyche and firm contact with a reliable spiritual tradition to visit the invisible domains safely. (Print. Date and origin unknown).

powerful and moving ritual. Standing round the configuration were people who had been through the process or were waiting to take part. They stood in silence as I described the levels and functions of the Tree and moved them on the path of the Lighting Flash up the Tree. After the ritual came observations and questions about the experience. The sharing produced a larger lens that only group work can create.

Later, the trust's course was moved to a country house and extended to five days. This was a residential operation which enabled people to be a 'School' for that time. Many people who attended became lifelong friends, even though they lived in distant lands. One result was the formation of groups in different parts of Britain and other countries. This is how the Kabbalah Society slowly came into being.

One of the exercises of the Summer School was to take people out of the lecture hall and into the wild wood just above the old mansion. Here I told the group to act as if they were a primitive tribe with myself as Chief and Shaman. Most people took on the rôle with great zeal. For example, one astute business lady said she enjoyed just being responsible for collecting berries, wood and herbs, while a young man enjoyed being the warrior protector of our clan. When we assembled in a clearing I invoked a greeting to the Nature Spirits. Many people, now deep into the experience, sensed a distinct response from the invisible watchers and some even saw and heard fleeting presences. After saying farewell in the Name of the One God we returned to the old house to share our encounter with these etheric entities. Some people went back to the glade later to make a personal connection.

In contrast to the practical exercises were slide-shows on the history of Kabbalah and related topics such as science. We examined the Trees of the body and psyche as well as those of astrology and many other related topics, such as stages of life, inner growth, death, the afterlife and reincarnation. After each lecture would come questions and a discussion on the subject being reviewed. Everything was referred to either the Tree or Jacob's Ladder. One session might be on the anatomy of fate, another an exploration of the mechanism of madness. The more traditional topics of angelics and demonics, as well as Hell, the two Paradises and the seven Heavens, were examined and related to human history.

One of the most popular sessions was when the astrological birth chart of an individual present was placed on the Tree to demonstrate principles. This revealed the strengths and weaknesses within the psyche of that person who usually was delighted to be an example.

However, sometimes they did not like to hear about their fatal flaw although most acknowledged it was a problem. An example of this was Mars in Libra in one birth chart, which meant the person found it difficult to make up their mind. People began to see how a horoscope was an 'end of term report' on the last life and description of what lessons had to be learnt. Such discussions were carried on in the free afternoon hours which allowed people to rest and reflect. This was a vital part of an increasingly intense course.

During the afternoon and coffee and tea breaks, people approached me privately. We would talk, while looking out over a very pleasant country landscape to the distant mountains of Wales. These conversations, I was told later, were often crucial to people who, in their home circumstance, had no one to talk to about their inner life. Most people left at the end of the Summer School with a deeper knowledge of Kabbalah and their own place in the Universal Scheme. One or two people from abroad became so committed to our work that they began to translate my books into their local languages. Over time, foreign publications of my works amounted to over seventy editions which included not only many European tongues but Japanese, Korean and Hebrew. I was astounded by this phenomenon. This had to be the hand of Heaven.

28. Confirmation

People often asked how could I write about such a vast subject as Kabbalah without a formal rabbinic or scholarly training. Some knowledge was clearly memory from previous lives and I had read a great deal. However, what came directly through my mind and pencil was the main source of what I wrote about. In the Bible there are those who are called the 'lesser prophets', that is, those who do not know what they are saying although it may be very profound. Many artists, writers and poets come into this category for, when questioned about their work, they say it is all about inspiration. However, I knew from experience that my case was a factor of another dimension.

This situation was clarified to me one day while meditating, when I became aware of a strong presence in the room. I had often picked up a psychic focus while writing, especially when I had come across a problem, such as a kabbalistic principle I did not understand or some missing link in Jewish history. The former might be about the relationship of the soul to free will or how Jewish *conversos* in medieval Spain escaped the Inquisition and secretly left the country. In the first case, the answer would come into my mind quite precisely in a silent exposition. I was told that the soul triad on the Tree was not under the laws of the physical World, or those of the spiritual, but completely psychological by nature and therefore flexible, within limits. This gave the soul its capability to make a choice. As regards escaping from Spain, an image came to me of a discreet escape route to various Mediterranean ports where Italian ships, owned by Jews, would take *conversos* to Italy, North Africa or the Turkish Empire where they traded. I found out later this was exactly how it happened.

Where did such information come from? Not from me but from someone who had access to the records of history. Tradition says that the Academies on High, in the upper part of Paradise, keep such accounts. Who, then, was this invisible being now standing just behind me as I meditated? I asked the question, 'Do I know you?' The silent reply was, 'Only by name'. 'How so?' I asked. Because, I was then told, I knew his work as an author, poet and philosopher.

FIGURE 57—MAGGID
This word, in Hebrew, is applied to one's spiritual mentor. All on the Path of Self-realisation must have one as a guide. They are usually discarnate individuals with experience in one's particular mode of life. In my case, it is a long-dead poet and philosopher whose task was to update the Tradition in terms of his time. He translated the mystical symbolism of Judaism into the metaphysics then being developed from ancient Greek concepts in Moorish Spain. A long prayer by him, describing Jacob's Ladder in poetic form, is a masterpiece and it is read in the Sefardi synagogue on the eve of the Day of Atonement. It is called Keter Malkhut, *meaning the top and bottom sefirot of the kabbalistic Tree of Life. (*Teacher and Pupil, *photograph by Jon Cooper Taylor).*

'Did I have any of his books?' I enquired. As the affirmative answer came, my eye was drawn to the bookcase and a volume my father had bought me some years before. This was the only book he had given me, besides a set of prayer books and the Old Testament in English and Hebrew. On the cover of this particular volume was the name of an eleventh century Spanish writer. To double-check that I was not fooling myself, I said, 'Place of birth?' I immediately got a picture of a southern Spanish port with a view of the harbour from a Moorish palace fortress with its pine trees, high above medieval ships from all over the Mediterranean. I was very struck by the fact that I was looking due south. This was significant, I was told. I then got up from my chair and looked up the birthplace of the author. It was Malaga in Andalusia. I then went to the local library and, to my surprise, there was a photograph looking south taken from the Moorish castle, with its pine trees, overlooking a harbour now filled with modern ships. It was essentially the same view, nine hundred years on.

Some years later, I went to Malaga and stood in the place that corresponded to my vision. His statue was at the foot of the Moorish citadel. It was a romantic image of the poet, quite different from how he described himself, as small and ugly, in his writings. His works were a mixture of Neo-Platonic philosophy, wise aphorisms and poems about life, as well as a poetic masterpiece called *Keter Malkhut* which described Jacob's Ladder in religious and astrological terms. This last work is read by Spanish Jews on the evening before Yom Kippur, the Day of Atonement. Its effect is to shift the mind from the personal to the universal and the Divine presence.

As I was paying my respects to my Maggid, by putting a stone from Jerusalem at the foot of his statue, I heard him weeping. I asked, 'Why?' He replied, in that inner, silent dialogue mode we had developed, that he had been excessively clever to make up for his lack of physical charm. This had caused him to be somewhat arrogant, which offended some of the people who might have supported him financially after his patron had died. He deeply regretted his conduct in that life. He was to be my mentor for many years, as a friend and companion of the light. After one lecture I had given, a woman came up to me and asked, 'Who was that oriental figure standing beside you?' I replied, 'my Teacher', as I knew he was present at that occasion. He turned up from time to time when needed with information that cannot be found in any book. I learnt, after our first encounter, that in Kabbalah such a relationship was not that unusual. I was deeply grateful for it.

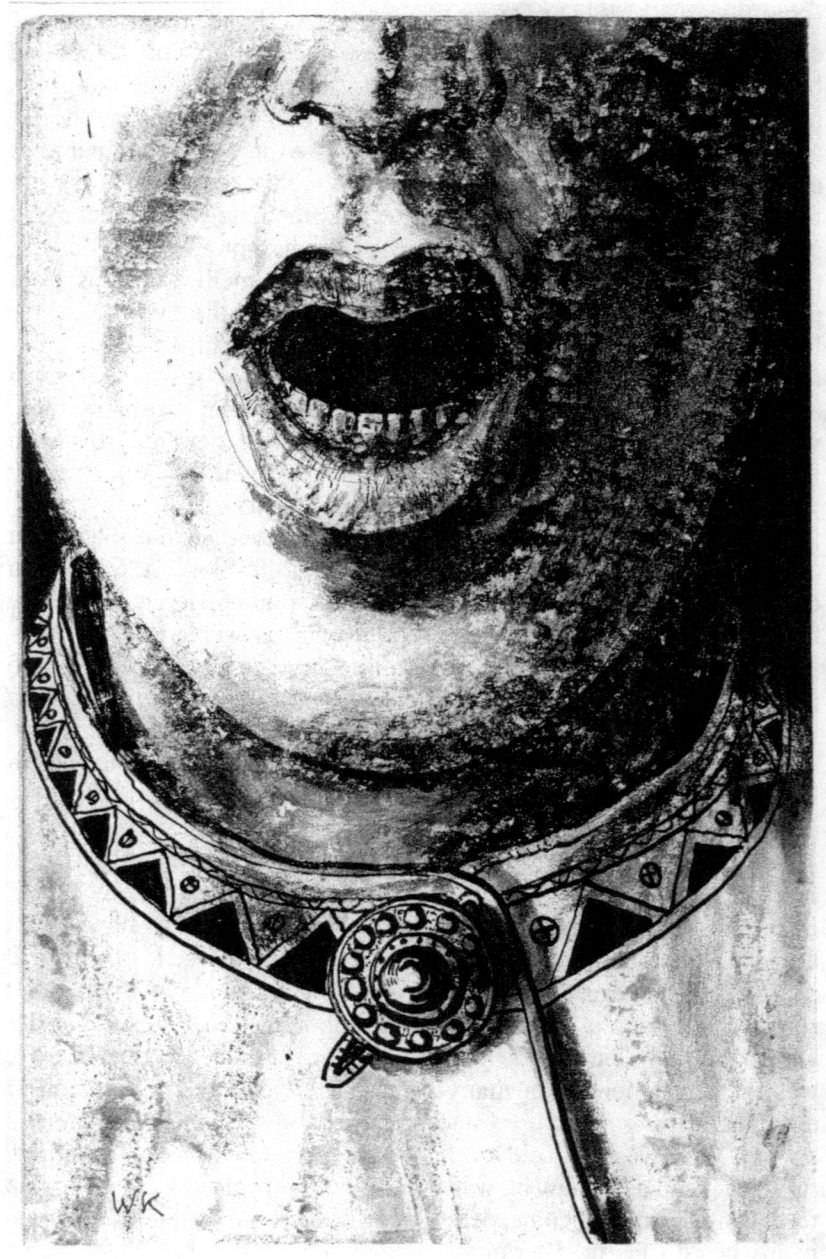

Another crucial psychic experience came when I was exploring a remote town in south-western France, where the medieval school of Isaac the Blind, one of the formulators of medieval Kabbalah, had been. I was in the *Rue des Juifs*, the street of the Jews where he had lived, walking up and down, trying to sense which of the old houses was his. One in particular appeared to be the place. It was then that I saw, in a flash, the image of a large man dressed in a prayer shawl smiling with an extraordinary radiance at me—and then it was gone. Just then the local historian, a doctor, came up the street to meet me as we had an appointment. He took me to the house I had identified as, possibly, the house of Isaac and knocked on the door. A woman opened it and said, 'Doctor, why have you come, there is no one sick here?' He brushed her aside and took me into a courtyard with an arch which no ordinary dwelling would have. He said that this house was part of Isaac's private synagogue and where he had his school. This experience convinced me that I was not suffering from an overactive imagination and that my psychic insights were genuine.

In Gerona, northeast Spain, the Jewish quarter was the centre of a most important kabbalistic school. It was here that Rabbi Azriel, an innovative scholar, formulated a Neo-Platonic version of Kabbalah so as to convince orthodox Jews that philosophy was not a threat to the religious tradition. At that time there was a fierce argument going on as to which was the true Teaching, revelation or reason. The books of the Jewish philosopher Maimonides were being burnt as heretical and the rabbis were excommunicating each other.

Azriel, who had been a student of Isaac the Blind and had, no doubt, gone to the local city university a street or two away from the Gerona synagogue, set out to meet the challenge.

He did so by presenting the educated Spanish Jews with a blend of the biblical, mythical and Jewish mystical teaching, with the

---

FIGURE 58 (Left)—VOICE
This is an illustration for an unpublished version of The White Ship. *It is the moment when the King, who had been waiting for his children on the English side of the Channel, learns that they have been drowned. No courtier dared to tell the King and so they trained a young boy to sing a dirge that he did not, in his innocence, understand, to give the dire news. This silent visual image symbolises how one receives psychic or spiritual communication. The process is similar in that one hears a voice from deep within. However, one has to differentiate between one's own imaginings and a message from one's inner teacher. The hallmark of such a transmission is its precise relevance and the ring of truth.* (Drawing by the author).

philosophical ideas coming in the form of Hebrew translations of Arab texts on Plato, Aristotle and Plotinus. Isaac the Blind disapproved of Azriel's project but it was too late. Kabbalah was now out in the public domain and became popular among the Spanish-Jewish intelligentsia. As I was sitting in the old Gerona synagogue, pondering the question of what can and cannot be said about the esoteric Jewish tradition in our time, I saw a figure come up the stairs with a bundle of scrolls under his arm. I knew straight away that it was Azriel coming to confirm what I was doing. As he vanished into an upper room in the old building, I felt a burden lifted from me.

The culmination of this ancient argument as to what can be said was sealed for me when I was in Israel, in the Galilean hill town of Safed. This is where many Spanish Jews came after the expulsion from Spain in 1492. It was regarded as *the* kabbalistic centre in the 16th century, because the tomb of Simeon ben Yohai is nearby. One day I was sitting alone in the old Spanish synagogue by the cemetery, where many noted Kabbalists are buried, when I overheard a conversation that I knew was not of this world. The voices were debating the old issue of what can be said openly about Kabbalah. One side was arguing for total discretion while the other declared that it was not possible to give esoteric secrets away, as most people would not recognise what was being given because they did not understand something that was beyond them. I knew, from experience, that this was the case. Only people above a certain level of development would comprehend what I had written; to the rest it would seem to be esoteric mumbo jumbo, boring or not of any real interest. I left the synagogue realising I had the support of some invisible mentors, as this soundless conversation had been timed for me to hear. It also warned me to expect more resistance from the conservative of my community.

Outside in the cemetery, I passed by the grave of Alkabetz, one of the founders of the Safed school of Kabbalah in the 16th century. I shuddered, as if someone had walked over my grave. I later discovered that I had a great affinity with Alkabetz. One of my students suggested that I might have been him. This I could not confirm, but there certainly was a connection. My reason for being in the graveyard was to visit the tomb of Moses Cordovero, an important writer who put together all that was known about Kabbalah up to that time. His *Garden of Pomegranates* is a dense volume that only scholars or Kabbalists can comprehend. After paying my respects, by laying a small scroll of Jacob's Ladder on his grave, I walked away. However, something made me turn and look back. I then saw a figure, in brown and blue robes blowing in the wind, standing by Cordovero's grave. I knew instantly that it was him. Then something struck me as very odd, because it was a calm day with not even a breeze. As I puzzled over this detail I heard the words, 'Your way is not my way, but then you live in a different time'. The figure then faded out of sight; so too did the wind.

All these experiences gave me an insight into the line of the Tradition. Each generation of Kabbalists has to reformulate the system in a way that is intelligible to their period. Ibn Gabirol with his Neo-Platonic approach was ignored by the conservative orthodoxy, while Azriel's more integrated version also met with some opposition. Even *The Zohar*, compiled by Moses de Leon, was attacked by rabbis who doubted his claim that the original text was written by rabbi Simeon ben Yohai of Roman times. There was good reason for this because his widow said, to Isaac of Acco, that her husband had composed the text out of his own head. The reality, as far as I could discern when visiting Guadalajara in Spain, may have been that the school there had commissioned him to synthesise all the mystical material then known into a great work. It was to be written in Aramaic, the language of ben Yohai's time, so as to give the book a feel of authenticity. The name of this ancient and respected sage would assure the success of *The Zohar*. To use a well-known name was common practice in early medieval times. A curious irony in reverse was to happen to me. One hostile scholar stated that I was a Christian convert, while another implied that my Hebrew name was just a *nom de plume*. Both were attempts to undermine any authority I might acquire. The strange paradox is that they spoke of texts being the only prime sources to be relied upon when, in fact, these are all second-, third- and even fourth-hand versions of mystical experiences. Direct cognition, I discovered, was the only genuine source of Kabbalah. All else is opinion and, in reality, many scholars, despite their claims to objectivity, are very subjective in their book-bound view. However, it must be acknowledged that without scholars what is gleaned by inspiration cannot be confirmed.

FIGURE 59—HIGH PRIEST
This illustration appeared in the original version of Kabbalah and Exodus. *It shows the four garments and the crown that the High Priest wore. These represent the four levels within a human being which correspond to the four Worlds. The crown, with a Divine Name engraved upon it, gives him his priestly authority while the square, hung about his neck, with its twelve precious stones represents the twelve tribes and Zodiacal signs. Knowledge hidden within the Bible and Jewish folklore gives many clues to the discerning about the esoteric Torah. (Drawing by author).*

29. Sacredness

The 1970s, when I was in my 40s, was a very productive decade. The creative flow was strong and I was writing a book a year. During this period Jupiter, the planet of emotional power, was moving through the 1st House of my birth chart. This meant that I had the strength and stamina to work very hard. It was also the time when I was asked to give public lectures in a synagogue and two rabbinic colleges. Such talks, given by someone who was not a rabbi or academic, were unusual but then there were other factors not recognised by most people. When the planets are in certain positions, innovation occurs. The reverse is true when a planet like Jupiter is afflicted, in a birth chart or general situation. This is the pattern of the Divine Plan. I was fortunate to be able to take advantage of a favourable period and present a modern view of Kabbalah to lay and rabbinic communities.

The next book to be written was to perceive the story of the biblical Exodus from Egypt as a process of physical, psychological and spiritual development, as well as the history of the Israelites casting off slavery and crossing the Sinai desert to the Holy Land. I did much research into Jewish legends and folklore, matching it to the Hebrew and English text of *Exodus*. I then interwove psychology and Kabbalah into the fabric of the story, so that the reader could relate their own life to the process of freeing themselves from conditioning of ingrained slavery.

The book began with the exposition of the Tree and Jacob's Ladder. It then went on to describe the descent of the Israelites into Egypt, that is, the soul coming down into the body, where it is dominated by instinct until the soul is aroused. The birth of Moses after centuries of servitude to Pharaoh, the symbol of the body's power, marked the beginning of this awakening. His training at the royal court, as the foster child of Pharaoh's sister, was the equivalent to a worldly education while his instruction under his father-in-law Jethro, about how to handle sheep in the Wilderness, was to be vital in his mission. He had to deal with what was, initially, a rabble of Israelites who were like a lost flock in the rough Sinai terrain. They represented the various aspects of an as yet ununified psyche.

SACREDNESS

The rest of the book was about the journey across the desert and how the slave-minded generation, who represented old habits, had to die off while a new, free, generation was born. In spite of having been given the Torah at Mount Sinai as a moral guide there were revolts, such as the worship of the Golden Calf, the symbol of material comfort. As one Israelite carped, 'At least in Egypt we had a degree of comfort'. The leaders of the rebellions symbolised the conservative sub-personalities within the mind that did not wish to change. To counter this problem the Tabernacle was built as a communal focus. This is called, by one esoteric tradition, a psychological 'Magnetic Centre' within a developing individual. This symbol of the Self can withstand the stress of growth and the temptation to revert into the old state of conditioned slavery. The book ends with the dramatic consecration of the Tabernacle, which represents the establishment of the Self as the centre of consciousness in the mind and the aim of reaching the Holy Land of the Spirit, despite what trials and tests might be met.

When I visited Mount Sinai I carried with me a copy of my book *Kabbalah and Exodus* which I wanted to give to the library of St. Catherine's Monastery at the foot of the mountain. At that time the area was under Egyptian jurisdiction. Even so, the local Bedouin people live much the same kind of life as they had done when the Israelites were there, some 3,500 years before, except that they now had four-wheel drive cars as well as camels. Many still lived in movable tents with their flocks and I sensed that they regarded us, and the Egyptians, as intruders. As we came closer to the holy Mount I experienced a feeling of awe arising within me. Upon seeing it, something shifted within my soul and I became alert to all that was about me. This meant that the people in our bus were but a fleeting episode when seen against the Bedouin and the stark rocky landscape.

Suddenly there was no time. The buildings at the foot of the Mount,

---

FIGURE 60 (Left)—MOMENT
This picture was taken during the few seconds I had my hands raised at the foot of Mount Sinai. I had gone off on my own, not only to present a prayer but also to avoid Egyptian officials seeing me. This was because they could arrest anyone doing something they considered to be unlawful. Some weeks before, a devout Christian had been imprisoned for conducting a short service. Even so, Providence arranged that one of our group was in the right place to take a photograph at that moment. When I was shown the picture, I saw it to mean that my submission had been acknowledged. I marvelled at the precision of the timing. Heaven had got everyone in just the right positions to see, or not to see, what was going on. (Photo by student).

including St Catherine's Monastery, disappeared and I perceived the presence of tens of thousands of people present before the high cliff-face of Sinai. Some of these presences were the psychic imprint left by the Israelites and many others who had visited the site over the ages. But there was also the impression of millions who came there via imagination as they heard about the event of Moses going up the Mount. This might have occurred over many centuries as people participated in their religious services. Thus projected psychic force added to the power of the Spirit that hovered about this sacred place.

I left my companions for a while, to wander about the loose rocks at the foot of the mountain, until I found a position where I felt I could not be seen, as we were being watched all the time by Egyptian officials. I had been warned not to perform any ritual as one clergyman, a short time before, had been arrested for carrying out some illegal act according to Egyptian regulations. The Egyptian government, at that point, wished to reassert its total control of the area, after it had been given back the Sinai by the Israelis following a disastrous war. Having found a remote spot, I then lifted my hands up to form a Tree of Life with my body so that I might receive any Grace that might be given. I thanked the Holy One for my life's work and prayed that I might continue to serve. This operation only took ten seconds, during which I perceived a very gentle and kindly response. There was no great revelation, just silence and a reassuring peace. A few weeks later, back in London, one of my travelling companions showed me a photograph she had taken when my arms were up. She must have been put just in the right place to get the picture. This I took as a sign that I had been seen and this photograph was to confirm the event. Not every encounter with the Divine is a stunning revelation. The Holy One is not as remote as people are led to believe but perceives everything, no matter how large or small. This is why in Kabbalah the Absolute is called *En Sof*—Without Limit. As we left Mount Sinai and I was about to board our bus, a small cloud appeared above the summit. I acknowledged this farewell as I climbed up the step as a cloud is a symbol of the Holy Spirit. There were no other clouds in the sky at that moment.

Upon one's first visit to the Holy Land, all the ideas and images that have been instilled into one as a child, be one Jew or Christian, initially overlay first impressions. These expectations, however, are soon dissolved upon realising that Israel is a country at war. This was not so much a shock for me, having lived through the Second

World War and witnessed the Blitz. But for those who were confronted with a biblical landscape filled with war machines and heavily armed troops everywhere, it required a psychological shift from a religious perception to the reality of everyday life in the present Holy Land.

This situation is underlined by the presence of soldiers patrolling the narrow streets of Old Jerusalem. There is a constant tension in the atmosphere, not unlike when the Romans occupied the city. And yet, despite this overlay of suspicion and hate, Jerusalem still has an atmosphere of spirituality as the focus of the three Abrahamic faiths. However, there are some places that are nothing more than edifices of religious superstition. By this is meant the accretion of myth and legend associated with a sacred site. All three religious authorities have built showpieces that are essentially exercises in propaganda to support not only the claims of each Faith but different sects within their tradition. Physical altercations between rival clergymen are not unknown and the dreadful Holy Wars down the ages bear witness to how the orthodoxy of each religion has forgotten what the 'Teaching' is about. No one can claim that they have the absolute truth because all have blood on their hands. This occurs when animal level people take over from the mystics.

The Temple site compound is a mixture of myth and history. Within the Dome of the Rock is the tip of Mount Moriah, where Abraham was required to sacrifice his son Isaac, or Ishmael according to the *Koran*. Here, Jewish folklore says, is the place where the physical universe began to come into being. Beneath the bare rock summit of Moriah are subterranean chambers that were part of the Temple. The atmosphere of these is haunted, as Moslems believe that the souls of the dead come there before their judgement. In contrast, the space of the Dome above, the place where Mohammed began his ascent to Heaven, is sublime, due to the quality of its exquisite structure. No orthodox Jew will enter this chamber, as it is seen as the site of the Holy of Holies.

In contrast I had a different kind of experience while exploring the Old City on my own. I had heard a great noise coming from the Arab quarter and I was about to cross into the area, to find out what the commotion was, when a voiceless voice within said 'Go no further'; Suddenly I realised the danger my curiosity might lead me into and I promptly turned around. A day later I read in the *Jerusalem Post* that someone had been shot by an Arab sniper from the Old City's wall. This sense of being watched over was with me when I went into the El-Aqsa mosque. The worshippers there were surprised to see a

Westerner and made it very clear I was not welcome, even though I had come to pay my respects. I left quickly. From that time on, in tricky places I took heed of my invisible guardians. One can only be protected if one is not stupid.

On one of my visits to Jerusalem I had a clear overall view across the Valley of Kidron opposite the Mount of Olives. While there I had a psychic impression of a radiance hovering over the domes, spires and roofs of the Old City. There was, however, below this light a dark shadow and the sound of conflict accrued over the centuries. Between these poles was a nexus of purity and integrity that arose from the millions of pilgrims, saints, sages and mystics who had visited and lived within its walls. I know no other place that has such a concentration of the best and worst of humanity. As I later walked through the crowds of Old Jerusalem I looked for the Messiah who I hoped might be there, but I saw no face to match the archetypal image I had of this most advanced individual on Earth. Maybe I did pass him or her by but I was obviously not at the level where I might recognise them. According to some, the Messiah or Axis of the Age, as the Moslems call this 'Buddha' of the time, may live in London. I am always on the lookout in its streets for what I would imagine would be a distinct radiant face. The reason for this is the story I once read of an 18th century Master Kabbalist travelling with a disciple. He stopped his pony and trap by a cottage deep in a Russian forest where he conversed for some time with an old man. As they drove away, the student, deeply impressed by his Master's obvious respect for the old man, asked, 'Who was that?' The reply was, 'The Messiah'.

30. Humour

Humour has been a vital part of my culture and development. A joke is when two incongruent elements are brought together and, in their juxtaposition, a new window and dimension is revealed. God, it is said, has a sense of humour, otherwise the Godhead would despair of humanity's stupidity. Out of a joke's punchline can come a refreshing sense of the ridiculous and a profound insight into the topic being portrayed. This can be practical, psychological and even spiritual. Stories and even jokes have been used by many spiritual traditions like Zen and Sufism. Kabbalah is no exception.

An example of the animal level of humanity is a poor Jewish migrant who comes to New York and cannot get any job because he can neither read nor write. The only one on offer is to be the caretaker of a synagogue. When the rabbi sees just a mark on the contract, he shakes his head and says he is very sorry but he cannot employ an illiterate. The Jew is in despair, until he remembers how he made a living in the old country. There he bought cast-offs for a rouble and sold them for two roubles to people who could make use of them. Working on this principle, within five years he became a millionaire but now by buying derelict land and selling when the market needed it. When he came to see his new bank manager to sign a deal, the banker was amazed to see just a mark on the contract. 'What would you have been, if you could read and write?' he exclaimed. The reply was, 'A caretaker in a synagogue'.

Another story about worldly wisdom is when Napoleon, after a great battle, came to see his wounded heroes in hospital. He asked the first man, who was a Frenchman, what he was before he joined the army. 'A peasant', was the reply. Napoleon said to his aide de camp, 'Put him down for a big estate as a reward'. To the second hero, a Pole, Napoleon said, when he heard the man had been a fisherman, 'Put him down to own a fleet of boats as a reward'. However, when he came to the Jew, Napoleon was told that the man used to sell pickled herrings from a barrel in a market. 'What would you like for a reward?' Napoleon asked. 'A pickled herring sandwich', was the reply. 'Send

FIGURE 61—HUMOUR
Humour is a tradition deeply embedded in Jewish culture as a counterbalance to the shadow of persecution. One joke is a typical example of the Nazi period. A Jew, desperate for employment, took on the job of dressing up as a monkey for the Berlin Zoo which was awaiting a replacement for the old animal that had died. He pleased the children particularly with his high swings on a rope. One day, however, the rope snapped and he fell into the cage of a very nasty-looking lion. When he was saying the prayer Jews utter before they die, the lion growled, 'Shut up! You are not the only Jew trying to make a living.' In this figure a Jewish trader is telling the latest joke while colleagues do a business deal. Some stories are centuries old but reset in a different time and environment. (19th century print).

out immediately for the biggest pickled herring sandwich that can be made', Napoleon ordered. After Napoleon had gone, the Frenchman and Pole said, 'Izzy, are you mad! You could have asked to be set up as a master merchant!' The Jew shook his head and replied, 'At least I know for certain I will get my sandwich.'

These two tales illustrate how the Jew is a realist in an uncertain world. The following reveals how the rabbinical mind works. The scene is on a train going from Moscow to the provinces in Tsarist Russia. A young man, obviously a Jewish student, asks a middle-aged Jewish merchant the time. The merchant shakes his head and remains silent. This shocks the student, who did not expect such discourteous treatment from a Jewish elder. The merchant, seeing the young man's puzzlement, then says, 'My boy, I will explain why I was so rude. When you got into the compartment, I concluded by your clothes and manners that you were going home from university and that you did not come from my small town, otherwise I would know you. Now, at our station everybody has to change trains in order to go on. I happen to know that repairs are in progress at the junction and that there are no trains until tomorrow. You therefore have to stay the night in my town. Now, if I get into a conversation with you I will be obliged, as a fellow Jew, to invite you home to stay until the morning. So it is inevitable that you meet my beautiful daughter Rachel. Upon seeing each other, I know, it will be love at first sight.' The merchant then sighed and said, 'To be frank, I do not want my daughter to marry a man who cannot afford a watch.'

A different story illustrates the ironic saying that Germans, Russians and Jews are traditionally anti-Semitic. The Jews have always laughed at themselves in order to offset the pain of humiliation. 'Better we mock ourselves', said one sage, 'in order to be able to cope with persecution'. This story tells of two Jews who, upon passing an Orthodox Church in old Russia, see a sign that reads, 'Jews, one hundred roubles if you convert to the True Faith'. One Jew then says to the other, 'Wait here, while I go in and see if what the notice says is true'. After two hours he comes out, not wearing his hat. 'Well did they pay up?' his friend asked. 'That's typical of you Jews,' the other said, as he walked by. 'All you think about is money.'

The root of this story goes back to the Middle Ages when the only profession open to Jews, besides petty trading, was banking. This occupation was forbidden by the Church and so some Jewish entrepreneurs became the financiers of Christendom. They generated

FIGURE 62—WIT
Benjamin Disraeli converted to Christianity in order to enter the English Establishment. He dressed like a dandy, was a ladies' man and made Queen Victoria laugh. When he became Prime Minister, he bought the Suez Canal so that Britain had a secure strategic route to India. Here he winks at the Sphinx about the deal. Disraeli's final joke was to be buried as an aristocrat in a very English country churchyard, just outside his country mansion. For the then-despised Jews of England, this was the ultimate ironic jest. His career opened the door for my grandfather and his like to migrate to England. (Punch cartoon).

much resentment, especially because they also collected taxes for the king, while their humbler and poorer brethren bore the brunt of hostility from those who called them 'Christ Killers'.

Jews also laugh about their own clergy. As we have no Pope, it is possible to parody rabbinic authority with relative impunity. Take the story of the two orthodox grandparents. Their grandson wants a 'Yamaha' for his *Bar Mitzvah*, that is, when he officially becomes a man at thirteen, according to Jewish tradition. The problem is that they do not know what a 'Yamaha' is. So they go to their orthodox rabbi and ask. He thinks for a moment and says it is not a Hebrew or Yiddish word and says they should go to his son, a conservative Jew and professor of Semitic languages. The professor ponders and says, 'Well, it is not biblical, rabbinic or modern Hebrew. Nor is it Syriac, western or eastern Aramaic, Coptic or Ethiopic.' He shakes his head and admits he does not recognise the word. The despairing grandparents are walking down the road when they see a rather nondescript building with a Star of David over the door. They ask the man sweeping the yard, if it is a synagogue. He nods and says it serves a Liberal congregation where the services are largely in English. Could they speak to the rabbi, the old couple ask. 'I am the rabbi', the man replies. The grandparents had never seen a rabbi sweeping before, but they explain that their grandson wants a 'Yamaha' for his Bar Mitzvah. 'What is a Yamaha?'

'Oh', says the rabbi, 'It's a small Japanese motorcycle'.

After the couple walks away, having thanked him, the rabbi calls them back and says, 'Tell me, what is a Bar Mitzvah?'

Even Kabbalah has its jokes. One is about Rabbi Cohen, who loves golf and plays it every day. One Yom Kippur, the most serious Day of Atonement when all Jews confess their sins, he goes out very early to play a round on the course. Elijah draws God's attention to Rabbi Cohen enjoying himself on the links before he goes to the synagogue. 'How can he be punished for such laxity?' Elijah asks. The Almighty replies, 'Just watch.' From that point on the Rabbi scores a hole in one for every shot. The Rabbi is delighted at the miraculous improvement in his game. Elijah says puzzled, 'What kind of punishment is this?' The Lord replies, 'Who can he tell?' The karma for our sins is sometimes more subtle than Hellfire and more effective.

Then there is the story of the Jew sitting on the roof of his house during a flood. A neighbour comes by in a boat and offers to take him off. He shakes his head and says, 'The Lord will save me'. Then comes a police launch on a rescue mission; but he turns them down with the words, 'The Lord will save me'. The water eventually rises, sweeps him away and he is drowned. When he gets to Heaven, he complains about how he was not saved in time. Elijah tells him, 'We sent you two opportunities but you did not recognise that they were in fact from the Lord'. This tale is about omens and options not seen.

Another story is also about choice. A certain man knew he was going to die soon, so he went to his local Kabbalist and said, 'I have not been that good in my life but neither have I been that bad. I believe, because I have free will, I can chose to go to Paradise or Hell. Can you put me in a trance, so that I can have a glimpse of Paradise?' The Kabbalist obliges and the man finds himself in a most pleasant place. It is like an exclusive country club with a nice class of people. Where better to spend the afterlife? Upon regaining earthly consciousness he asks, 'Out of curiosity, could I have a brief vision of Hell?' 'Indeed, that is your choice', says the Kabbalist and puts him back into a trance. The man then finds himself in a place like the gambling city of Las Vegas with its brilliant lights, girls and all manner of excitements. Somewhat reluctantly he returns to his body and says to the Kabbalist, 'I've decided to choose Hell. Paradise, in comparison, is very boring.' When he dies, the man finds himself spitted on a griddle over a hot fire, being poked by demons with very sharp forks. 'It wasn't like this, when I came last time', he screams. 'Ah', says one of the demons, 'Then you were a tourist'. Here is free will in action.

Finally there is the thought-provoking joke about spiritual inflation. Two very important rabbis are praying in the synagogue. As they sway to and fro, like a flame that represents the fire of Divinity, they chant in Hebrew, 'Lord I am nothing! Lord I am nothing!' This is a kabbalistic mantra. The synagogue's caretaker, who is sweeping in a corner, hears them and he too begins to chant, 'Lord I am nothing'. This goes on for a minute or two, until one eminent rabbi whispers to the other, nodding towards the caretaker, 'Look who thinks he is nothing'.

I have used these and many other such stories in my teaching to illustrate kabbalistic principles. The human mind works well with either ideas or symbols, that is, the left and right pillars of the Tree and the two halves of the brain. The joke is a mode which requires a degree of higher consciousness, to discern the incongruity of the situation and its resolution in an insight. I have observed, over the years, that neurotic people often cannot get the point of a joke because they are locked into a one-dimensional universe of their egocentric world. In contrast, evolving people often get the message before the end of the joke, as they see exactly what is coming. The joke is a very useful tool in discerning someone's level, in counselling or presenting another dimension by a crazy parable.

The Universe is full of humour. One only has to consider the various strange kinds of different plants, animals and people there are. Life presents ridiculous situations that make a point about development, such as looking where you are going. Without laughter, humanity could not survive. This is why we love the court jester and joker who can expose the Truth in a witty comment. Most cartoons are based upon this principle, be they political or domestic. Consider all the jokes about courtship and marriage. For example, take the Jewish view on before and after the wedding. 'Love is kissing on a sofa—marriage is arguing about which sofa to buy'. Or, when an old couple were asked if, in their fifty years of marriage, they had ever considered splitting up. They both replied, 'Murder yes! But divorce? Never!'

FIGURE 63—SPINOZA
I always felt a sympathy with this lone philosopher and mystic. The Jewish community rejected his 17th century rational interpretation of kabbalistic ideas because it was not in traditional terms. When I visited his cottage I felt a great kinship, as I had the same problem with the rabbinic establishment. His study was much like my own. He, too, had groups which were made up of people belonging to different faiths seeking for the truth. (Spinoza's home, 19th century drawing).

31. Visits

After one of my books had been translated into Dutch, I received an invitation to lecture there. Out of this came the first overseas group which still continues today. The Dutch are very religious for a nation of traders. Having so little land and so few natural resources, aside from the sea, they have a saying, 'God made the world but the Dutch made Holland'. This is literally true, as much of the country is below sea level and could easily be swept away if the dykes failed. I concluded that this threat made them acutely aware of fate at a collective level, which inclined them to be both philosophical and religious. As a people they are said to be ruled by the Watery and psychic sign of Cancer, which makes them very receptive to the mystical.

I felt a great affinity with the Dutch, who are a small nation. Like Palestine, their land has been fought over many times as the great powers of Europe used the Netherlands as a battleground. Upon gaining their freedom from Spain the Dutch became, despite being fiercely Protestant, the most tolerant of societies on the Continent. This allowed Jews from Spain and Portugal to settle there and become part of the commercial establishment during the golden 17th century, when the Dutch were Europe's leading traders. This was a providential event as the Jews, a Capricornian people, are the astrological complement to the Cancerian Dutch. Indeed, both prospered as Jews had relatives throughout the known world who could further Dutch commercial interests.

Rembrandt, the greatest of Dutch artists, lived in the Jewish quarter of Amsterdam. He often depicted biblical events, using the local people as models. Most of these spoke Ladino, a medieval Spanish dialect. With their Iberian culture came Kabbalah. The Dutch intelligentsia were particularly interested in this, as it was seen as the lost teaching of Jesus who undoubtedly knew the Jewish esoteric tradition. This was revealed in such phrases as the 'Kingdom of Heaven', which is the meeting place of the three lower Worlds on Jacob's Ladder. The place of the Messiah and the site of the Heavenly Jerusalem are the 'Kingdom of God'. Because the Jews possessed such Knowledge, the Dutch intelligentsia sought out rabbis who could reveal the inner Teaching of the Bible. I suspect that this need was the reason I was invited to Holland. It was very familiar to me, especially the Jewish quarter of Amsterdam.

After each weekend I spent in Holland teaching, my hosts would take me to wherever I wished to explore. Besides the Great Synagogue in Amsterdam, which has an extraordinary atmosphere, I also visited Anne Frank's apartment, where she and her family hid until they were betrayed by a neighbour. This was a very moving experience as the presence of her family was still there. She was an old soul, whose fate was to record the situation in German-occupied Holland. Her sensitivity and belief in the best of human nature indicated that she might well have volunteered to be born in that time and place, to bear witness to the Holocaust. Not every old soul returns to Earth to enjoy the fruits of their development but to carry out, as in her case, a very difficult mission.

Another old soul, Baruch Spinoza, who lived in 17th century Holland, also had a difficult time but for different reasons. He was a Spanish-Portuguese Jew who was born in Amsterdam where he had the standard rabbinic education. At that time, the Protestant world was opening up to wider horizons not permitted in Catholic countries. The French philosopher Descartes' approach of rationalism was then taking over from medieval scholasticism which had atrophied from religious dogma. Spinoza set out to cast the Kabbalah in rational terms. Unfortunately, analytical method was beyond the rabbis who saw his abstract ideas as godless when, in fact, they were the very opposite. The community excommunicated this remarkable mystic because they felt that the Dutch authorities might see him as a heretic and a threat. This could curtail the Jews' delicate position in Holland and so he was isolated.

The philosophically-minded Spinoza retreated to a small house near the university town of Leyden. Here he earned a living as a lens grinder while teaching a small protestant study group the metaphysics of his system which was based upon kabbalistic principles. Alas he died relatively young, from glass dust. His home, however, has been preserved exactly as it was. I went to visit it. The place was very quiet, full of books, his furniture and workbench. It had the feeling that he had just left the room and would soon be back. The silence was almost overwhelming, as I had picked up that some of Spinoza's most profound revelations had occurred in this space. I felt a great affinity with him, as he had set out to update Kabbalah in the terms of his time. I hoped I might get a 'visitation' from him while there but this did not happen.

Another country to which I was invited was Belgium. This had quite a different feel. It was essentially Catholic, as many there had chosen to side with their Spanish overlords. One result was the split between the French- and Flemish-speaking populations. Here was the front line in Europe between the Catholic and Protestant communities as collective memories had not faded in the passing of the generations. While in Belgium I sought out to find out more about the medieval school of the soul, called the 'Brothers and Sisters of the Common Life'. These were Christian lay people who lived under a remarkable spiritual discipline which allowed them to lead everyday lives. They clearly had an esoteric teaching as one of their number, the painter Bosch, demonstrates. He was educated by the Order and produced a picture of the soul, immediately after death, floating up a dark tunnel assisted by angels towards a figure standing against a background of Light. This was a classic image of what happens upon dying. Recent research into 'Near Death Experiences' confirms Bosch's depiction of this post-mortem phenomenon.

Another famous product of this school of the soul was Erasmus, the illegitimate son of a monk. He was well acquainted with Kabbalah and one of the first 'Humanists'. However, while he was for the reformation of the Catholic Church, he did not wish to destroy the best aspects of this ancient institution. His book, *On Human Folly*, reveals a balanced insight into 'sleeping' people who live in a semi-dream state and pursue delusions, such as believing in buying a guarantee from the Church that they would be allowed into Heaven. The clergy, especially, did not escape the witty barbs of his criticism. I later discovered that the Society of the Common Life still existed but in a modern form. It did, however, hide its presence until a suitable candidate was invited to join its company.

In my early days studying Kabbalah, my Instructor had mentioned the line of the Common Life, as he had a connection. At some point he asked me if I would like to join the fraternity. Needless to say, I was most intrigued and agreed. I was then told to take a train to a town, just outside London, and go to a certain public building at a specific time. There I would be shown into a room, hired for the occasion, and be asked to wait. I had heard of such initiation ceremonies in the occult tradition, where a candidate's commitment is tested by asking them to

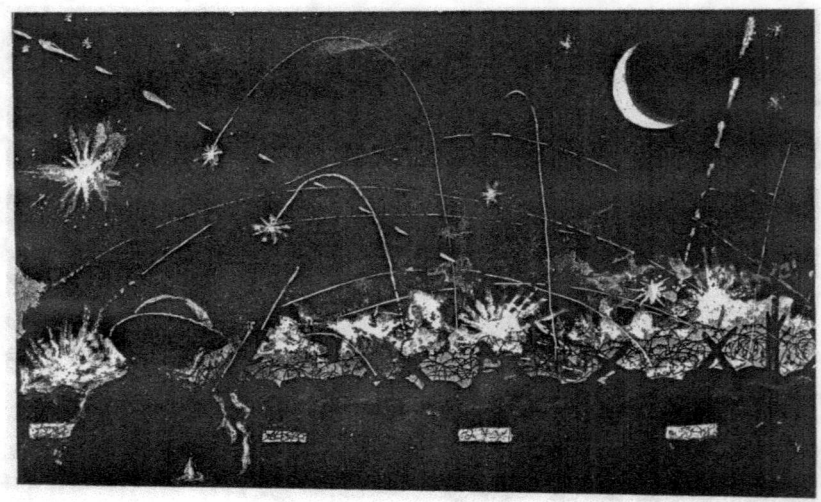

FIGURE 64—TRENCHES
I have no memories of the First World War. While I was deeply moved when I visited the battlefields in Belgium, it was not personal. I believe that I died sometime before this conflict, as the pre-Great War clothes and styles are very familiar to me. It is clear that I was not meant to be incarnate during this dreadful time. However, I was born in England in 1933, the year Hitler came to power, and lived to witness the Second World War. The reason for this, it would seem, was to be ready for the rise of interest in the esoteric after the war, when many who had been killed returned and matured in the 1960s and sought to understand what life was about. (Impression of a Great War battle by the author).

meet some unknown person in a distant place at an awkward time. I agreed to be at the appointed place and hour and waited in the room as directed. After a moment or two someone entered whom I did not know. They asked me if I agreed with certain statements, which were then read out. I agreed with them because they were both ethical and practical as regards spiritual work, which I liked. I was then given an arrow. The person then suddenly turned and left the room, leaving me alone with this symbol of shooting straight.

On the way home on the train I examined the arrow. It was the kind used for target practice, not hunting. This led to the realisation of the implication of its meaning. Truth was the target. I was delighted by the analogue and the thoughtfulness behind it. In later years I came to know which of my friends and acquaintances were members of this Order. I dedicated the book *Adam and the Kabbalistic Tree* to them. They are still present but very discreet and we have travelled together, each on our own paths, for many decades.

A particularly moving experience in Belgium occurred when I visited the old front line of the First World War. This was in the section called Sanctuary Wood which had been carefully preserved. It was composed of a stretch of trenches in a wood whose original trees had been blasted away by shell fire. Standing on the site, I picked up the atmosphere of terror and carnage that still hung over it. It was here, in soaking uniforms and soggy mud, that soldiers stood guard, slept and were killed. Many of them must have realised the madness of that war but few deserted, as the collective conditioning of the period, to fight for one's country, had a total hold on people's mind. A few who did realise the conflict was insane did indeed go mad. Those who kept their nerve and refused to fight were declared cowards, tried by a biased military court and shot. Here was a classic example that most of humanity, the vegetable level, is psychologically asleep and easily led by animal people who are half-awake but subject to their need to dominate. It was only those who tried to be fully human that saw what was really happening. Many millions died as a result of this international folly. Erasmus was right.

I had read of a psychic who came to this place, after the Great War, and saw the apparitions of many dead soldiers, still hanging around the trenches awaiting orders. They had not realised that they had been killed because there were so many others like them who appeared to be alive. Now all but a few had gone, as I could pick up their sad presences around. Upon leaving the battlefield I pondered why the two World

Wars had happened. When I asked my inner teacher this question, the answer came back, 'Karma'. Europe had exploited the populations of every other continent and, due to the law of 'Measure for Measure', the West inevitably had to suffer. 'Why had God not prevented such events?' I asked while viewing a vast military graveyard. My teacher's answer was that this would deprive humanity of both collective and individual free will. Mankind, it seemed, had to learn the hard way, like a wayward child. However, all who had died were soon reborn, some, alas, to wreak revenge for their defeat in the Second World War. This brought about a lesson, that wars bring no profit to anyone. All this went into my deepening understanding of history from an esoteric viewpoint.

32. Testings

Since my break with the 'Anima' lady who, I believed, had been the great love of my life, loneliness had become a problem. I would work all day on my books but the evenings were empty. I would visit friends but that was not the same as having a partner and there was a limit to spending time in someone else's home. As leader of the group, people would come to see me about their birth charts or to discuss a problem, but never for social reasons. I realised that this was the situation of every captain of a ship, be it in esoteric or exoteric work. The boss of whatever enterprise cannot talk to just anyone. This is because few can understand the complexity of leadership with its many levels, ranging from the overview to fine detail. I would often consult the I Ching, which was like having a wise father to talk to, but I needed an intelligent and committed lady with whom I could discuss anything to balance off my life.

There was no lack of women in the group whose female instincts attracted them to the alpha-male archetype. Unfortunately this is largely a romantic projection which a male leader has to deal with, even if he has a partner. Another problem was that many women of that time belonged to the feminist generation who fought for the right not only to be equal but also to compete with men. One result was that they often found themselves without lovers or husbands because most men turned away and chose feminine girls of a younger age. This still-youthful set had seen how their elder sisters either had no partners or teamed up with a weak man they could control but for whom they had little respect. While most of the women in the group were concerned with development, some were unconscious of the grip that the feminist movement had upon them.

Some male teachers I came across succumbed to the temptation of women offering themselves, in their delusion or desperation, to the 'Master' archetype. One Guru I met slept with several devotees in a month, while another had a current 'queen', until he became bored with her or she began to lose her 'shine', due to the stress of the rôle and the envy of her rivals. Needless to say, this destroyed the integrity

FIGURE 65—SOUL MATES

*According to many esoteric traditions, we all have soul mates. The reason for this is that, in the Garden of Eden, each cell of Adam Kadmon is divided into a couple. Each couple, in turn, belongs to a particular soul group, dependent upon from which part of the Divine Adam they came. When first incarnated on Earth the pair is, initially, part of a tribal family. Here they get used to terrestrial conditions. This takes many lives but there comes a point when the clan breaks up. Then the male and female souls go off in different directions to individuate. They may encounter each other in later incarnations but not to come together until they are spiritually mature. Then their fates merge into a mutual destiny in which they perform their ordained mission. (*Garden of Eden*, Medieval woodcut).*

of both teachers and eventually precipitated their downfall. I was once at a meeting of such a 'Master' and saw how he deliberately enchanted his followers with sacred songs on a guitar. I then perceived the apparition of a tall figure standing just behind him, shaking its head. Dressed in the traditional robe of that group's tradition, the teacher's normally invisible mentor was in despair. His protégé, who was extremely gifted, was not only destroying himself but also estranging many seekers from the 'Work', as well as emotionally hurting several women.

After the meeting, I left with a mixture of sadness and anger, as this remarkable man had succumbed to the Lucific test all teachers face. Halfway home, I was stopped dead in the street and told, by a disembodied voice, to go back to the house where the man was staying and warn him. I found him in the kitchen with a mug of whisky, already well inebriated. I told him of the message I had been given to pass on. He looked alarmed but took a gulp of his drink as his eyes glazed over and he turned away to speak with someone else. I saw him some months later, on a rainy night, walking drunkenly along the gutter of a London street in a deep depression. I learnt later that his earthly instructor had cut the man off from his school and taken his honourable title away from him. From that time on, slowly over the years, the man dissolved from a charismatic spiritual figure into a shell of what he might have been. He finished up alone in an old folks home, long before his time.

My test came in several direct offers from nice and some very pretty and well-meaning ladies. One asked if we were soul mates, in what I thought was meant to be an astrological consultation, while another, in a social situation, hinted that she was devoted to me. I tactfully refused both proposals, although I was tempted by the beauty of the latter. Another lady tried the direct sexual approach. During a visit to her flat she actually pushed me down onto her bed. I froze to her passion and she suddenly realised that she had made a terrible mistake. I used all my diplomatic skill to extract myself and alleviate her embarrassment. She soon left the group because she was seeking a husband, rather than the Truth.

There was one woman, of my many acquaintances, who did attract me. She was a very statuesque and fiery character whose lover had left her upon getting her pregnant. The opportunity to help a lovely damsel in distress, together with the fact that we were from the same Jewish culture, prompted my instincts. I was now well into my forties which made me consider her as a possibility. Such is the subtlety of the Lucific temptation.

At first I did nothing as I knew it would cause problems in the group because the conventional rule is that a teacher should not court a student. And so I held back. However, when the time came for the child to be born, she invited me to be present at the birth as a stand-in for the absent father who would have nothing more to do with her. I had seen death, but not birth, and so I could not say 'no' on any account. Together with some of the women in the group, I went to the hospital to give support and set up the astrological chart for the moment the child was born. The midwives in the labour ward assumed I was the father and accepted my presence. After hours of waiting and noting the positions of the Sun, Moon and planets moving minute by minute, I was eventually called in to the delivery room actually to see the child being born.

This was an extraordinary experience. Besides the nurses and doctor working on the mother-to-be, I observed four huge shimmering columns of blue fire surrounding her bed. I took these potent but silent pillars to be a protective field-force. I assumed that they were there to prevent any lost soul in Limbo seeking to take over the now-complete embryo by displacing the incarnating individual. At the top of this psychic 'channel' I could just make out several figures who appeared to be helping someone into the head of the great funnel made by the columns. There was a pause and then the infant came forth from the womb. The figures above then faded. The shimmering funnel remained in place for a while until the umbilical cord was cut. It then dissolved. My attention was now drawn to the child.

The little girl's eyes were very bright as she looked around the delivery room at each person present. Her gaze was that of an adult, not a baby. The mother then directed the child to be given to me to hold. At that moment I felt the power of the higher Worlds flowing through her being and into mine. If I had been the father, I think I would have been overwhelmed; but I was not. I had had no part in the parents' relationship and so I could be relatively objective. Even so, I perceived the force of Nature that 'might' bind the mother, the child and myself together. Was this Providence, I wondered? After all, Pythagoras had married one of his students. Was this to be my fate?

Once the child was taken home and the routine of life set in, I observed the 'Jewish mother' archetype manifesting when the lady stated that she wanted three daughters. This was, to me, an omen. It was an understandable instinctive desire and, as there was no husband to hand, I might fill this rôle. I soon found myself being increasingly involved with her and the child as my memories of a happy family life arose to feed the feeling of being part of the Jewish tribe again. Initially, our relationship worked well because we had a collective culture in common. However, the lady still loved the absent father. This was the second warning. I realised I was at that point just a very good substitute.

I disregarded this thought because I was charmed by the prospect of perhaps being the father of a settled and secure family. However, I had had a controlling mother and three powerful and possessive aunts, as well as a very strong-willed sister-in-law. Traditionally, Jewish women are not delicate flowers. This dates back to the Bible when Moses gave in to the demands of the daughters of a dead man whose legacy was going to be given to the girls' uncle. This decision about inheritance not only became law but put women in a non-subservient position. This is seen in the Jewish joke about a fiftieth wedding anniversary. In this the husband, in his speech to friends and family, declared that he and his wife never quarrelled. This was because she made all the small decisions, like moving a home, while he decided the big ones, such as Israel's military and political policy.

As the romantic stage of our relationship faded, it became increasingly apparent that there were big problems ahead. I was poor, with no prospect of having a nice, middle-class home for two or more prospective children, while she made it clear she could not be a teacher's devoted lady. She was too much of an artist and a bohemian to fulfil such a demanding role. This, I recognised, was an honest admission of her limitations. Added to this, her interest was now primarily focused on her child. I was sharply reminded, time and time again, of the classic conflict between Jewish spouses. This was summed up in a joke about the husband who said to a friend: 'I married Miss Right but I did not realise her first name was Always'. Fortunately the relationship came to a natural end. Shortly after she had left the group, she married a man who gave her two daughters.

So here I was on my own again. This was increasingly hard as many of the people of my age now had grown-up children and I felt that my prospects were rapidly shortening. My birth chart, as noted, said marriage would be a problem and, indeed, it was the case. Nearly all the women I had courted did not want to live like a student, as I did, although they enjoyed the idea of being the lover of a writer.

Moreover, some wished to keep their independence because they were strong, talented and intelligent. The irony was that, in later years, two of them regretted this when they saw I was doing well. One had married a weak but wealthy man and the other was alone and past her time to bear children.

At a certain momentous moment, while out for a walk in Holland Park, I decided to leave the whole 'wife' problem to Heaven, where true marriages are said to be made. This can only occur, according to kabbalistic tradition, when the two people meant to be together are mature enough to be a match. Then they can carry out their mutual destiny. Until that time I had to accept being alone and wait and see who would come.

33. New World

About this time, I was invited to run a course in New York City. It was the first of many visits to North America. My image of New York was based upon books, movies and television, so what I expected was not real. For several days I walked the streets waiting to be mugged until someone pointed out that the way I dressed, in an ex-army jacket and jeans, I looked like a mugger and was more likely to frighten New Yorkers. I realised that I had ceased to be a tourist after several visits when I stopped looking up in awe at the skyscrapers and someone, a tourist, asked me where the nearest subway was. New York was in many ways like London and soon I felt quite at home. It was only by a trick of fate, perhaps, that I had not been born in New York, as my paternal grandfather had been on his way there.

As a result of a series of lectures over several years, a New York group was founded. However, it was not without resistance from some of the many orthodox Jews who lived there. At one talk, a man stood up and asked how I could teach Kabbalah without speaking Hebrew. Some of the audience nodded and waited for my answer. I was about to reply when someone else stood up, turned to the man and shouted, 'You just heard a damn fine lecture on Kabbalah. Why don't you just shut up?' This was clearly New York and not London, where one is polite even in delivering an insult. The questioner ran out of the lecture hall. I learnt later he was a Jewish dope junkie who envied me the attention I was given. My response to this kind of opposition is the biblical injunction that the Jews were meant to be 'A light unto the Nations' and I was fulfilling my Levite calling.

Another sign of resistance was when I went to visit the ultra-orthodox community in Brooklyn. I had gone there to see the Hassidic *Rebbe*, said by some to be the present Messiah. While waiting in a queue to enter the Study House, where he was to conduct the afternoon service, a Hassid saw a copy of one of my books in my hand. I had the delusion that it would be a nice gesture to present the Rebbe with a copy, to show what 20th century Kabbalah was doing. He had been to university in Paris before the war and was well aware of modern secular and

FIGURE 66—REDSKIN
This name was used by some Europeans to correct the misnomer 'Indian'. When I encountered them on my travels around the United States I felt great compassion for them as their destruction echoed the story of my people. Their defence was stoicism and this protected their culture and esoteric tradition. I encountered this in a medicine man, dressed in blue jeans, who instantly recognised the Tree of Life scroll I showed him. He saw that we were both children of the Great Spirit. A common problem was recognised when a group of young Native Americans showed me a film about the extermination of their people. When I told them about the Holocaust they became silent and respectful. (Drawing by the author).

scientific attitudes. The Hassid standing beside me, observing that the book's title was in English, muttered something in Yiddish which was clearly contemptuous. This omen made me give up the idea of giving it to the Rebbe. In a different situation another rabbi, I was told, said that I was not Jewish. My informant about this incident told the rabbi that he knew me personally and that I was a Jew. The rabbi said that he had his information from the highest source. A few weeks later he was injured in a car crash. Whether this was karma is open to debate, but what is not is that he was clearly denying the truth which, in his responsible position, was a sign that he was not a man of integrity.

Once, while travelling by the Canadian-American border, I met a Native American medicine man on an Indian Reservation. I showed him Jacob's Ladder, which he immediately recognised. He said, 'Ours is in the form of a circle'. In contrast, I had a quite different experience when I was taken to the Reservation museum. Here, a number of angry young men showed me a video of how the whites had massacred their ancestors. However, when I said I was a European Jew who had had six million of my cousins murdered, not only recently but down the centuries, they changed from being hostile foes into sympathetic friends. I had the sense that this incident had made them realise they were not the only oppressed minority. Years later in New Mexico I met a Red Indian, as he wished to be called, who had been in Australia and visited the 'Black Fellows' there. He now knew that persecution was a worldwide problem for indigenous minorities. He identified his people's plight strongly with the Israelites in the Bible, whom he had learnt about from Baptist missionaries.

I found New England delightful because its landscapes, towns, names and people were like home. Indeed, when I gave some of the Vermont Kabbalah group an example of the English country accent I had as a boy, they declared it could be easily mistaken for the local Vermont dialect. This cultural affinity was very helpful because on most of the courses I taught abroad I had to adapt to the local culture. However in Boston, the most British of cities, there was no problem of communication. In San Francisco I had to cope with a strongly feminist audience up to the point when I said I was a Jewish European white male-chauvinist pig and that they would have to take this into account. This caused great laughter, even among the women who now accepted me as a perhaps worthwhile patriarchal monster. The Spanish South West of the United States was of particular interest, as I have Spanish-Jewish ancestors and easily related to the Latino

FIGURE 67—SOUTH
I painted this mural for a London restaurant. The Disney-like image and its jolly figures did not match what I experienced when I visited the Deep South. The memory of the Civil War was still present. The Black community was still subdued and, while the Whites were outwardly gracious, as was the nature of the old aristocratic culture, there was still an unconscious resentment of the Yankee North. One fact fascinated me. Many of the poor Whites were descendents of convicts from London's prisons. They had the same fair hair, blue eyes and pale skin of the 'Cockney' who had Viking ancestors. These raiders had settled in London's East End. I was told that the South had more Whites in prison than the North. Reincarnation had changed nothing. (Painting by the author).

culture. The 'Anglos', as the white Americans were called, even though they might be Polish, German or Russian in origin, were of a different order. Many belonged to the psychotherapy community of the Santa Fe area. This group invited me to speak to the Jungian society about Kabbalah and psychology which was a revelation to some psychologists. One result was that one of the students began to teach Kabbalah at a local synagogue, even though he was not Jewish. This was extremely unusual and occurred because the rabbi felt that Kabbalah had something important to say. He was a very rare kind of rabbi. But then he, I believe, had been a 'hippy' in his youth and was open to the spiritual dimension in addition to Talmudic studies.

Once, when I was sitting in a Santa Fe restaurant, the waiter who served us just looked like a Sabra, an Israeli-born Jew. When I asked him, out of curiosity, if he was Jewish, he replied yes but he was now a Baptist. I had heard that Jewish *conversos* had fled to Santa Fe to get away from the inquisition in Mexico and this was confirmed by an old graveyard with the names of Cohen and Levi appearing on several tombstones. The waiter told me that his grandfather used to take his prayer shawl and prayer book out to the nearby mountain and pray in secret. This was ironic, as the range is called *Sangre de Cristo* or the Blood of Christ. As I drank my coffee I thought of the secret Jews who had been arrested, tortured and executed by the Inquisition.

I, like many Europeans, had a romantic view of the old Wild West. When I visited an old mining town, which had been preserved and was now inhabited by people dressed up in 19th century clothes, the idealised image dissolved. On the main street there was just a veneer of civilisation. Violence, I was told, was commonplace as men, roughened by hard labour and lack of women, would kill each other over some trivial issue. And yet there were good people present at the same time who ran the school, church and the synagogue. The Jews were the merchants of the period who brought in, by mule and steam trains from the settled areas, tools, gadgets and even fashionable clothes, as well as prefabricated houses that could create a town within a decade. This was the American dream at its best, as a new kind of nation was being born. Here was evolution at work in the Divine Plan.

Seeing this dimension made me think of the millions who crossed the oceans to build a new kind of society. These were usually animal-level people because the vegetable stratum of the Old World's population preferred to remain at home in poor but relatively secure positions. Most of the migrants who came to America set out to become rich, acquire land or live according to their political and religious ideals. This made the United States a unique country in that, unlike the other European empires, its people were relatively free from rigid traditions, codes and conditionings. Here was humanity at a new point of development. There was, however, a contradiction that was inherent in the American birth chart. Mars in Gemini on the Ascendant together with Uranus meant fraternal conflict. Here was the shadow side of the country.

The issue of slavery in the 19th century precipitated the American Civil War between the Northern and Southern states. The Geminian factor fought over the issue of equality and opportunity. When I stood on the Civil War battlefield of Bull Run in Virginia and picked up the hauntedness of these seemingly tranquil meadows, I thought of my visit to the house of Thomas Jefferson, the son of a poor London woman. This was a large and beautiful mansion, based upon an English aristocratic country manor. Here he had many slaves and a black mistress. The 'Land of the Free' had a kind of schizophrenia which was to plague America, with its destruction of the Indian people and its acquisition by war of much of Mexico's territory. All this went on while denouncing European imperialism.

In Washington D.C. I ran a course at a Masonic Lodge. This was a very interesting operation. It was the result of one of our School, then resident in Washington, writing an important book about Freemasonry with Kabbalah as a hidden framework. He was to be one of several people from the Kabbalah Society who founded various study groups in the United States. Some of these arose quite spontaneously, using my books as a guide. This proved the inspiration I had been given to produce a series of kabbalistic textbooks in a modern idiom which gave seekers anywhere access to the Tradition. With more and more foreign editions, the Kabbalah Society's version of the line became available to students all over the world.

There was one providential incident associated with America that is worth recording. Before setting out for the airport in New York to go home to Britain, I received a telephone call to say my flight had been cancelled and that I was to report to the prestigious Concorde desk for its supersonic flight. I was delighted at this news and looked forward to flying home on this remarkable plane. However, when I got to Kennedy Airport the airline knew nothing about my change of schedule. As I had missed the flight I was supposed to be on, I was in a most difficult position. Recognising my plight, the British Airways people said that it so happened there was an empty seat on Concorde. Soon I was flying at supersonic speed at a height where I could see the curvature of the Earth. It seems someone, with malicious intent, had set up this cruel hoax but Providence had intervened and turned it completely around. A world traveller friend remarked, when he heard about this incident, 'I could never afford to fly on Concorde. Heaven must be taking care of you.' Indeed it was and I was deeply grateful for this very precise miracle.

FIGURE 68—SIGNS
The design of the Zodiac is not based, as usually believed, on the constellations. These star markers have long moved on out of position, due to the precession of the Equinox. The origin of Capricorn, for example, is a symbolic picture of that specific time of the year and the kind of general temperament born then. The Fish-Goat represents the Sun's shift from its lowest point and the beginning of its climb. The Fish is below and the Goat above the surface of the solstitial image of the transition. However, there is much more to be read in this archetype. The fish is cold- and the goat warm-blooded, which gives an insight into the Capricornians' complex temperament. (Painting by author).

34. Astrology

The next book was to be about astrology and Kabbalah. By this time I had mastered the former and no longer needed to refer to books, except in unusual cases. This was because I saw how kabbalistic principles worked within the astrological system. In this new volume I wanted to show how the two systems could be applied to psychology and the pattern of a life, hence the title *The Anatomy of Fate*. In the preface I set out the aim of bringing in the spiritual dimension without which astrology has no depth. Most people do not know that its purpose is to be a working method of development and not just a character reading or insight into what might happen on this or that day.

The first chapter outlined the cosmology of the ancient world and aligned astrological principles with those of Kabbalah. Then the various human levels of vegetable, animal and human degrees of evolution were defined together with the nature of the celestial gods. After this came the metaphysics of Existence and the Divine Plan for the macrocosm and the microcosm, and their interaction. This was followed by a description of the psyche in terms of the Sun, Moon and planets, and their archetypes, on the Tree, leading to a look at how astrology affects history, taking the birth chart of the United States as an example. The descent of an individual from the 'Treasure House of Souls' into the body was then described, with an examination of the resultant horoscope. This not only set out the nature of the person's temperament but the pattern of fate from birth to death. The process was demonstrated by an example birth chart in the light of how that individual would exercise, or not, the prerogative of free will. Disease, crisis and decisions, as well as degrees of choice, were discussed, so too was the theme of sleeping or awakened Sun or the Self. The soul and the spirit were then explored in terms of astrology, as well as the problem of evil, together with themes of Providence, destiny and death.

Many of the conclusions in the book were influenced by my doing numerous charts of well known and historic people but, more importantly, those of individuals who came to see me to have their

FIGURE 69—ASTROLABE
This medieval instrument was used for locating both terrestrial and celestial positions. I made this one from a photocopy of a medieval model, which was then cut out and set on wood. One of the early Kabbalists I admire was Abraham Ibn Ezra, who used to carry an astrolabe wherever he went so as to draw up horoscopes. He was a Spanish Jew who lectured on the Bible, astrology and Neo-Platonism to the various Jewish communities with whom he stayed during his travels. He spent some time in England, in London, and no doubt visited Oxford where Jews taught Hebrew at the new University there. Some have suggested that I might be a reincarnation of him and, indeed, we have much in common as regards temperament, especially regarding his unconventional approach. (Photograph of the author's model by Peter Dickinson).

charts done. Most were people in the Work and therefore open to the notion of different levels of astrology and development. In the case of people not on the Path one could tell, by their demeanour, whether they lived off their Moon or Sun, that is, their ego or their Self. By applying the birth chart to the Tree, it was possible to see the configuration of the psyche. For example, an afflicted Saturn would incline a person to be cautious, while an afflicted Mars could make them obsessive. Conversely, a favourably-angled Saturn and Mars might make them industrious and highly disciplined. The art was to interpret the various combinations of the luminaries and planets in relation to the Zodiac and the House system. It is similar to a physician synthesising all the symptoms presented and coming to a diagnostic conclusion. It took many years to learn how to see the overall pattern and not to be lost in detail.

There were occasionally some very interesting encounters. One day, I had a psychoanalyst to tea. Out of curiosity, I asked if I could take a look at her horoscope. After about four minutes of defining the chart's main features, she became very agitated. This was unusual in a person trained to be psychologically objective. She said, while controlling some powerful emotions, that I had identified in a few minutes her main problems. This was extraordinary. She said with some feeling that it had taken her many years of analysis, and a great deal of money, to arrive at the same conclusions. She added, with a grim humour as she recovered her composure, that had we lived five hundred years ago, she would have had me denounced to the Church and burnt at the stake for witchcraft. Ironically, as a result of this conversation she became a committed member of the group.

Another case which did not have such a pleasant outcome was an engaged couple who came to me to see if their birth charts were compatible. As I went through the procedure of comparing their horoscopes, it became apparent that their mutual attraction was due to their harmonious Ascendants and Moons. This meant that they aroused each other sexually and got on well at the social level. However, the positions of the Sun and planets indicated that they would initially get on well but that conflict would ensue when passion began to wane, despite being outwardly suitable as man and wife. Inwardly there would be a hard disagreement on long-term aims and the currently dependent woman would grow strong and dominate her essentially weak husband. I suggested a long engagement, so as to give time for the inner difficulties to manifest and perhaps cause them to call off the marriage. Alas, the instinct to mate was too strong. They married and had several children before an all-out war broke out. They separated in a bitter divorce. On hearing of this, I thought that perhaps I should have said that I foresaw disaster—but then, would they have taken any notice? Here was an example of choice.

Another difficult lesson I had to learn was not to do the charts of children. This was because it fixed the minds of parents as to what to expect, not allowing the child to develop its own potential. One example was a woman who came to see me with a young boy. She asked me to tell her what his character might be when he grew up. As I described what kind of man he was likely to become, her face became bright red. The person I was describing according to the chart was a good looking, talented Casanova. She then said, through gritted teeth, 'Just like his damn father!' I learnt to be more discreet after this. I did, in an exceptional case, write a brief account of the possible character of a child but put it in an envelope, saying to the parents that it must not be opened until he was at least twenty-one. By then his fate would have been well established. I trusted the parents because they were on the Path. However, people are human and I do not know if they kept their promise. I decided never to do this again.

As regards prediction, again I learnt that one had to be very careful. Cosmic time is not the same as human time. A cycle for the Moon is a month, for Mars two years and Saturn twenty-eight years. So, in making any prognostication, one has to take into account several factors and even then one cannot be that precise. In one instance, I predicted to a person that a certain event might occur in the first week in September of that year, according to the position of a particular planet in a specific sign and mundane House of the client. This was some months away, so I forgot about her until I got a note saying I was quite wrong, the event occurred in the last week of September. It is this kind of projection that gives astrology a bad name. A week or two out is but a second or two in cosmic time.

Quite a different use of astrology is when one applies it to the 'present'. In ancient and medieval times kings, generals and merchants would take into account celestial conditions in crucial situations. This was the norm until the so-called Age of Reason and materialism overshadowed the esoteric view of the universe and science obliterated astrology. From then on celestial influences were seen as purely mechanical and of no account beyond the tides and seasons. A whole body of observations and conclusions formed over thousands of years was all but forgotten even though Sir Isaac Newton, the definer of gravity, was a committed astrologer.

In my case, Providence presented me with a unique opportunity to practise horary astrology. I lived in the same Kensington road as the then British foreign minister. I did not know him personally but I was acquainted with his wife as a neighbour. At one time there were some very difficult negotiations about independence going on with some of the African colonies. According to the news, they had reached an impasse and the talks might break up. On that day I happened to meet his wife in the street. I said to her, because she had an open mind, to tell her husband that there was an eclipse on the morrow and that he should defer any decision until it had passed. It was a bad moment to complete or start anything. She replied that he would not take such advice seriously but that she would mention the event to him. I heard on the radio, later, that he had postponed the final meeting by a day due to various administrative complications. The next meeting occurred on the New Moon and, to everyone's surprise, the parties decided upon mutual co-operation. All went home with some satisfaction.

Such discreet events are never reported by the media, although they might get into the history books centuries later. To possess the capacity to influence such decisions is not without danger. There was the story of a certain ruler who had a Jewish astrologer. He would advise on when and when not to implement a political or personal policy. However, the ruler began to feel that his astrologer knew far too much about his own and state secrets, so he decided to get rid of him. Being a tyrant, he thought it would be an amusing idea to take the astrologer to the top of a tower and push him off but make it look like an accident. As a cruel man the ruler could not resist tormenting his victim by asking him if he knew the day he would die. The shrewd astrologer, knowing what was about to happen, replied, 'Sire, I will die just one day before you die'. The ruler not only refrained from his plan but made sure his astrologer was, from that time on, under his personal protection.

This story brings to the fore the notion that fate is not absolutely fixed but can be modified by a conscious decision. I have known a number of people who should have died at a certain point, according to their birth charts, but had lived beyond the date. The reason for this was that they were too useful to Providence as there was no one else, as yet, of their calibre to take their place. In contrast, the factor of free will has shortened the lives of some people because they have misused their potential. This I have seen in the sad endings of several Gurus who abused their power. However, it can occur at the ordinary level with drink, drugs and any excess. Providence can only protect those who come under its cosmic laws and to qualify for this one has to be of some use to human evolution.

35. *Opportunity*

One day, on my way to teach at the Royal Academy of Dramatic Art, I passed a striking looking girl as I came out of the underground station. In London this is not unusual, but there was something familiar about her. I surmised she was a student at University College nearby. What was unusual was that although she was clearly a very English and upper-class girl, there was something Chinese about her. I had a deep love of China and its culture as well as an old memory of spending time there in the Middle Ages as a Jewish merchant and traveller. When I turned to have another look at her, she had gone but a deep impression remained.

Some years later I was invited to a party where, for fun, I did a very superficial birth chart reading for the people present. The flat where it took place was the home of a young woman who had recently parted from her husband and had an infant child. When she appeared there was a feeling of familiarity but I could not place it. When I did her birth chart it revealed a highly intelligent, sensitive and determined character who came from a privileged background. I said to her, in a joke, that she had been born with two silver spoons in her mouth. She laughed nervously, but I did go on to say she had great potential as a writer which pleased her, as she was obviously not in a good psychological state. After the party, she was the person I most remembered and this connected with the student I had seen long ago near the underground station.

I met her several times, over the years, through mutual friends. One told me later that they had said to her, because I was then free, that I was the man for her. She had written an impressive book on Chinese mystical philosophy, the oriental complement to Kabbalah and my books. On hearing this I decided to explore the possibility of getting to know her better, especially because she had been in the Steiner school and studied Jungian psychology. She was then about thirty-two and I forty-seven. One day I called on her and we had tea. I learnt then that she had been a student at the London University around the time when I had encountered the memorable unknown girl by the underground

station. I bought her book on Chinese symbolism and metaphysics and was deeply moved by its clarity, scholarship and vision. I said to myself, 'This is the woman I am going to marry'. Soon a serious love affair began and we became very close. I got on well with her daughter who, initially, was resistant to a stranger because while her mother had had lovers, our relationship appeared to be very different.

Intellectually we were of the same calibre. We could share and compare ideas as well as deep emotions and passions. After a month or so of great happiness, she turned up one day unexpectedly at my flat and said, 'My psychotherapist believes we could have an Alchemical Marriage'. I was somewhat taken aback and said, politely, that it was the man who should propose. My reaction was due to my experience of controlling women and the Chinese notion that the female is the Yin principle she had written about so well. However, she was no Jewish princess but a refined Anglo-Saxon Protestant girl who was used to getting her way as she was beautiful, intelligent and had a private income, which meant she had never had to work or be an employee. But she was everything I desired in a woman and most of all she was seeking out the Path. The opportunity could not be missed.

As I had by now fallen in love I proposed to her a few days later because the relationship seemed to have the hallmark of Heaven about it. I had lived in my small flat for nearly twenty years and the thought of spending the next twenty there alone was now horrendous. Why should I deny fate and refuse such a chance for happiness, with someone I now adored? She insisted that we should be married as soon as possible but my Capricornian caution noted some astrological problems. Saturn was then moving through my 7th House of marriage and so was Mars. This indicated that serious conflict over principles might occur. I disregarded these considerations, like anyone in love, but there was another warning omen. She said, shortly before we were

FIGURE 70 (Left)—DISASTER
Every marriage begins with the hope that it will fulfil an ideal. Alas, this is rare and most marriages are good or bad compromises. I believed that, with the remarkable qualities of my first wife, our liaison would be a great adventure on the Path together. Unfortunately, this was not to be. As an ardent feminist, she insisted upon her views being acknowledged. I, who had come from a patriarchal culture, tried to adapt to the 'new woman'. However, when she decided to become celibate and asked me to accompany her to America, it all broke down. I said that my life's work was in England and that I would not desert my post. Unfortunately, she decided to leave England. After only eighteen months of marriage she wanted a divorce. Here began my 'Dark Night of the Soul'. (The Wreck of the White Ship, graphic by the author).

to be married, that she would not take my family name as she wished to retain her own identity. I did not argue as the feminist movement to which she was committed was very strong at the time. While I agreed that she was indeed a person in her own right I did feel uneasy, as the refusal indicated something about commitment. I disregarded this thought as things were going very well, with plans for me to move into her larger flat and set up my study in a big room where the Thursday group of about twenty would meet.

In the week immediately leading up to the wedding there was a continuous downpour of rain. However, on the day, it suddenly stopped. The break of sunshine I took as a good sign before it soon began to rain again. After the civil formalities, we had a private ceremony in which a candle fell down. Then at the very start of our honeymoon we nearly missed the plane because a cab was late. I recall thinking that this was not a good beginning, even though we did have a wonderful time in Spain. A third omen came when we missed the return flight home because, on that day, the clocks had been changed to Summer Time. Something was out of joint.

The first manifestation of a problem came in a conversation when she talked vehemently about how Chinese women had been downtrodden. As I listened, it occurred to me that we had known each other in medieval China where we had either had an affair or actually been married. Either way, karma had brought us together again to complete some unfinished business or combine our work in a spiritual project that could bring the Orient and Occident together. However, it soon became apparent that the former reason was the case. Once I had moved in, it was obvious that the only space I could really call my own was my study. Then, some weeks later, a change came over her which made me think that I had done something wrong. She said she wished to sleep alone, not only because I snored but also because she wished to be celibate for an unspecific time. I decided not to make it an issue and be patient, as I loved her deeply. Over the next few months I slept in my study. However, I inevitably became increasingly desperate, not only because of the lack of intimate contact but also for affirmative emotional interaction. Was it because she believed she became pregnant on our honeymoon, when she was not? I recall thinking that the soul who might have been our child foresaw what was coming. The tension began to undermine my patience and we started to quarrel. From then on the situation began to deteriorate rapidly. A turning point came when, during a heated discussion I saw, out of the corner of my eye, a hazy figure with a green reptilian head, dressed in a bizarre costume, standing to my left and observing us. I blinked and looked again to make sure it was not just my imagination but the apparition was still there, although it appeared to be quite unaware that I knew of its presence as its eyes were on her. This event shifted my level of perception as I realised that there was more going on than the breakdown of a marriage. It was an assault on my work and upon her, perhaps to prevent her from finding her true self, which very much preoccupied her. Later she wrote in one of her books about a grotesque green entity in a dream that sought to harm her. This confirmed what I had seen. She also described, in this same volume, a thinly-disguised image of me as a judgemental husband, without saying why he was angry.

From that time on I knew I was not just dealing with a strong, independently-minded woman but also a corrosive psychic intrusion. This crisis was now regarded by me as an esoteric trial. If we could get through this initiation, our relationship would indeed be an 'Alchemical Marriage'. The resolution would either move our relationship on to another stage or destroy it. We had to unite or separate or both our missions would be aborted if we failed the test. Either way a battle was on and I decided to stand my ground.

One day a Buddhist abbot came to our home to have his birth chart done. I went up to my wife's study and asked her if she would come down and greet our guest. She replied that the abbot should come up to see her! I was astounded by this feminist statement which was quite contrary to her normally courteous manner. I said to her very sharply, 'You are the lady of the house. Is this how you treat a distinguished guest?' Her genteel upbringing then came into play. Reluctantly she went downstairs to greet him with much grace, made tea and was a perfect hostess. However, from then on she became openly hostile.

This surprised me as she had said, during our courtship, that I was a rare type of man who gave her hope and a sense of stability. This was the reason, I believe, she wanted to marry. However, when it came to the reality of living with me, my patriarchal solidity provoked an unexpected feminist response. This was strange as she despised weak men. Then came the suggestion that we were in competition as writers which I did not understand as this was not what our marriage was about. I realised that we were caught up in a set of contradictions. But I still had hope.

During a periodic truce, she asked me if I would come with her to

America where she wished to complete her psychoanalytic training. I replied that this was not possible as my work and place was in London and I could not desert the group. She may have anticipated my answer, as it would be a valid reason to separate. From then on she treated me like a lodger. This view, eventually, reached the point where she said that she wanted me out of her flat. I replied that it was also my home, in which I had contributed two-thirds of my savings as an act of faith to convert it into a marital nest. I would only leave when I was ready and not before the group stopped for a holiday break. More important, where were I and my possessions to go? My old flat, which I had rented, was gone.

Needless to say, both I and my cat were very distressed by all that was going on. Fortunately, one of my students kindly offered a place in his house for a refuge. I took up the offer and Hymie and I moved into a little room where I reconstructed my study. It was nice but it could never be like the home that I had had in Holland Park. Because of the disturbing changes, all within eighteen months, Hymie soon sickened and died. While adjusting myself to the reality of my new situation I talked to my wife's first husband, who said he had had a similar experience. Their marriage had lasted, because of their child, just a little longer.

A week or so after I had settled in, my wife phoned to say she wanted to see me. I thought, judging by her sense of urgency, that she realised a serious error had been made and might want me back. But it turned out just the reverse. She wanted a divorce. I was shocked by this impulsive request because as a psychotherapist, I thought, she should at least examine why the breakdown had occurred and come to some kind of understanding with me. But this was not going to happen. She, against others' advice, wanted to leave the country as soon as possible. I remember thinking: was this the karmic price I had to pay for, perhaps, deserting her in China? No, I thought, this is something of greater gravity. As she sat opposite me in my little room my face must have revealed the shock I felt as I foresaw the possible

---

FIGURE 71 (Left)—TEST
Here is the face of the King as he realises that he has lost his children in the 'White Ship'. This image expresses the grief I felt after the breakup. For a long time the pain was almost unendurable, at the level of ego, but the Self observed the process while I continued to write and take the group. This discipline held me steady. The situation continued until one day, upon seeing my melancholy reflection in a train window, I realised I must not allow this disastrous episode to destroy me or my work. From that point on, I began to recover. When I started to look at graceful and intelligent women again, I knew I was on the mend. (Drawing by the author).

consequences of this decision which would disrupt the Work. She had neither taken that into account, nor the effect the split up would have as regards her own fate. She saw my grim reaction as the judgement of an Old Testament prophet when, in fact, it was the manifestation of deep concern for both of our respective futures.

When she arrived in America, the immigration authorities would not, initially, allow her to settle there. This I took as a possible sign for her to return. However, such was her determination that she hired a lawyer to get legal permission to live in New England. There, I was told, she took a lover. Two years later she returned to London on a family visit. She asked to meet me in her parents' flat to discuss the final business of divorce. While we talked, I had a strong feeling of mutual attraction. I did not succumb to the temptation because by that time there was a nice lady around who, I thought, might heal the rent in my heart. I realised, as I left a suddenly melancholy ex-wife, that Providence had timed a romantic possibility to coincide exactly with our meeting. This was to ensure that I would not be drawn back into the old situation. She called me the next morning, on a pretext, to see if the lady was with me.

Because there was still a connection, we exchanged occasional letters and telephone calls over the following years. These were usually just about news. However, one postcard that came was of a lone pine in the desert. I knew what it symbolised. This was confirmed when she sent me the price of an air ticket to the USA. I did eventually visit her in New Mexico, to where she had moved, as I was to run a weekend Kabbalah course there. Again the attraction was present, especially after she stretched herself out on a sofa in her mountain home, saying how harmonious it was between us. I left as soon as I could because by that time I was remarried. She then moved on again, buying land in Colorado where she built what was to be a spiritual centre which never manifested, even though a lot of effort and money were spent on it. Some time later she called me up to say she wanted to salute me, because I had been true to my mission, and that she loved me but it was too late. A wonderful opportunity to travel the world, meet remarkable people and help found a school of the soul had been missed. She now lived in a beautiful but remote part of a Pacific island after a third short marriage.

While these events were still far in the future my present position, then, was one of devastation. I had a roof over my head but, at the age of fifty and with little money, my prospects were grim on all fronts. After the separation I felt hurt, angry and betrayed, having been promised a taste of Paradise which had then been suddenly withdrawn when solemn vows were broken. I went into a state of deep depression. Only my writing, which now was going badly, and the group meetings kept me in relative balance. However, one day while sitting in a London underground train I saw my reflection in the carriage window opposite. This visage of grief woke me up with such a jolt that I vowed then and there that I would not be beaten by a demon that sought to crush my spirit and destroy what I had been given to do. I remembered the old school friend who had been fished out of a pile of dead children in a Nazi concentration camp. If she could survive that and live a normal life, I could endure my ordeal and move on.

36. Novel

The marriage, despite its failure, did produce a novel and a unique experience. While we were on our honeymoon I worked out the plot of *The Anointed*. This was a story set in medieval Castile. Toledo, where we stayed, was my model for the imaginary town of Zeona. Once the capital of Spain, this city had been a political and ecclesiastical centre as well as being a city of high culture where the three Abrahamic religions met. It was also the place where Hellenic philosophy came back into the mainstream of European civilisation. It was here, in fact, that the Renaissance began. There had been a school of translators in Toledo where the Greek texts, which had been turned into Arabic and Hebrew, were translated into Latin. At that time Toledo was a cosmopolitan city to which people came from all over Europe to study not only philosophy but also science, medicine and mysticism.

As I walked through the Christian, Jewish and Moslem quarters, visited the old synagogues and mosques that were now churches, caught glimpses of half-hidden courtyards that still had their arabesque decorations, the plot for the novel slowly grew in my mind. The old Jewish marketplaces, now no longer bustling with produce from the Orient, were still full of ghosts. From there I went south out to the Toledo mountain, about a day's donkey ride from the city in the Middle Ages, to where I was to create an imaginary town of Zeona. Here I took note of the severe Castilian landscape which could be covered in snow, because of the high altitude, or blasted dry by hard

---

FIGURE 72 (Left)—CONVERSO
This is a portrait, by El Greco, of a Jew who had converted to Christianity in Spain. Many did so in order to remain in a land they had called home. The alternative was to be expelled in 1492. In the novel The Anointed *Don Immanuel, whose character is based upon this picture, converts in order to bring about an understanding between the three Abrahamic faiths. Having failed to offset the expulsion of the Jews from Spain, he retires to the town of Zeona where he forms an inter-religious group that studies the Teaching through the mode of astrology. When he becomes the target of the Inquisition he takes on the role of the Messiah of his time. The novel is about this process. It was eventually published after fifty-three rejections. (Portrait of an Unnamed Gentleman,* El Greco, 16th century).

summer light. The landscape had a particularly powerful impact on me, bringing back many memories of another life of long ago.

The period of the story was set just before the fall of Granada, the last Moslem kingdom, and the expulsion of the Jews in 1492. The chief character in the book was to be Don Immanuel, a Jewish scholar, married to a Sufi's daughter. She had been killed in a religious riot in Cordoba, his home town, leaving him with his now eighteen-year-old beautiful daughter, Rachel. He had moved to Toledo and become a Christian in order to work for religious harmony within the Spanish court where, he thought, he might be able to influence events. Although he reached the high position of royal advisor, he found the politics too difficult to endure. As a man of integrity who followed the spiritual path, he concluded that it was impossible to change the mindset of the Catholic ruling caste. He decided to retire from the capital to the quiet town of Zeona where the three Faiths lived in relative peace. Here Don Immanuel founded an esoteric group, composed of individuals of each tradition, where he used astrology as a common and acceptable mode of studying esoteric ideas and practices.

With Don Immanuel, as the Tiferet-Sun of the group Tree, I made each member of the group to represent one of the other sefirot or planets, with Rachel as the Venusian or Nezahian principle. All went well until the Inquisition arrived, seeking out Jewish and Moslem converts who had secretly relapsed back to their old faith. Their prime target was Don Immanuel, who had made enemies at court. In Zeona, the envious and weak aristocratic Christian governor set out to destroy this 'New Christian' noble upstart. This precipitated a set of tensions within and between the major and minor characters of the story, who now began to play archetypal parts in a much bigger cosmic drama. Don Immanuel realised he was to be the 'Anointed', that is the Messiah of that time. Meanwhile his daughter fell in love with a feckless handsome officer of the Militia Christi who guarded the Inquisitors. One member of the group was an ex-soldier, symbolising Mars or Gevurah. He loved Rachel but, because of his spiritual discipline, held back from telling her that the officer was a womaniser. A crisis developed as a transformation occurred in all of the characters, as the people of the town took sides either for or against the Moslem and Jewish conversos. The Inquisition forced everyone to choose between truth and falsehood, good and evil, and face the consequence, while Don Immanuel transcended events and, in his sacrifice, moved history on to a period when religion no longer had a deadening hold on the Western mind.

The novel went to fifty-three publishers before Penguin, an important British company, took it on. It was later translated into French, German and Portuguese. This book was seen by those, who had read my other books, as Kabbalah in action. In many ways it was more explicit about the Teaching, in the symbolic working out of each character and situation. For example, the chapter where Don Immanuel's spiritual presence transformed a grimy prison cell into a place of purity and peace, affecting the jailer so deeply that he treated him as a guest of honour, touched a number of people, I was told. The reviews of *The Anointed* were very good and several people wrote to me to say it had altered their perception of history and, in one case, had turned someone's life around. I was delighted; at last I had written a successful novel. Some film people were interested and commissioned a script but the movie was never made because, as a Hollywood agent said, 'Its time is not yet right'.

Before we separated, my first wife and I went to Egypt. Its ancient culture was of particular interest to her in her study of symbolism. I could not afford the trip but I knew, if I was meant to go, the money would come from somewhere. I remembered the promise by the 'Voice' on the empty top of a London bus many years before and waited. On the last day it was possible for me to book a ticket, as my wife was going anyway, a package was pushed through our front door. It contained just enough cash to cover the cost of the journey. I was amazed. The 'Promise' had been kept. I discovered, years later, that an old friend knew of my problem and decided to solve it as she had lots of money at that point. I paid her back, many years later, by having her come on one of the Kabbalah Society's trips to Spain, for free, when she was broke. I recalled a saying from one of my teachers, 'If you put the work in for Heaven, the money earned is stored in someone else's pocket until you need it.'

Egypt is a unique culture. Its collective mind is Islamic but the ancient Egyptian and Greek influences are just below the surface. We went first to the Pyramids which are awesome in size and atmosphere. As we entered and penetrated what is said to be a tomb but was also a place of initiation, I picked up many strong presences. When we came to the King's Chamber, it was packed with Japanese tourists. However, suddenly they were gone and we were quite alone. This, I believe, was arranged by Providence so that I could place a stone from Jerusalem there. When I raised my arms up in the form of the Tree of Life and said, 'Greetings from the House of Israel to the House

of Egypt', Time and Space changed. The image of a large, beautiful, green face appeared before me with piercing but not unkind eyes, accompanied by the sound of tinkling laughter. After a millisecond, the vision dissolved and we were in silence for a long moment before more tourists came. When I got home I questioned a friend, who wrote books about Egypt, about what I had witnessed. She said that the face corresponded to that of Osiris and the laughter to that of his followers who are known by this phenomenon.

Later we visited the Valley of the Kings, the great ruined Temple of Rameses and the famous two huge statues that sing in the wind. These were impressive but sad places which were full of the shades of long dead people and the atmosphere of once being a great spiritual centre. My wife spoke of how familiar the area was and, upon seeing some of the inscriptions and chambers, something stirred deep within her to make her weep, which she rarely did. I was not so much moved but impressed as there had obviously been a priesthood who possessed esoteric knowledge.

While coming down from the stony hills overlooking the Nile, I took it into my head to take a shortcut while she descended by the usual path. As I paused to jump down a steep embankment, a voice said within my head, 'Egyptian hospitals'. I suddenly had a flash of having a broken leg, far from home, in conditions that might not be up to Western standards. I took a step back and climbed slowly down to the road below, chastened by my stupidity. Heaven will protect one, it seems, as long as one is prepared to listen.

When we were in Cairo, I went to visit the oldest part of the city where the medieval Jewish community had lived. I got there by taxi and found the area to be a derelict place. The original synagogue was still there but all locked up. It was here that the great Jewish philosopher Maimonides had had his home and served as court physician to Saladin. I picked up, psychically, the echoes of the past. Having gleaned all I could, I decided to walk back to the hotel. As I passed

---

FIGURE 73 (Left)—EGYPT
I have memories of Egypt, especially Alexandria. I did not visit the modern city as I knew there was nothing left of the great Museum where I recall standing, out of the sunshine in one of its porticos, with a Greek companion who, in this life, is my oldest friend. The pyramids and temples of upper and lower Egypt were familiar, but alien. However, I did encounter the presence of Osiris in the King's Chamber in the Great Pyramid and experienced how the Sphinx sees Eternity and history as a 'passing show'. Here, the Moon and Venus mark different rhythms in time as the Sun goes down. (Drawing by author).

through a clearly poor district, people stared at me in a very strange way. Puzzled, I asked an Egyptian in the hotel about these slums. He was horrified and told me that this was a criminal stronghold and said, 'You must have been protected by Allah'. I again shuddered at my naïvety and was grateful for the patience of Providence.

On a visit to the Great Temple at Karnak, where huge pillars and vast halls dominate the site, I felt I was in alien territory. I had a flash of memory of not wearing cotton, as the ancient Egyptians did, but a woollen robe, the garb of an Israelite. The sense of living in the ancient Egyptian time came up at another temple. Here we met an Englishwoman who said she had been a priestess in the time of the pharaohs. To prove her case, she told us how she had directed some archaeologists to locate where a large cistern of water had once been and, indeed, that is what they found. As a girl in England, she had had such a strong affinity with this particular temple that she migrated to Egypt, upon becoming an adult, because she felt this was her homeland. I could concur with this affinity as I had experienced a similar connection with certain other countries. Strange as it may seem, I never felt drawn to India, that great and ancient spiritual centre, as many of my friends were. I presume it was either my destiny never to be born there or some traumatic event put me off visiting the subcontinent. I had a strong aversion to Russia, where I have a dim recollection of being interrogated by a Tsarist secret police officer which made me fearful whenever I had to deal with officials.

37. Fruits

At the age of fifty I found myself, and all my possessions, in one small room in a friend's house. It was a beautiful Victorian building with a view over many back gardens. It was a safe haven but I had lost a home and a wife. Outwardly, all seemed well. My books were being translated into several languages and I was being invited to teach yet more, at home and abroad. But inwardly this was my dark night of the soul. The situation weighed heavily on every aspect of my being. What had I done to deserve it? This is a question every Kabbalist has to ask themselves when things go wrong. I had not committed any obvious crime, betrayed anyone or broken any rules that I could recognise. Of course, I knew I could be in denial about something. But what?

Meanwhile I had to deal with the reality of the situation. Handling the outer world was no problem. Everything in my room was fine, as all my books and pictures were in order. I could hold meetings in my space, which expanded to accommodate whatever number attended the group with people sitting on the bed, table and chest of drawers. After the meeting we could go downstairs and eat, drink and socialise, for a while, before going home. The social aspect was an important part of group work, so that people could get to know each other and work together and even begin a romance. However, our unofficial Kabbalistic Marriage Bureau never worked, as developing people are too choosy in what they want in a partner. In contrast, our Kabbalistic Divorce Bureau was very successful, with myself as the leading example. This was because some members of the group inevitably outgrew their spouses if they did not also grow alongside their partners.

My cat, of course, always came with me to wherever I moved. She had a very hard time, not only adjusting to different environments but also to two other cats in my new home where she had to fight to establish her own territory. As she was now getting on in age she was not very happy except when she was with me under a blanket when I had a siesta. Here were familiar smells and textures—and her master. This did not prevent her from becoming increasingly unwell. One day

FIGURE 74—ENDURANCE
This image of a U.S. Cavalryman of the Old West depicts the attitude he had to take in the harsh conditions of terrain, besides the deprivations of a soldier's life. His sullen, weather-worn face expressed how I saw life at this time. He and his horse were the symbols of my animal soul carrying me up into and over the mountains of despair, towards a sunny valley I knew I would eventually enter. At this time I recalled the Book of Job *and its message. In my case I was not righteous like Job. I was, no doubt, paying off some karma of a past life.* (Drawing by author).

she climbed up on my chest and licked my face all over, purring all the while. It was one of the most moving expressions of love I have ever experienced. It was a kind of farewell as, shortly after, she suddenly became seriously ill. I took her to the vet who said she should be put down because she was in great pain. I reluctantly agreed and, while my hand was on her pain-stricken body, the vet gave her a lethal injection. After a gentle shudder, she was gone. However, when I got home and laid down on my bed to recover, I detected her presence in the room. I then felt her jump up onto my chest and lie there for about a minute until the sensation faded and she was gone. I greatly missed her company. We had shared a life for thirteen years.

One thing a Capricorn is good at is a disciplined routine. We are tortoises, not hares, although I have a Geminian Moon which gives me a Mercurial quickness when needed. My day had a distinct cycle of breakfast, meditation and work, followed by lunch, a siesta and then work again, until around five pm. I then had an early supper and went out to see friends, take a group or just relax, with or without feminine company. There was also a weekly cycle. On Friday I would scrub my table, have a bath and light the Sabbath candles with a kabbalistic form of *Kiddush*. On the Saturday I would perform a similar ceremony, wearing my hat from Bukhara and my old prayer shawl. I would then open an Old Testament, at random, and read what the chapter said and symbolised. The reading was always relevant to my situation. The process was a kind of Jewish version of the I Ching. I would then ponder the meaning, whether it was about an interior process or outer events. This exercise was most useful in getting another view of my situation. After a rest I would go out and visit some friend or go to a museum. I also had an annual cycle of celebrating the Jewish festivals of Rosh Hashanah and Yom Kippur. I did not go to the local synagogue because it was usually packed with people who had not seen each other for a year and the occasion was more to do with social custom than religious reflection. Often, when I celebrated these important events alone, I sensed that I had an invisible presence for company. Sometimes members of the group would come and share this experience with me. These routines carried me through a very distressing period.

About this time I was invited to Mexico. This country is a curious mixture. The majority of people there are Catholics on the surface but underneath there is the ancient pre-Columbian culture. Here the old gods have been turned into Christian saints while the churches, despite

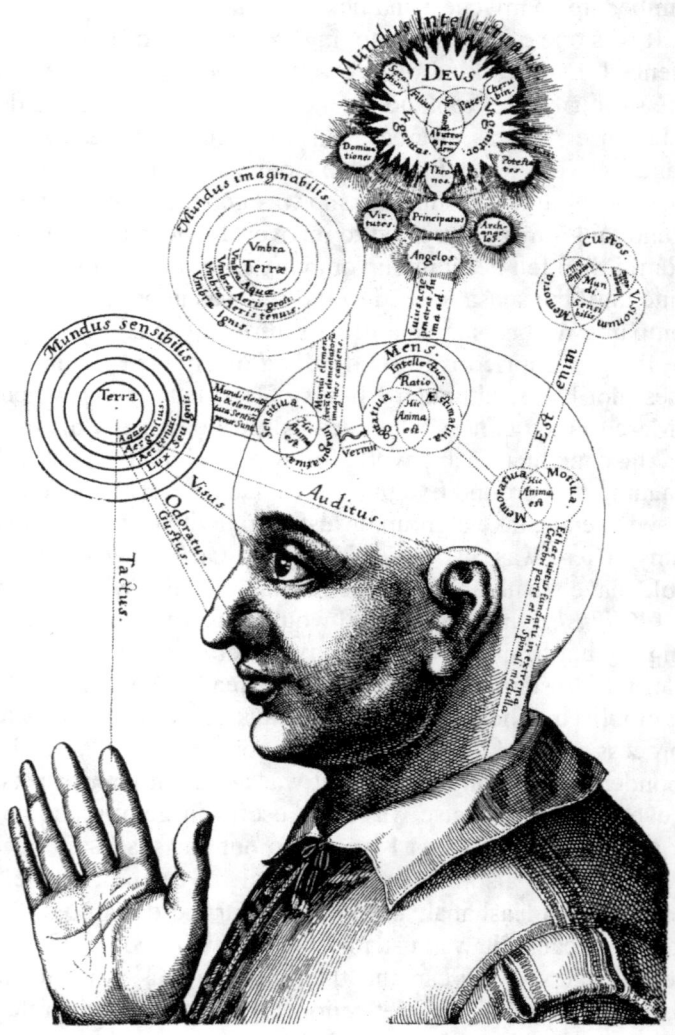

FIGURE 75—INTERIOR
As this illustration indicates, there are other levels within a human being besides the body. While the depiction is not accurate, the concept is correct with the Tree at the top. The psychological vehicle, called the astral body by some traditions, is where we have our memories, emotions and intellectual faculties. The experience of many lives is held here, as is the general state of development. This picture on the wall of my study is as powerful, in its way, as the psychological, metaphysical Tree in that it touches the mythology of the mind, through imagination. (Engraving 17th century. Robert Fludd).

their elaborate baroque interiors, are in fact semi-Mexican temples with Jesus as the human sacrifice. The people I met were of the old Spanish colonial class as well as North Americans and Europeans who lived there. They had a deep hunger for spiritual experience. Some had taken to local drugs in order to explore the invisible realms, while others came to my courses to learn about the slower but more solid path up Jacob's Ladder which would enable them to enter the higher Worlds safely.

Many people soon recognised that Kabbalah was a genuine esoteric system. As a result, a core group was built up over the years. The level of commitment was manifest in its leader who had a garden laid out in the form of the Tree of Life. One year a concert was given there on the theme of Creation, with dancers acting out the Tree and the four Worlds. This was a sacred ceremony, transforming the garden into a Temple and us, the spellbound audience, into a congregation. This event indicated that the Kabbalah Society was not just a series of courses but also was producing an art form as well as literature. Indeed, some of its members around the world were now writing books on various topics such as science, healing and history as well as development.

One experience in Mexico, which echoed my life at that point, was the great earthquake of 1984. I was in the car of my hostess in Mexico City, when she suddenly halted it saying, 'We are in an earthquake'. At first I could detect nothing, as the springs of the car absorbed the shockwaves moving through the ground, but I could see the lamp-posts swaying and electric cables flashing as they dipped and contacted each other. When I got out of the car I could hear the earth roar like a giant underground train beneath us which made the car rise and fall like a small boat riding on a rough sea. The power released below my feet was awesome. Later, we learnt that around ten thousand people died that day. One building had simply sunk into what had been the sandy bottom of the lake upon which Mexico City was built. Providence had it that we were driving over a solid area of rock at the time. The impact of this event remained with me when I returned to England. For several days, whenever I went out for a walk, my body was ready to adjust to the ground moving up and down. This echoed my personal situation.

Such an event made me realise that my psyche was essentially stable because of the discipline of Kabbalah. I could ride out my own earthquake. One result was that I decided I must move on and begin to think about a new kind of life. Meanwhile I got on with a new book, entitled *School of the Soul*, drawing on my experience over the years of teachers and traditions that I had encountered. This was to examine not only the light invoked by such institutions but also the shadow side of esoteric work and its hazards.

38. Emergence

My Dark Night began to end when I moved out of the house I was staying in because my friends now had two children. It was time to go. That was not easy, as my instincts did not wish to undergo the trauma of packing up yet again. Moreover, there seemed to be no suitable place to resettle, as the rents in the nicest area in London were too high while those places which were affordable were not good. At fifty I did not want to return to living in a rundown place, the conditions I had accepted as a young man. Unfortunately, nothing seemed to be working until a turning point was reached.

After viewing a big Victorian house, which had been taken over by hippies, I sat down outside the local Spanish-Portuguese synagogue and wept. I could move into one room that was available but it was not secure. The people living there were mostly in their twenties. Moreover, they were largely drifters who would eventually be evicted once the house's ownership had been decided by the courts. I uttered a prayer ending in an old Jewish saying, 'Lord, if this is how you treat your friends, who needs enemies?' Immediately after this statement the name of my 'Sister' came into my head. This was the woman, now married, who had recognised that Kabbalah was the Path for her when she first saw my room in Holland Park many years before. She lived nearby, in a kind of commune. However, this small community was made up of people in the Work. It had never occurred to me to approach her because the large flat where they lived always seemed to be overflowing.

Following the lead given by Providence, I went at once to see her. To my surprise she said, 'Why did you not ask before? We did not offer a room because we thought you needed solitude to write, rather than a place full of people.' I replied that 'good company' was exactly what I needed. I had spent far too much time on my own. She then told me that, as it happened, one of the big rooms was about to become vacant as someone was moving on. I thanked Heaven and said I would take it over.

My new home was perfect, as I could have my privacy and the

FIGURE 76—CHANGE
This Wheel of Fortune symbolises how each of the planets, Sun and Moon have a brief period of being at the top, bottom, ascending and descending positions of influence. In 1985 Neptune, the planet of realisation and delusion, entered my sign of Capricorn while Saturn, the ruler of Capricorn, touched my Midheaven. Triggered by Jupiter in Capricorn, my life took an upturn. It was then that I moved into my 'Sister's' commune where I experienced home, friends and children. This was very healing. The pattern of my fate began to assert itself again and I started to write once more. From then on things really began to happen. The group in London became the nucleus of a world-wide school as I began to travel widely to teach people who had read my books. (Medieval woodcut).

pleasures of a family and kindred souls. It was with great pleasure that I was able to invite my father and his new wife to have supper with us. There were at least twenty people, many of whom were my students, to welcome him. My father was at the centre of attention which, as an old patriarch, he loved. When asked what he had learnt from his long life he replied, 'Nothing'. This delighted those present as here were the wisdom and integrity of a man who had recognised just how ignorant he was. His comment on the dinner, a week later when I went to visit him, was that it was very kind of these Christians to take me in. He had not approved of my marriage to a Protestant. I told him that there were also Buddhists and Sufis present. This made him very thoughtful as his image of non-Jews was based upon the anti-Semitism of old Russia and Nazi Germany.

Once settled in, I started work on *School of the Soul* by putting together all I knew in terms that could be applied to any esoteric tradition, although cast in kabbalistic terms. This was possible because I used the Tree of Life and Jacob's Ladder as models. After defining the structure of an esoteric organisation, I described the various starting points, levels and false paths to be encountered by seekers of Truth. The book then went on to explain the dynamics of a school and different types of students and teachers. Using examples, but no actual names, I illustrated how people came into the Work from different directions. Then came a chapter on the kind of problems that can arise within any hierarchy. One example is when the honeymoon period of finding the Teaching is over and real effort is required, as well as the 'star student' syndrome when a clever 'undergraduate' believes he or she knows more than the tutor. Here crisis management has to be very subtle because an exposed learned fool-turned-rebel can disrupt a school of the soul. Where there is light the shadow of opposition appears. This section was followed by working methods and interior exercises that lead to direct mystical experience.

The dangers and shadow side of spiritual and esoteric work involves being acquainted with magic and the misuse of power and sex which can bring about the fall of a teacher, the destruction of a school and the disillusion of some students. To avoid such disasters requires a degree of psychological skill and a code of ethics. If these factors are ignored, an organisation and its hierarchy can become more important than its original spiritual aim. When service to the Divine is forgotten, then animal level people move in. This is what happens when priest-craft takes over. A genuine school is supposed to free people, not to bind them.

The book also dealt with 'dull times', when the Work is sheer slog, in contrast to the excitement of beginning to climb Jacob's Ladder. Here real effort is required. The book goes on to explain how to set up a conference, build a Temple and run a retreat, which is important if a school is to operate in the wider world. All this information, I hoped, would be of use to people in describing how to identify a false school from a true operation, as well as recognising a dying or dead institution or starting a new one. This last section helped people in remote areas to found their own groups, without the aid of a living guide, because help came from above if they were of the Path.

It was during this time of writing that I went with a Sufi group on a trip to Turkey. This was important for me because my Spanish ancestors had passed through Istanbul on their way to southern Russia, which was then part of the Ottoman Empire. My first impression of Constantinople was that it was dimly familiar to me. The vast church of Santa Sophia, with its steps worn down by feet over a thousand years, was most impressive. I marvelled at Roman engineering as its massive dome was still standing after many earthquakes. I could understand how overawed the Crusaders were by the city's magnificence, wealth and sophistication, compared with their own crude Western culture. The old Jewish and Italian quarters were particularly moving to walk through, as there was potent feeling of Orient meeting Occident in the streets and people. The great and ornate Topkapi palace, the home of the Sultan, had, in contrast, a sinister atmosphere of corrupt power. It was here where each new sultan had all his half-brothers murdered, as they might claim the throne, their mothers having been concubines to the same father. The harem was full of the ghosts, like most of the city with its layer upon layer of history. The ancient capital was a shell of its former power, like the tomb of a great conqueror.

The city of Konya, where the Sufi Dervishes were, had quite a different atmosphere. Here I witnessed the Turning ceremony, where

---

FIGURE 77 (Left)—MUSIC
Folk-song has always had a great appeal to me as it is usually based upon real experience of life, work and love. The melodies of the 16th century English, 18th century Irish and old Jewish Ladino, as well as secular and sacred medieval music, have always had a strong resonance in me. No doubt they stirred up old memories of other lives. Certain modern orchestral pieces also affected me deeply, such as Debussy's La Mer *(The Sea) and his* Girl with the Flaxen Hair. *Vaughan Williams'* The Lark Ascending, *which evoked memories of lying in the grass in the Chiltern Hills watching this joyous bird, always brought me great pleasure. (Illustration to* The White Ship *by the author).*

the participants in flowing robes spin on the axis of themselves. This school had been in existence since the Middle Ages and it was clearly alive and well. The tomb of the founder, Rumi, had a particularly powerful presence like the tombs of the prophets and sages in Israel. When we visited the ruined city of Ephesus with one of the wonders of the ancient world, the temple of Artemis the Moon-goddess, I became aware of a very strong psychic field-force. It was here that I had an experience in the market place, for a vivid moment, of what it was like when it was full of people two thousand years before. Such flashes made history books and texts alive and, in this case, gave an insight into the mystery schools of that classical period. This in turn opened up a vista to the schools of Athens and Alexandria because of their shared Hellenic culture.

Two people with whom I shared the flat were also good travelling companions. When we went to Morocco, I was struck by how different the Islamic collective mind was from medieval Christendom and the modern West. Once we left the Europeanised coasts and went into the interior, we found many small towns and villages where life had not changed much since the Moslems came. The old markets with their donkeys, snake charmers and people beating out brass trays took me back to a previous life in Andalusia, when southern Spain was ruled by the Moors. This feeling was especially strong in the city of Fez which, in the Middle Ages, had a university complex where students not only studied the Koran but also Hellenic philosophy, medicine and astrology. Many Jews came to Fez after their expulsion from Spain in 1492. Here they lived in the same semi-oriental manner, keeping the keys of their houses in Spain should they ever return. Now there were only a few Jews left, the others having migrated to Israel. This visit explained why the elderly Moroccan Israelis studied Kabbalah in the old way. They still had the medieval mindset. To them *The Zohar* was a holy book to be revered, not studied. This is usually a sign that the inner teaching has been lost and the tradition drifts into religious superstition. Many kabbalistic texts are seen in this way by both orthodox Jews and academic scholars but for different reasons.

Upon returning home I made a special visit to the street called 'Old Jewry' in the City of London. This square mile of the financial district was the area covered by Roman and medieval London. Until 1290 the Jews lived in this street and had their synagogue there, which is now marked by a plaque. As I stood in the misty and damp street, a stark contrast to the desert-dry air of Fez, I saw for a second the modern buildings disappear and a row of low stone houses loom before me. This was unusual because most domestic structures in medieval London were built of wood. I also saw dim figures, standing about dressed in long robes and pointed hats. This was the dress code of the medieval Jews, required by law. However, my attention was distracted by a particularly pretty girl walking up the street at that moment. The vision abruptly vanished but not before I heard a silent inner voice say, 'You have not changed much since you were here long ago'. I both shuddered and laughed. Maybe this was why I had such bad karma with women.

39. Meetings

The Thursday night meetings continued in my new home. They started at 8.15pm and finished at 9.30pm, followed by refreshments bought by a volunteer who was given a small sum by everyone. This was about the same price as a cup of coffee. Anyone who wished to donate to the Bet El trust, set up to support my work, could either put something in a donation box or make a standing bank order. Bet El gave me a modest annual grant which was a great help. Another weekly volunteer wrote a brief report on the evening's meeting and the theme discussed. These texts were put together in a book of records, covering most of the years the group had existed. Later, someone brought in a small recorder and a library of discs began to be built up. All this material will have to be sorted out sometime, when myself and the senior members of the group are gone.

Those of us who lived in the flat held a smaller meeting, from time to time, to do 'Merkabah Riding'. This is the traditional name for the exploration of the higher Worlds through the eye of conscious imagination, which is quite different from dreaming. Taking the model of the method used in the Second Temple, we sat in a circle in silence for a while before I spoke the Great Invocation. This was:

> 'Let us gather together. Let us draw together. Let us form a Vessel, to catch the Dew of Heaven. Let us rise up and go to that Holy Place of Meeting and gather there with the Companions of the Light. Let the Veil of Heaven be drawn back. Hear this: Malkhut, Yesod, Hod, Nezah, Tiferet, Gevurah, Hesed, [silently] Daat, Binah, Hokmah, Keter.
> Lord, Thou art the LIVING ALMIGHTY. Thou art YAHVEH-ELOHIM, the HOLY ONE. Thou art, I AM.
> If it be Thy Will, let Thy Holy Spirit descend upon us, that we may know Thy Presence.'

The use of the Holy Names is not forbidden by the Torah. The commandment is 'not to say them in vain', that is, without knowing of WHOM one is speaking. We would then go deep into ourselves and visualise what was called the 'Upper Chamber'. Here we would perceive who was there to meet us. Usually there were one or two beings but occasionally more. These we took to be our *maggidim*, or spiritual guides. In the case of my 'Sister', it was a Christian abbess and for her husband, an African wise man who carried a great staff. Mine was my old spiritual mentor. The one among us, elected as spokesperson, then began to transmit answers to the questions each of us in our circle had presented. The responses were relayed by the spokesperson, listening with great inner intent to what came into their mind, before any personal thought or emotion intervened. This art took some practice to acquire. The replies were usually short and to the point, from the appropriate maggid. Sometimes a gesture would suffice, like when the African chieftain would raise his staff indicating, 'enough of talk, action was required'.

These sessions were very informative, as they often clarified some problem or gave a wider insight into a personal or general situation. The operation would go on for perhaps an hour, until all that could be asked, at that point, had been answered. Then an Inner Teacher would indicate the convocation was over.

We would finish the session by the following invocation:

> Most Gracious God, Thou art YAHVEH-ELOHIM. Thou art the LIVING ALMIGHTY. Thou art the LORD. Holy, Holy, Holy art Thou, God of Hosts. Thy Glory fills all the Worlds. Amen.

After a moment of silence, so as to make contact with the physical reality, we would then discuss the answers we were given. Out of this came an increased understanding of perhaps an idea or an experience, or a solution to a current problem. These evenings were extremely fruitful as we were informed about things not found in books. They also developed a deeper connection with our invisible companions.

Every third week there would be a formal meditation for the group at large. This would take place in different members' houses. While the Thursday group usually numbered anything from thirty to fifty, the meditation session was around fifteen to thirty of the more committed people. The inner exercise began and ended with the Great Invocation but each time there would be a different format, usually led by myself. There were standard meditations, like the *House of the Psyche*, to

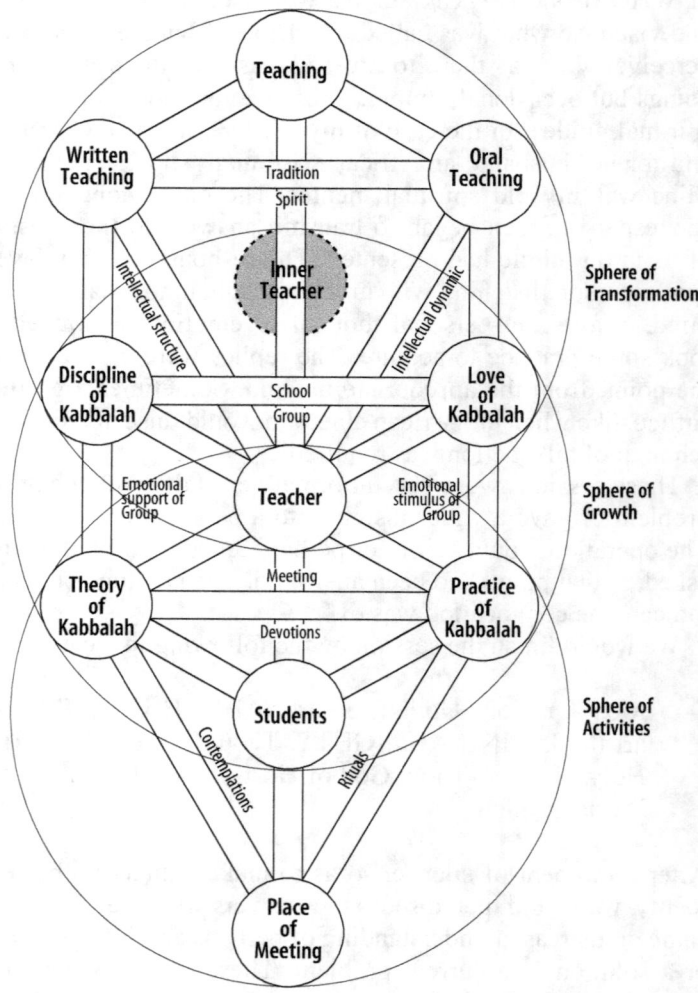

FIGURE 78—SCHOOL
I composed this Tree on the basis of what I had observed over many years. There always has to be a place of meeting, students and a teacher. This, together with the theory and practice of a genuine line, always follows this classic pattern. The devotions, rituals or intellectual modes may differ according to culture. There are always the outside pillars of structure and dynamic with the column of consciousness at the centre. One or more groups may make up a school which, in turn, belongs to a particular tradition. However, if there is no connection with the esoteric Teaching it is no more than a religious, philosophical or magical university. (Tree of a school by author).

ascertain the current state of one's mind by the symbolism of the rooms and the mood of the people who inhabited them. These archetypes were most revealing, as they showed very precisely what was going on in the unconscious. For example, one person saw a struggle between the soldier, who represented Gevurah, and a seductress, who symbolised Nezah. This denoted a conflict between discipline and passion which was an issue for the person at the time. In another case the Grandmother figure or Binah indicated, to the person who saw and heard her, that she should consider her long-term life aim.

Then there was the journey that took us first down to the centre of the Earth, before ascending like an arrow from a drawn bow through the rock's mantel to the ocean floor, then rising through the various grades of the submarine world before coming ashore at the mineral level of sand. We then viewed the vegetable and animal kingdoms before coming to the stratum of humanity. Here we traversed the different orders of living people and entered the Limbo realm of those who had just died or were about to be born. Beyond this zone are the lower and upper levels of Paradise. Here we viewed what we were permitted to see, before approaching the Heavenly Jerusalem. If it was willed from above, we were allowed a glimpse of the Seven Heavens and occasionally Adam Kadmon. From this apex of mystical experience we then came slowly down the same way until we re-entered our bodies via the animal, vegetable and mineral processes within our physical organism. Upon opening our eyes we came back into the physical space where the session was taking place. After this exercise observations were made about the inner journey and questions asked. A discussion would then ensue, bringing together our shared personal and collective perceptions. The exercise was then fully earthed by food, drink and socialising before going home.

The group, now over thirty years old, was made up of many types of people. They came for all sorts of reasons; some out of curiosity, others looking for a mate or because Kabbalah was the Path for them. We did, however, sometimes have some very odd visitors because we were open to anyone who seemed really interested. In one case it was two plain-clothes policemen who came to check if we were a subversive 'Kabal'. They reported, I was told later by one of our members who had contacts in government service, that we were classified as harmless cranks. This visit may have been triggered by enquiries by both Israeli and Arab intelligence agencies who heard that our group had both Moslem and Israeli members. The Mossad

agent who telephoned gave herself away when she said she was very interested in Kabbalah but she did not know of the famous Watkins esoteric bookshop in London that sold my books. Someone from Lebanon also enquired by phone about our activities but quickly lost interest as we were clearly not a political cell.

We also had the occasional sociopath. One came with the deliberate intention of disrupting the group. She openly admitted that she disliked anything organised. The solution to her psychological problem, she believed, was to project her chaos on to others. However, she found that she could not challenge what we were doing as she had no idea what was actually going on. She only came to one meeting. Then there was the man who simply wanted to be the centre of attention. He once sat on my high stool before I came in to take the meeting. He stepped down when I entered but made a big show of it. I had allowed him into the group to give him a chance to order his life but this behaviour was quite unacceptable. He then threatened to leave the meeting, believing he had something important to contribute. I said he was welcome to do just that, to everyone's relief. However, he returned afterwards to partake in the social time and refreshments. I then got two of the heftiest men in the group help me escort him out. At the door, I said he was not to return until he had a job and a woman, knowing this was highly unlikely. He was a 'poor rich kid' who had been ruined by being left a fortune by his grandparents. He, I heard, eventually finished up in an asylum when his fantasy of being a Guru had come to nothing. While some felt sorry for him, I pointed out that our meeting was not a psychotherapy group. Our work was about inner development. There were plenty of highly-skilled practitioners to help such people, that is if they really wanted to be healed. It is said that there is a risk of going insane in studying Kabbalah but that is possible even with marriage.

One periodic activity was the making of Tree scrolls. This meant drawing up the Tree of Life and Jacob's Ladder on canvas and painting

---

FIGURE 79 (Left)—EXERCISE
Kabbalists see the psyche as the vehicle by which to enter the higher Worlds. Here the mystic's physical body remains inert while his psyche, which carries his consciousness, ascends into another reality. This practice can be used to explore distant places and times, in a form of astral projection, and to rise up through the seven lower Halls of the World of Formation and enter the upper Halls of Heaven. This can be done only by individuals under a strict discipline who are familiar with Jacob's Ladder. Discrimination is vital in order to distinguish between vision and delusion. Misuse can lead to psychosis. (Redrawn from a Chinese Scroll by author).

them. These diagrams would hang up in the student's own home where they could be studied at leisure. This was a very useful exercise, as it made people become increasingly familiar with the kabbalistic scheme. Anyone who has not made their own Trees has missed out the process of integrating the system, as it takes great attention to get the geometry and lettering right. With this work comes the bonding with the diagrams as an interior experience. Having them in one's home makes them a constant presence and a point of reference. Sometimes, when I have a question, a glance at the Tree of Life or Jacob's Ladder has led my eye to the appropriate place to get the answer, as the unconscious resonates with these images of Divine principles.

Besides these activities, we had occasional lectures by experts among us on their field related to Kabbalah. One talk was on alchemy, another on history and yet another on poetry. There were also private trips to the French and Spanish towns where Kabbalah was studied and small seminar groups in people's holiday homes during the summer break. We used the academic cycle of spring, autumn and winter terms to give me time to rest, travel and lecture abroad and the group space to reflect. There were also the Jewish festivals, to which non-Jews were invited. One was a kabbalistic Passover in which its symbolism of escaping from the bondage of conditioning was enacted. Some people accompanied me when I ran courses abroad.

My father, who was now in his eighties, had come to a point when he was weary of the world and his own life. He said to me, 'I want to go home!' This was a real breakthrough as he had always been sceptical about an 'Afterlife'. One Thursday morning I got a phone call, from the old folk's home in which he was staying while his second wife was visiting American relations, that he had just died. I went immediately there and, as I approached the home, I heard his voice say, 'About time too'. When I said the Jewish prayer for the dead over his body, I felt a deep relief in his hovering presence. That evening, at the group, every chair except the one at my feet was occupied. After the meeting a lady came up to me and said, 'Who was that old gentleman sitting just below you?' I replied that it was my father who had died that morning. He had come to see what his idiot son was doing with his life.

According to Jewish Law, he had to be buried before the Shabbat and, as my brother was in China on business, I had to be responsible for the arrangements. On the Friday morning after the meeting, while I was meditating before going to the cemetery, I felt his strong presence. I asked him what he wanted? I heard his voice say loud and clear, 'Are you going to wear a suit and black shoes?' I responded with, 'Yes, but is that all you are concerned about?' Having got his answer, his presence disappeared. However, I was very pleased he did now know there was an Afterlife. Over several years he did make himself known from time to time, but then no more. I presumed that he had been reborn somewhere in the London Jewish community, like my mother. I knew my mother had been reincarnated because of an interesting incident. Many years after her death, I asked in a meditation how she was as she no longer came to berate me over my first marriage. On that day I decided to visit a park near the most Jewish quarter of North London. My attention was alerted when I saw that the road by the bus stop at which I got down was called 'Wycombe'. This is where we lived during and after the war. I then saw a young orthodox Jewish family of four; the little girl of about seven was the image of my mother with her eyes, face and black hair. I was tempted to call out 'Esther', but I realised the parents would have thought me mad. I walked on, not having had my conclusion confirmed.

FIGURE 80—HAVEN
Not all my journeys were pilgrimages to distant places. Some of the most important revelations came when I visited the English countryside of my boyhood to rest and reflect. Sitting in a field at the edge of the Chiltern beech wood, far from bustling London, would allow deep inner processes to surface. In contrast, sometimes I would go to the British Museum to make contact with the past. Objects from Ur in Mesopotamia, the ancient home-town of Abraham, would evoke insights not found in books, while contemplating the Greek section would bring about a deeper understanding of the Hellenic genius that invented Western philosophy, psychology and science. (Painting by author).

40. Pilgrimages

A Jewish American businessman, who had retired in his forties, set out to find me after he read one of my books while flying at 30,000 feet over the Atlantic. Kabbalah's metaphysics were a revelation because they pointed to a resolution of some profound questions that perplexed him that science could not solve. He had been wandering around the world on his retirement, looking for he knew not what, but now he had a key to aid the scientific method. Being a scientist by training, he had a very sceptical view of all things esoteric but Kabbalah was part of his religious tradition which, up till then, he saw as a faith. The book *Adam and the Kabbalistic Tree*, which set out the scheme of Existence, both in its micro- and macrocosmic dimensions, suddenly brought together in his mind an ordered system of Existence. He saw that Kabbalah was where his path lay.

Many years before, a psychic friend of mine foretold of an American who would come to support our work. So his appearance at one of my New York courses was not a surprise. It soon became clear that his skill in enterprise and organisation would be of much value. When he came to one of our London meetings for the first time, he happened to come through the door at the same moment as a Jewish South African architect who had been a student of mine for some time. I told the South African, who had lived and worked all around the world, to take care of the American at the meeting. As a consequence they became very close friends, not only at the personal level but as a team working for the Kabbalah Society. The timing of them coming in the door at the same instant was too precise to be an accident.

It was these two worldly-wise individuals who organised Kabbalah Society trips to Spain, France and Israel. They checked out routes, hotels, transport and financial costs. The American would then set up the project, arranging for guides, tickets and all that was needed, supported by the South African who spoke several languages and had a diplomatic charm which was a perfect balance to the more assertive American man's approach. This difference was manifest in their physical appearances. The diplomat was small and nimble while the

entrepreneur was large in every dimension. An incident sums up their dual image. Once, when checking a hotel's facilities of Cordoba, the staff appeared to believe that the American was a Catholic Cardinal incognito and the South African his aide de camp, which meant they got the best service. I became the third member of a middle-aged 'Kabbalah Gang', as we saw ourselves. None of us, when young, had ever belonged to a gang because we were all 'loners'. Together we made up for this boyish gap in our wide experience as we enjoyed many trips around the world discussing, arguing and joking. This was possible because we all shared the same ancient culture, even though we came from three different continents. These two men have been my good companions and peers for many years and I thank them for their support.

On one Kabbalah Society pilgrimage to Spain we had people from America, Mexico, Canada, Holland, Britain, Japan and several other countries. On this trip we visited places where Kabbalah had been studied and practised. In Gerona, we held a meditation in the medieval synagogue complex, where the kabbalistic group of Azriel probably met, and visited, next door, the house of Nahmanides, the famous scholar and member of the circle. While in his garden, I looked down into the well, saw my reflection and remembered the old saying, 'Truth is at the bottom of a well'. This was an awesome moment as I experienced the SELF of the Self. While on this journey I would periodically call out to the group the Hebrew word *Shema*, which means 'Listen' or 'Pay attention'. Some people in the group would then became aware of another dimension. This happened to many in the old Jewish quarter of Malaga, where we became conscious of souls still hovering around the streets and houses. Our South African said the Hebrew prayer for the dead in an impromptu service, hoping to help these long dead to move on.

In the important synagogue of Maria Blanca in Toledo, which had

---

FIGURE 81 (Left)—WALL
This outer wall of the Second Temple, built by Herod, is one of the most sacred places I have ever visited. This is despite the fact that everyone hated this brutal king who even murdered members of his own family. It is an irony of history that this wall has been the focus of Jewish collective consciousness for centuries. My own experience with the Wall is that, despite its solidity, it is a gate into another realm. It is saturated by millions of prayers from near and far. My prayer, on one visit, was that a lady companion would come along soon, as I felt very alone. Within days a letter from Finland arrived from Rebekah. (19th century print of the Wailing Wall).

been converted into a church after the Jews had left the city, many people felt the invisible presences of discarnate Kabbalists who came to hear Kabbalah discussed within its walls again. It was an extraordinary experience to be connected with the guardians who had remained to watch over this beautiful building. A similar event occurred when we went to visit the off-the-tourist-route town of Lucena, which had been a major centre of Jewish learning in the Middle Ages. Here I asked our party to put their hands and foreheads on the walls of the old synagogue, now a church, and feel what they could pick up at the psychic level. Some experienced the walls becoming transparent in that they could hear and see shadowy figures inside the building performing Jewish rituals. The local inhabitants, not used to foreigners, clearly thought us a very odd kind of tourists. These experiences brought us close to understanding the period in which Kabbalah flourished. Such exercises were very informative as we keyed into the history stored in the field-forces of these sites.

On this and other Kabbalah Society journeys many interesting things happened because the unfamiliarity of the situation and the School's discipline woke people up out of habit and conditioning. While on the coach or in a hotel, conversations about life with people from different cultures opened up new vistas. Many international friendships began on such trips because people shared the same kabbalistic frame of reference and aims. In one case, a trip was a crucial turning point. An American, who had been with the Dutch group for some years and was about to leave for home, was not sure where he should resettle. As we sat in the coach on our way to Granada in Andalusia, I said to him, 'Ask the Holy One and see what happens'. This he did. When we approached the city he opened his eyes as we passed a sign saying 'Santa Fe', an outskirt of Granada. On returning to the United States he set up a home in a town of the same name in New Mexico. There he founded a Kabbalah group which has flourished for many years.

Similar personal events occurred during our visits to Israel but in a very different way. For example, sometimes the religious image of the Holy Land, acquired as a child, is dissolved by the reality of the country. This shock precipitated a crisis in one of our number who had been brought up as a Catholic. After he went into the Church of the Holy Sepulchre he came out quite shaken because the priests of various Christian sects were arguing over whose was this or that part of the building. A similar trauma hit Jewish members of our group when they saw how the ultra-orthodox community were fixated in the past. In both cases there was no place for spiritual development. Ironically, these experiences cleared the way for individual evolution in that people were freed of unnecessary cultural clutter. They saw the accumulation of centuries of religious customs which were no longer understood or relevant to our time.

The Wailing Wall, below the Dome, is a remnant of Herod's Second Temple. Here Jews from all over the world come to pray. While it is only a retaining wall of the Temple Complex, it has a spiritual dimension. To make a kabbalistic Tree with one's body and lean against the ancient stone blocks is to open a door, not only into the past and millions of memories but also to the invisible higher realms. This is the function of sacred sites. For Jews it has been the focus of prayer from near and far over thousands of years and the 'Wall' has absorbed every prayer of praise and petition into its fabric.

One of the ancient customs of the 'Wailing Wall' is that one may write something on a paper and insert it into a crack in the wall. The rabbis say it will be then transmitted directly to the Deity. Many people come to Israel especially to post their thanks or requests, which may range from the mundane to the deeply spiritual. On one visit to Jerusalem, I went specifically to the Wall with a petition about my 'problem'. I knew, because of my birth chart and experience with women, that difficult partnerships were part of my fate. However, in my early fifties I had had enough of trying to sort this out by myself. In my request I asked for a beautiful, intelligent and agreeable mate, 'If it was the Holy One's will'. A few days after returning home, one of our communal household got a letter from a girl in Finland who had been to one of my courses in London. Now she was coming to London to spend some holiday time with us. Was she the answer to my prayer?

FIGURE 82—PRECOGNITION
This is a sketch for a painting I did about the age of twenty. The image was based upon a beautiful piece of piano music, The Girl with the Flaxen Hair. *It was meant to be the epitome of youth and yet have a certain sadness and seriousness as to what would come in the future, when the innocence of girlhood gave way to the experiences of love and everyday life. The girl is Scandinavian, rather than Semitic, which seems to have been an unconscious foresight into the future. The attraction of Viking girls may have been a reaction to the volatile, black-haired women of my own clan.* (Drawing by author).

41. Marriage

Tanja, as she was then called, was a typical Scandinavian. This could be seen in her tall slender figure, blue eyes and high cheekbones. She grew up on a remote farm in Finland and had learnt to work from an early age. She led the cows to and from the meadow, morning and evening, and carried out many other farming duties. She loved drinking coffee and playing cards with grown-ups but resented not being allowed to smoke. She learned to read at four and by the age of ten she had worked her way through the local children's library and moved on to the adult department where she read classical novels and poetry. The farm was surrounded by birch and pine woods and huge rocks, left by the Ice Age, were her playground. Keen to see the wider world and practise foreign languages, she did not embark on an academic education but chose commercial college so that she could go and work in Germany and Sweden. When she settled back in Finland, she joined poetry circles and art classes. She had read a wide range of esoteric books and eventually joined study-groups for yoga and the Gurdjieff system and found good companions. She also studied and practised astrology.

Our connection was, at first, quite indirect. She had read my books in English and wondered how she could know more about the Tradition. An opportunity came when she saw an advert in a New Age magazine that I was to run a weekend course in London. She came to the place where I was to teach and waited to see what she believed would be a venerable old man called Halevi. When I arrived at the venue, with the canvas scrolls of the Tree and Ladder under my arm, she thought I was one of Halevi's senior students. She was taken aback, as I was then fifty-four which, for a Capricorn, is no great age. On my part, I was also taken by surprise because she was the Scandinavian type that matched my anima-projection. Being aware of this I was sceptical of my attraction to her.

However, during a coffee break I asked one of the companions I lived with to invite her home for lunch. The excuse was that she was a stranger in a foreign land and we were showing her hospitality. In

FIGURE 83—FULFILMENT
Although a Levite on both sides of my family, I never felt the obligation to marry a Jewess and continue the line. My brother had done this. When Rebekah came, as a result of my petition put in the Wailing Wall, I knew she was the right one to be a companion. She came to London to meet me, having read my books. She was supportive and did the things to be done without fuss, taking care of our home wherever we lived. She also typed and edited my manuscripts while her comments and suggestions were tactful and helpful. She was also great company. In this photograph she sits having a picnic in the woods where I spent my boyhood. This was a long way from Finland but not too different from the forests of her homeland. (Photograph by author).

fact, I wanted my kabbalistic family to look her over, as my judgement was well off-centre because of my mixed feelings. And yet, her having read my books and come all the way to London was too coincidental. After the course we drove her around the great sights of London and then took her back to her hotel. When I got home, the consensus of my companions was that she was a very nice girl but she did live a thousand miles away. I was somewhat relieved at this, as my mind balked at the idea of a long distance romance and I wished to avoid any fantasy stimulated by this delightful anima figure on which I could hang a dream. I had been bitten twice by women who had enchanted me. This was partly due to having Neptune in Virgo in the House of partners, which makes beautiful and spiritual women particularly alluring to me.

After coming back from Jerusalem and having put in my petition about a wife, I was somewhat shaken by a letter from Tanja saying that she wanted to spend Christmas with our small community. Her request had not been addressed to me and so I was under no personal obligation to say yes or no. My companions, however, sensing that Providence was up to something, replied that she should come. When she arrived I, as the only bachelor in the flat, took her on walks around where we lived. Soon it became very apparent, when we shared our stories of lost love, that we were in a very similar situation. Her teacher, whom she adored, had, like my first wife, rejected a major opportunity to have a partner to walk the Path with them for life. I was deeply affected by her story, as it resonated so closely with my own. I felt not only drawn to her but also had a sense that we had been brought together for some reason. Had my petition in the Wailing Wall been answered? I was initially very careful not to jump to any conclusion.

Both Tanja and I soon recognised, during our walks, that we had indeed been brought together to heal each others' wounds. Indeed it became apparent, within a few days, that we might marry but we were both extremely cautious because neither wished to be caught up in a hopeful delusion. We concluded that the best solution was for her to come to England for three months and see what would happen. This suited us both, as I did not have to move to Finland and have my work disrupted whereas she was at a point where she had explored all the possibilities of where she presently lived and was ready to move on. Her choice was either to go to the capital city of Helsinki or come to London. At the age of thirty-six, the prospect of being alone in Helsinki or becoming part of a kabbalist family produced a clear-cut decision. She decided to take the opportunity in which there seemed to be no choice.

No one with whom I had been involved so far in my life had ever offered such a commitment except my first spouse, who broke her promise. All the other women either had their own path to tread or wanted a lifestyle I could not afford. But Tanja understood what the 'Work' was about and wished to be part of it. She was quite prepared to live in one room in a flat where there were five adults and three children. Moreover, she was ready to live very modestly with me for the rest of her life. She was the first woman to say to me, 'I want to help you.' All the others wanted me to support them in some way, which I was prepared to do but not at the cost of neglecting my mission.

When Tanja came to London, she not only fitted willingly into the community but was a major asset in what we were doing. Now I could give up grieving and transform my negative emotions into positive ones. This was not a relationship based upon passion, although this was present, but a genuine and true sense of partnership. Together we went to visit the groups in Mexico, America, Brazil and Holland where she was warmly welcomed as my partner. It is said that when one travels with a friend or lover, one either becomes closer or further apart. In our case it soon became apparent that we should marry.

When we married, she became known as Rebekah. In the Bible story, this matriarch came from a distant place to marry Isaac, the son of Abraham. It was also a symbol of a transformation in her, as she took on a wifely role which allowed me to devote all my energy to writing and teaching. We lived in our one room, packed with books, pictures and esoteric objects, for several years, enjoying the good company of the companions. Over the communal dining table many important conversations took place about Kabbalah and life while the three children of the household slowly matured in our midst. They would sometimes be present at our 'Ascent' sessions, sleeping in the room while we explored the higher Worlds. Their mother, my 'Sister', who had clearly been a Mother Superior in previous lives, took care of all those who came to our 'hostelry' and created a loving and secure environment which I, Rebekah and many others needed. It was a most happy period for several years.

However, there is always a time to move on. This was now possible because, since Rebekah's arrival, my income had suddenly increased. This was partly because the Trust for which I ran kabbalistic courses was dissolved when the founder died. I continued to run the courses doing my own administration but now I got the full financial benefit which, before, had gone to the Trust. Also, now being known worldwide, I could charge a professional fee for a course at home or abroad. At the individual level, I did not charge for a consultation but, if people did offer, I would accept a fee. However one teacher, envious of my work, said that I should not charge for spiritual services. Meanwhile, he was living off state benefits. My response was that in the Bible my ancestors, the Levites, were supported by the community giving them one tenth of its wealth in tithes. I did not require this. All I asked for one hour, if I was paid, was what people could afford.

Rebekah and I now could afford to move into a flat of our own which would allow us to expand in every way. The apartment came, without question, to us by Providence. The husband of a student of mine was a property speculator. He had a place he could not sell because it was in a poor area and it needed refurbishing. As a favour he had it rebuilt, according to our specifications, plus a balcony for plants, as we both felt isolated from Nature. On one side was a house full of gays, in the flat below people smoked cannabis that came through the floorboards, while above and on the other side of us there were periodic outbursts of loud music from young tenants. In the street, drug dealers did their business while within our building there was the ghost of a dead woman who had committed suicide and wandered, with her freezing cold presence, through our flat from time to time. Initially we put up with these negatives, as this was 'our' home where the groups were held which, to a degree, neutralised the immediate environment. The positive aspect was the cosmopolitan life of the area which gave it a lively atmosphere with its ethnic shops and every kind of culture. Most important, it was near the centre of London and very accessible for people to visit or participate in our group.

42. Memory

My next book, *Astrology and Kabbalah*, covered similar ground to *The Anatomy of Fate* but to a deeper and more subtle level. This was due to the further decades of experience and analysis of birth charts. When one begins to study and practise astrology, only the obvious is seen and one goes by the book. However, this depends upon which particular book one favours. But there comes a time when one has one's own angle on astrology. In my case, it was kabbalistic. By this is meant that which is beyond the mundane and psychological. My particular viewpoint was about spiritual development as revealed in a birth chart.

The book began by defining esoteric knowledge and its place in human evolution. This led to a brief exposition of the Tree of Life, the sefirot as the planets and their positions on Jacob's Ladder. Then came an outline of the microcosm of a human being who contains, in miniature, all four Worlds and so resonates with the macrocosm. The concept of soul-groups was then presented, followed by a detailed account of the signs of the Zodiac in relation to the triads of the Tree and the influence of the planets upon them. The horoscope of the United States was analysed, as an entity. The difference between the lower and upper faces of the psychological Tree was illustrated from an astrological viewpoint. After this came a description of transits and what might arise during their occurrence. Observations about choice, crisis and schools of the soul were then made as well as comments on personal relationships and problems when placed on the Tree. These were considered in psychological terms, together with the factor of free will. The book concluded with chapters on development, transformation and nemesis as well as Providence, destiny and history, closing on the theme of Self-realisation.

This was a technical work, written for astrologers, but anyone who knew something about astrology would be able to follow the text and perceive the relevance of the two ancient traditions to modern psychology. This would enable the reader acquainted with these subjects to key into archetypal and universal principles and so get additional insights into the human and cosmic situations. There is a Divine Plan and the Universe is not the result of some random set of physical elements that accidentally produced stars, planets and people. Out of this realisation, it was hoped, would come some reflection upon the reader's own fate and purpose within Existence.

One of my astrological heroes is Abraham Ibn Ezra. He was born in the 11th century, in Spain, but wandered far and wide over Europe and the Middle East. He was an original thinker, as far as Jewish scholarship was concerned, and also a poet, Neo-Platonist and astrologer. Wherever he went, he left a mark on the people he encountered. He sought out scholars of every creed to discuss philosophy, as this was a time when Jews, Moslems and Christians were greatly involved in the debate whether Revelation or Reason was the highest Truth. Up to that point in history, most people in all three Abrahamic religions accepted what their scriptures said without question. However, with the advent of the Greek analytic method and Hellenic philosophy coming into their cultures, through translations coming from the House of Wisdom in Baghdad, every thoughtful person had to reconsider their position. This caused great controversy and even split some communities. People were excommunicated and books were burnt as they were considered heretical.

Ibn Ezra, being unconventional by nature, openly challenged the accepted views regarding the Old Testament. He wrote from a philosophical angle as well as the allegorical and literal viewpoints. Well-schooled in the Neo-Platonistic approach, he made many scholars begin to think about the Bible in a new way, causing them to look again and perceive the Torah as an organised system and not just a random collection of religious symbols, meaningful stories and wise sayings. His novel conclusions were to influence even the most conventional rabbis in the long run, as the philosophical viewpoint became vital in defending Judaism against an intellectual assault from the other two Abrahamic lines which sought to prove that Judaism was redundant and their own creed was superior.

At one point Ibn Ezra came to London and spent about three years there. He left, it is said, because of the cold, damp and foggy weather but more likely he moved on because he loved to wander. I had, at one point in my study of him, a vivid picture of him walking through High Wycombe, where I had lived, with his brass astrolabe in his bag on his way to Oxford. A Jewish community there served the university, by renting out rooms to students, and Ibn Ezra possibly stayed in Oxford

FIGURE 84—ASTROLOGERS
In medieval times Christian, Moslem and Jewish astrologers co-operated to improve the art of understanding celestial influences. Here the Jewish observer is identified by his forked beard and unusual collar. Abraham Ibn Ezra was an 11th century poet, scholar and astrologer who wandered about Europe and visited England. He was familiar with the medieval form of Neo-Platonism and introduced a philosophical dimension and novel views into his rabbinic conclusions. He lived, for a time, in London where he had been invited by the community's rabbi to expound his unconventional ideas. I felt a strong kinship with him and he became my model. (Medieval woodcut).

and taught Hebrew at the university. According to some scholars, he returned to England and died there, possibly on his way to Cambridge where a new university was being founded.

As I felt much in common with this man, I decided physically to trace some of his journeys. I first visited Béziers in southwestern France, where he left such an impression that people talked about his visit for several decades after he had gone. This was the area where the Pope carried out a crusade against the Cathars, a breakaway sect of fundamentalist Christians. Some of these dissidents were burnt to death in the church just opposite the Jewish quarter in Béziers where Ibn Ezra had stayed. As men, women and children screamed out, it is recorded that a soldier said to a priest, 'Some of these people may be Catholics'. To which the priest replied, 'Christ will know His own'. As I stood in the square by the ruin of the old Jewry, opposite the now rebuilt church, I shivered with horror as the psychic field-force still retained the cries of those being burnt. From there I moved on to the towns in the area where the medieval version of Kabbalah had been formulated. No doubt there was Ibn Ezra's influence as well as translations of Hellenic philosophy.

My most personal journey in following Ibn Ezra's trail was in London. My own pre-this life memory of walking up from the dock of Billingsgate, in medieval times, enabled me to perceive what the city was like then. The fact that the original City of London's street plan has hardly changed, despite the Great Fire of 1666 and the Blitz of 1940, allowed me to find the Old Jewry with ease. There I saw, in a series of psychic flashes, the shadowy figures of Jews dressed in their distinctive robes, standing near the site of their vanished synagogue. From here I went out into the main street of Cheapside which, in the Middle Ages, was a busy marketplace. I then walked westward until I came to where the small river, the Fleet, once flowed. This is now buried beneath a Victorian road. There had once been a small monument and bridge across the stream but these had long gone. Interestingly, the street where the local prostitutes of the time plied their trade was still there and so, too, was its grotty atmosphere, despite being overshadowed by a magnificent 19th century viaduct.

I then walked Ibn Ezra's track west through Holborn, once an Archbishop's garden, to Oxford Street, now one of the world's great shopping centres; past Tyburn, where they hanged highwaymen, and on by Hyde Park to Notting Hill, then known as Nutting Hill, because of its many hazel bushes. As I went beyond what had been the village

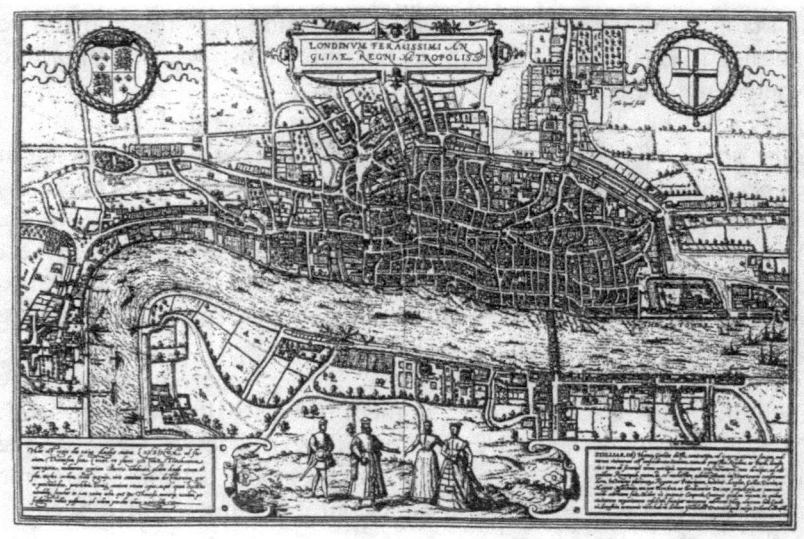

FIGURE 85—LONDON
This map was made before the Great Fire of 1666 burnt down most of the city's wooden buildings. The Jews lived here until 1290. Going back to that time, I can recall landing at Billingsgate Wharf, by London Bridge, and smelling the fish as I made my way up to the street now called Old Jewry. It was either in the late 12th century or early 13th. This is where I must have heard the story of the wreck of the White Ship. Then I might have been a trader, which was a common Jewish profession, as we had family and business connections in every great city from London to Jerusalem. My speciality was illuminated books and astrology. (16th century print).

of Shepherd's Bush, on the road to Oxford, I looked for remnants of the medieval countryside that must have existed when Ibn Ezra passed that way. Indeed, there were patches of woodland that had not been built on because of rough terrain or waterlogged soil. These areas gave me a clue to the conditions he would have experienced. This perception was particularly sharp when I reached a river-crossing, just outside Uxbridge, then a small town about twelve miles from London. The small river Colne with its ancient trees, grasses and wildlife was the kind of scenery he would have encountered all along the road to Oxford, as he either walked or rode a donkey. Only the nobility were allowed horses in that time.

As I traversed what was, even now, still countryside, I passed hamlets and villages that Ibn Ezra must have seen. The houses then would have been made of timber and wattle with thatched roofs. These had now gone but the old names were still there, evoking the Saxon, Danish and Norman periods of this part of England. As I moved northwest along the ancient road, I saw the hills and woods he would have traversed, much of it unchanged as this is the 'Green Belt' that surrounds metropolitan London. However, as I approached High Wycombe, where I spent my boyhood, I became increasingly alert, especially when I saw the ruins of a medieval hospice called St John's where travellers could stay *en route* to Oxford or London. As I walked by this familiar landmark, in the grounds of my old art school, I began to visualise what the town must have looked like in Ibn Ezra's time. Besides the wide main street there had been, at that time, a square in front of the church. On one side there was a row of buildings where, I believe, two Jewish families lived until they were expelled in 1290. They took care of Jewish travellers going to and from the capital. This realisation reinforced the impression of my having been there in the medieval period. It is very odd that my parents had chosen to live in High Wycombe during the Second World War when there were dozens of other places to choose from. Was I being told something about my past? This opened up a whole new vista about an earlier life in Norman England when Jews were invited to settle there as they were a literate middle class.

The next portion of the journey was through a flat rural area, after leaving the escarpment of the Chiltern Hills. This was more or less unchanged since the Middle Ages, except for the hedges introduced in the eighteenth century. As I approached Oxford, my psyche again became very alert, as it had done when I had first visited the city as a young boy. When I crossed the bridge by Magdalene College, which stood on the site of the medieval Jewish cemetery, I felt as if I were entering familiar territory. As I had a map of where the Jews lived in the city before their expulsion, I tracked down the site of the Jewish quarter and where the synagogue was, by the gate of Christ's College. Here, again, I had psychic flashes of the faces of Jewish figures standing around the area that seemed extraordinarily familiar.

Now, it has been suggested by kabbalistic colleagues that I may well have been Ibn Ezra. We certainly have much in common in our work and travels. But one can never be certain in such matters. It is easy to identify with a character whose life is similar to one's own but one must be cautious. Even so, my aversion to rabbinic orthodoxy and writing my own esoteric understanding of the scriptures had some resonance. We certainly shared a love of astrology and Neo-Platonism has a great resonance with me when applied to Kabbalah. Whether I was Ibn Ezra, or not, does not matter. However, what we did have in common was the aim to propagate a fresh view of the Teaching and bring it up to date with the leading edge of knowledge of our respective periods. My pilgrimage, following his tracks at home and abroad, gave me much insight and encouragement to carry out my assignment.

43. Encounters

When I was invited to Portugal to teach, I looked forward to getting a sense of a country that took in Jews exiled from Spain in 1492. Portugal is said to be ruled by Pisces, a Watery and Mutable sign, in contrast to Fiery Sagittarian Spain. Indeed, this essentially Atlantic country was initially very sympathetic, as the Jews brought in many skills useful for a then-expanding maritime nation. The Jews were safe for a while until Spain began to pressure this smaller country into persecuting not only Jews but everyone opposed to the Catholic Church. This was the time when Western Christendom began to be torn apart by the Reformation.

Many Jews converted to Catholicism, as they were weary of being persecuted, while others fled to Holland or Brazil, Portugal's American colony. As I wandered around the old Jewish quarter, now a slum in Lisbon, otherwise a most elegant city, I thought of the Kabbalists of the time and how they might have seen the situation. I suspect, when Lisbon was later reduced to ruins in a great earthquake in the 18th century, they might have considered it as karma, not only for betraying the Jews but for transporting millions of Africans to South America. This order of national retribution was one of the themes of a new book, called *A Kabbalistic View of History*, which I was now researching.

There was one place in Portugal, I discovered, which was undoubtedly a school of the soul. This was the Academy of Navigation founded by King Henry, called the Navigator, in the 15th century. He was half-English and half-Portuguese and encouraged his mariners to go beyond the limits of the known world to find a sea route around southern Africa to India and China. When Columbus discovered America, the Portuguese moved in and settled what was to become Brazil. Like people, nations have their great moment. For Portugal it was relatively brief but the work of the Academy of Navigators opened a new dimension for other seafaring nations and proved that the Earth was a globe. In my reflections on world history I concluded that a particular soul-group of explorers was at work. They would be incarnated at certain times to open up new frontiers. In contrast,

another soul-group might be artists, as seen in Renaissance Italy, and yet another in Britain to create the Industrial Revolution. There appeared to be many such soul-groups, each having a different mission within human evolution.

As fate would have it, I was invited to Brazil to run a course there. The result was the start of a group in Rio de Janeiro, the great port on the Atlantic seaboard. Here I had a salutary experience. I had been warned that Rio was a dangerous place for any westerners who, it was assumed by the local criminals, were all well-off. Most of my time I was well protected by being in a hotel or private houses, sometimes guarded by fierce dogs. However, one morning I decided to go for a stroll along Rio's famous beach.

I decided not to leave the thousand US dollars fee I had been paid for the course in the hotel safe in my room, as I had been told thieves could steal it while posing as staff. So I tucked the notes into my money belt and went down to breakfast. As I drank my coffee, a story I had once heard, of an Austrian who had wandered into a Mafia zone of Naples, kept running continuously through my head. I could not think why this persistent theme should come to mind. I recalled that the Austrian had been suddenly confronted by a friendly Mafioso who said that the Austrian would be robbed, and possibly killed, if he did not promptly leave the area. I was puzzled by this recollection which I put down to an instinctive reaction to the reputation of Rio's infamous street gangs who dominated the slums of Rio.

As I walked along the beautiful beach, around nine o'clock in the morning, all seemed normal with people swimming, sunbathing and playing football. At one point in my walk I saw a large dead fish in the sand but that was not unusual. However, a bit further on I came across a dead seagull. This stimulated a train of thought about the biblical image of the Fish of the Sea and the Birds of the Air, representing the angels and archangels. As I pondered the kabbalistic significance

---

FIGURE 86 (Left)—OMENS
In the course of everyday life, we act according to our conditioning. However, sometimes an unusual event draws our attention. For the Kabbalist the question is, what does it signify? The phenomenon of synchronicity, or happenings that have something in common, often indicates that something important is imminent, needs correction or even requires immediate action. Providence sends these signs but we can miss them and sometimes, only years later, we realise that such an episode was a warning to stop or a sign to go ahead. Some people regard such a view as superstitious but I have never disregarded what were often important omens about a situation. (Illustration from *The White Ship* by the author).

FIGURE 87—NAME
This icon is made up of the Hebrew letters Yod, He, Vav, He. *That is,* YHVH. *Set out in a vertical mode, the letters compose the figure of Adam Kadmon, the image of the Deity in a symbolic form. It has three pillars, four levels and it forms the basis of the Tree of Life. This figure is said to be the vast radiant being seen by Isaiah seated upon a Throne in the Temple. In early medieval times this* Kavod, *or Glory of God, was defined in mathematical terms to give a sense of the dimensions of Existence. This formulation seems to be contrary to the commandment to make no graven images and yet it became part of the Jewish esoteric tradition.* (Calligraphy by the author).

of the symbolism the ocean, which was quite far away, suddenly produced a large wave which swept up around my feet. I was being told something. But what?

A boy of about twelve, one of the street children common in Rio, then came up and asked the time, in English. I thought, 'How polite', as I stopped to view the seafront with all its smart hotels. As I turned to see a group of youngsters digging something out of the sand, the boy suddenly jumped on my back. Although I was totally surprised, an old wrestling technique that my brother had taught me as a child came into action and I threw the boy over my head. As he picked himself up, he was clearly as shocked as I was. He looked over to the young beachcombers for support but they were too preoccupied with their mystery object to notice the incident. He then panicked, as people around me came running to my aid, and sprinted away as fast as he could. The first adult to approach me was a doctor in his beachwear. He said, in perfect English, 'I have never known such a thing to happen this time in the morning.' To my surprise, he advised me not to go to the police on the waterfront as they were corrupt and might lock me up, accusing me of molesting the boy, unless I paid them something. I walked briskly and somewhat shaken back to my hotel. It was a sharp lesson not to be so naïve in strange places and take even more note of the omens that Heaven sends in moments of danger.

Two other distant places in which I was asked to teach were Australia and New Zealand. These visits were like stepping back in time. Both countries had a British style of culture which was like that in which I grew up as a boy. However, there was a distinct difference. The Australians, some of old English convict stock, were becoming more American while the New Zealanders, by contrast, were very conservative, possibly due to a strong Scots Calvinist presence there. This was an interesting observation, as it gave an insight into how the collective mind of a people is influenced by the terrain in which they live and their origins. This was to be seen clearly in Latin America where the Iberian civilisation overlaid but had not destroyed the native culture. Nations clearly have souls and fates which must fit into the Divine Plan of development.

When one of my students, a physician then living in South Africa, asked me to talk about Kabbalah at his synagogue in Cape Town, I could not resist the offer. I had been to Morocco and Egypt, and stood on the fringe of the Sahara desert looking south towards Black Africa, but had never thought I would go there as I had no previous life memories of African culture. This was a chance to enter quite a different collective consciousness. I also wanted to experience, once again, the southern hemisphere of the Earth from where a different kind of sky could be seen. For an astrologer it was an intriguing exercise to see the Sun at its zenith in the North and the Zodiac from a new dimension.

The southern tip of Africa, with its Mediterranean climate and European culture, made me feel quite at home. In Cape Town, the house in which I stayed was spacious and beautiful. This was in stark contrast to a nearby Black township I visited. This imbalance between wealth and poverty I saw could not possibly last forever. I had the sense of a time bomb that would explode if the situation was not balanced. I warned my friends to be prepared to leave, if the omens began to indicate a dangerous turning point. Alas, most of the Europeans did not heed my words as they lived in comfort with their black servants. The fact that most people are psychologically asleep was all too apparent.

The lecture at the local synagogue went well with a large audience asking many good questions. However, I noticed a rabbinic figure seated at the back with a very sullen look on his face. I had encountered such hostility before, with regard to my blend of ancient, medieval and modern approach to Kabbalah, but this rabbi's body language indicated that he was, indeed, exceedingly angry. Why such hostility, I was not sure. I was not a threat to his territory because this was not even his synagogue. As an act of diplomacy, my friend the doctor offered to arrange a meeting with the rabbi, in a neutral place, with himself as a mediator. This I thought might be an opportunity to meet as individuals and assuage his anger.

We met in the genteel atmosphere of an English teashop in Cape Town where I began to explain that Kabbalah needed to be updated. However, he kept interrupting me. I asked him to hear me out but he said that I had no right to teach Kabbalah. I paused and said, very quietly, that he was being discourteous. At this he started to shout so that people in the teashop began to look at us. I politely quoted one of the 613 commandments which says that one should never humiliate a fellow Jew in public place. At this he stopped, jumped up and ran out of the teashop. My friend and I were astonished by such conduct. Some months later I heard that the rabbi had been dismissed by his congregation for being excessively pedantic. This is unusual, as most synagogues, especially in distant places, will put up with a difficult rabbi because they are hard to replace. What he had done to outrage his congregation I do not know, but there was clearly a karmic reason for such a nemesis. Over the years I have noted that anyone who seeks to deliberately block, distort or discredit the Teaching often hits, sooner or later, a hard time.

44. Hostility

Leonardo da Vinci observed that there was never a bright light without a deep shadow. Anyone who has attained a degree of achievement is soon faced with this phenomenon. In the vegetable and animal kingdoms competition is normal, as part of the evolutionary rule of the survival of the fittest. The same occurs in those levels of human society. In everyday life, generally, the strong and attractive get the best mates while the most cunning and clever secure the best positions. This is all they need and want. However, there are those at the stage of transition between the animal and human levels who compete with those who no longer seek to dominate whatever field they are in but perform a higher transpersonal service. They do not have to be great saints or sages but men and women who have a calling, however humble.

When I was at art school there were many students who were exceptionally gifted. Only one or two of these became successful artists to a lesser or greater degree. Of the others, some soon gave up seeking fame, because they did not get instant recognition, while the remainder turned their talents to commercial design, film, television and even writing. One contemporary of mine became a well-known writer of spy stories while another became a top fashion photographer. I met the latter in the street a few years ago. By then he was no longer interested in the ephemeral world of fame, turning his creativity into a range of modest but worthwhile occupations. Both retained their humour, humanity and integrity despite the seductive trap of glamour.

FIGURE 88 (Left)—WRECKER
In the story of the White Ship, this rock could not be seen at high tide. The captain taking the prince and princess across the English Channel was too busy watching his youthful passengers' antics to notice that he was steering the ship on to a collision course. So it is on the Path, if one is forgetful of the dangers of being distracted by all manner of temptations. A lifetime's work can be destroyed such as that of Merlin, who was seduced by a beautiful woman, or Dr Faustus who risked his soul in a deal with the Devil. These temptations are obvious. The most dangerous ones, however, are those within oneself. The highest treason is to do the right thing for the wrong reason. I have seen several brilliant people wrecked by this hidden rock. (Illustration to *The White Ship* by the author).

FIGURE 89—INSIGHT
A boat is a symbol of the soul. In a kabbalistic exercise one is asked to imagine a vessel with one's name on it. The size and type are very informative, as is its condition. The question is then asked whether it is well run, in need of repair and what is on board. It may be cargo or people. What is shown reveals the state of the soul. In one case I encountered a disturbed person who had a pirate galleon, which described very precisely his psychopathology. In another a devout nun had a well-kept clipper ship carrying people to the Promised Land. In this figure, the hero is becalmed revealing, in its symbolism, that he has to wait for the wind, or Spirit, to move him on to his destination. This gives him time for reflection, perhaps to reorient his course. (Drawing by author for an unpublished novel).

One of my encounters with the temptation of inflation was when I went into an esoteric bookshop, with a foreign visitor, to buy her one of my books. The man behind the counter, to show that he was 'in the know', leaned over and said very confidentially, 'Halevi's name is really Warren Kenton.' I was tempted to reveal my identity but refrained. I said to my friend, after we had left the shop, that what I might have said in equal confidentiality was that I knew this as I slept with Halevi's wife. It is as well I kept my mouth shut. Then there was the incident with a socially climbing lady who, upon hearing that I might be a famous author, turned on her full sexual charm despite having her husband by her side. This is an instinctive reaction to any supposed leader of whatever social pack they head. Many a well-known person has fallen into the delusion that they are special and live out the projection of their admirers. In Kabbalah this is known as a Lucific test and initiation.

However careful one is to avoid such pitfalls, there is also the problem of envy. People may admire what one has done and yet seek to undermine it, even though unconsciously. One can dismiss outright criticism as simple jealousy but comments from well-informed people such as 'Quite good' are known as 'damning with faint praise'. My father had warned me about friends becoming enemies, which now began to manifest. At first I resisted recognising the fact. But, over time, negative comments by some people I regarded as on the same journey of Self-realisation as myself began to filter through. In one case an occultist I had known for many years remarked, I was told, that I knew nothing about meditation. His speciality was ritual and guided imagery and so he regarded my interior exercises as intruding into his territory, even though the Universe is vast enough to accommodate millions of meditators.

Perhaps the most difficult situation to accept was when one of my original group of companions, who resented me writing about Kabbalah, believed I was giving away esoteric secrets. He was a bright ex-Oxford scholar who was very angry, as he planned to write a book himself but had not yet begun. He felt that I had usurped his rôle as the expert on Kabbalah. Needless to say, such an event precipitated a break-up of our original circle. One or two members were very annoyed with me because they were older or had been in the Work longer. This revealed their real motivation as regards rank. However, most of my old companions proved to be the best of friends in this Lucific test of integrity. They saw my work as aiding in the aim of their own path and helping others.

The most difficult crisis of this period was when my Instructor began to find fault with my work. This I could accept when the criticism was valid. I had made note of any needed corrections but, when I heard from a friend about his judgmental and personal comments about me, it was most hurtful. I pondered, at the time, what was really going on. Could his observations be right? I did not openly confront him as we had shared much over the years. Perhaps, I concluded, he was going through an inner crisis as he had not fulfilled his potential because, by his own admission, he was lazy. I decided to wait upon events and hoped he would realise what damage he was doing, not so much to me but to himself.

We continued to meet every so often and I hoped his crisis would be resolved. However, one evening he told me how he had always sought to surpass others. I took this as a challenge. My reply was that I sought to learn from those who were superior in their field. He then began to write a book himself. It was published but it did not sell well. Two later volumes had the same problem. One result was that he declared that I did everything better than him. From here on, he openly swung between being a companion and a competitor. In normal circumstances this situation would be quite unacceptable. However, it became increasingly apparent that he was struggling with his shadow side and he needed all the support he could get. The problem was that, despite his great knowledge about esoteric matters, he confessed to me that he was not really interested in his own psychology. It was ideas that fascinated him. I was now caught between my loyalty to him and my right to protect myself. During a particularly provocative evening, he actually got up from his armchair with a clenched fist, as if to hit me, but then sat down realising that he had crossed a line. I was stunned by this action and left his flat, a place full of memories of wonderful conversations, with great sorrow. Later, when it was reported to me that he had said I was on the wrong path, I decided never to go back as my presence seemed to provoke a very negative reaction. This I did with great reluctance as I was beholden to him for many things and still felt a deep affection for an old colleague. He was by now in his seventies and suffering from a lifetime of heavy smoking.

About two years later, I heard he was in hospital and dying. This opened my heart to him again, especially when I heard that he was in great pain. When I went to see him in hospital I found the physical wreck of the man. However, his mind was just as sharp—but he had changed. He was quite philosophical as he had no fear of death which, he believed, dissolved all individuality. In this we had disagreed. When I bowed to him, as a mark of respect as I was about to leave, he smiled, clearly delighted I had come. All his animosity had gone and I felt great love for him again. We talked as in old times and this healed a deep wound. However, he said to me before I left him for the last time, 'So who won?' I could have said, 'We both lost', but replied, 'You did'. He smiled and said, 'Liar'. I bowed to him again. He then said, 'Thank you for coming'. He died shortly after.

His funeral was a cremation. All his friends, including myself, came to say good-bye. In my short contribution I said that he had been a kind of Socrates, whom he closely resembled, and that I had no doubt he would seek out, like Socrates, several long dead sages he would like to debate with. As the service proceeded I had a flash of him standing by the coffin, in a perplexed state, amazed at all the people who had come to see him off. After the ceremony I spoke to many acquaintances I had not seen for years who, like me, now had white or less hair. Among those present there was one of my chief detractors who was no longer hostile. Indeed he appeared to regard me as an old friend. This was an ironic closure to a difficult episode.

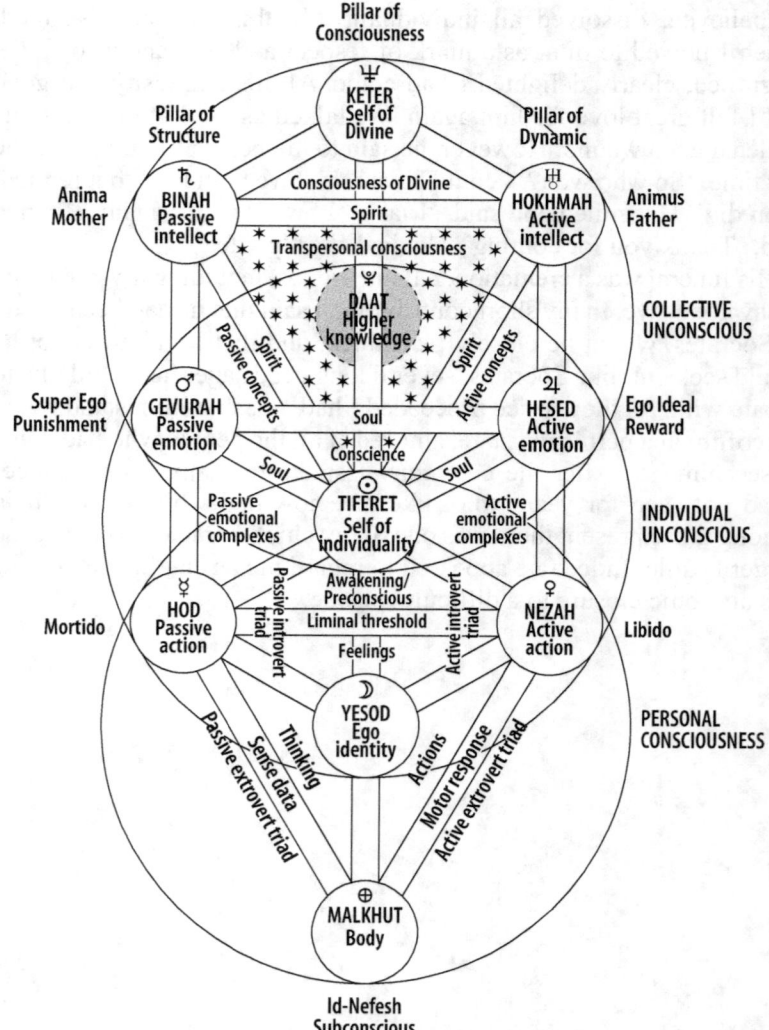

FIGURE 90—PSYCHOLOGY
The kabbalistic view of the mind was very important to the groups I taught at home and abroad. They observed that while Kabbalah's account of the higher Worlds was necessary, one had to live life on Earth. The psychological Tree revealed how its principles could be applied to the personal and the transpersonal aspects of the everyday world. The nature of the soul and free will were of particular interest, as it meant one could master one's fate to a degree and identify one's destiny. This was vital in the process of Self-realisation that involved all the Worlds. (Tree of the Psyche by the author).

45. Development

The book *Psychology and Kabbalah* is about the path of inner development. It begins with the two approaches of observation and revelation as regards the psyche, which is the focus of the study. It then sets out the structure and dynamic of the Tree and Jacob's Ladder before defining the four levels within the human being. Then comes the concept of reincarnation, followed by a brief account of the difference between fate and destiny. The process of death is examined, followed by what happens before the next life, looking in detail at the stages of gestation and birth. After this comes a chapter on astrology and its relevance to the psyche and incarnation.

From here on, perception, orientation and the foundation of the ego lead on to the sense of identity, learning skills and relating to society at large. These circumstances are examined, as is education and the stages of maturation into physical adulthood. Following this is an insight into the power of instinct, the composition of the Ego and the Super-Ego-Ideal. The psyche, as a working system, is then explored in detail, together with its defence mechanism and the Unconscious. Dreams are considered, as are psychopathology and crises. Freud's and Jung's views are taken into account regarding the various functions of the mind, the Individual and Collective Unconscious as well as the Archetypes, the Persona and the Shadow. These aspects are put on the Tree with the Self at the centre. The interactions and syntheses within the mind are explored, as is the notion of individuation. This leads on to the process of evolution from the physical, through the psychological to the Spiritual and Divine levels.

This is everybody's story from the cradle to the grave and beyond, through many lives. In Kabbalah the soul's present incarnation and its evolution over many centuries, perhaps with the same family soul-group and culture, is considered. Most people are still at the vegetable level of survival and propagation, before reaching the animal stage of seeking to be the best or the most dominant until they realise that worldly success is quite ephemeral. The English poet Gray observed that, 'The paths of glory lead but to the grave'. Nothing can be taken

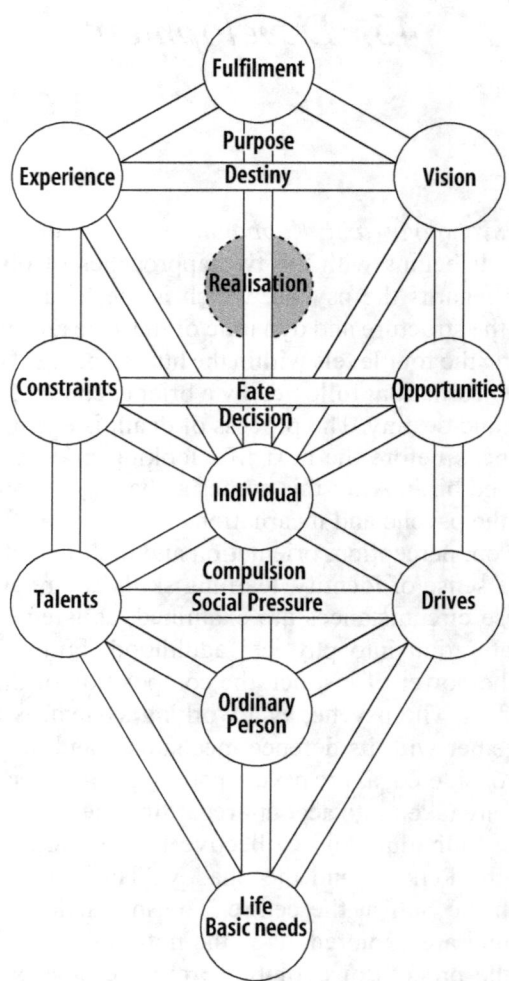

FIGURE 91—OPTIONS

It would appear that each of us is born into a circumstance that is best for our development. However, everyone has the option to make the most of their fate. In this Tree the choices are set out. At the ego level instinct and conditioning rule, in contrast to the Self and soul where we can start to individuate. In my life I had to recognise what I could and could not do. This took some time, as the delusions of youth had to be dissolved and certain talents developed. This led me to the realisation of what my purpose might be. To cling on to one's fantasies is to miss the moment when Providence opens doors for greater possibilities. (Tree of Possibilities by the author).

beyond this life except our karma. However, the animal level is the first step to individuation, that is, to being truly ourselves.

I recall as a child realising that, while I was in a loving family situation, I was not one of them. Even so they were not alien to me, as my past lives had been generally within Jewish culture, and so the values and customs were not unfamiliar. Deep within I decided to keep a low profile and act out the rôle of an obedient son until I reached adolescence. When the hormones began to exert the instinctive need to find a mate I forgot my soul for a while and yet my rebellion, in going out with a Christian girl, was an unconscious statement about being my own person. I began to wear, to my parents' horror, what were, to them, unconventional clothes such as a long black coat that, my mother said, made me look like a member of the Gestapo.

Youth tends to go to extremes and seek out an ideal cause that goes against the establishment. In my case, it was going on anti-nuclear marches and refusing to join the military when my national service came up. I opted to work in a mental asylum and a general hospital. By the time most of my contemporaries reached their mid- and late twenties many had regular jobs and had married, which was the norm in my time. However, I decided to remain single as I saw my friends' dreams of being artists and writers being eclipsed by homes, children and mortgages. In my processes of individuation I chose to live like a student until my late forties, as this was the only way I could keep a real control of my life and learn what I had to in order to carry out what had become, by then, my life's work.

What I did with my relative freedom was to develop the psychological component of the Self. This was done during the many hours of reflection that people have who live alone. This allowed the opportunity to grow inwardly. As a writer on esoteric topics I could combine my profession with my personal process of individuation. This was not just fortunate but the result of what I had learnt at the School, the Society and from Kabbalah. With this training I exploited what talent I had and worked hard to develop it. The novels rejected by many publishers bore witness to this. I also made use of my instinctive drives, in that if they were not used to support a family or a high lifestyle, their energy went into my books and the groups I ran.

As regards fatal decisions, by forty I was mature enough to recognise the limits of my capacities. I had hit various limits and constraints, such as no longer drawing, which made me realise that certain doors were closed to me. I was clearly no all-round genius like Leonardo da Vinci.

Such a moment of truth came when the art director of a publishing firm said, upon going through my portfolio of drawings, that while I was good he would not remember my work because it was too general. He only remembered artists who were specialists in babies, animals or certain subjects such as war, history and architecture.

Concerning what particular talent I did have, I developed my Geminian and Capricornian abilities to analyse the complexity of a subject, see the overall pattern and then explain the essence of the matter. This was a very useful skill in unravelling the obscurities of Kabbalah, the old texts of which were complex and sometimes distorted versions of the Teaching. When I applied my capacity to synthesise to my esoteric training, things began change in both my inner and outer life. Suddenly the way was clear to get on with my destiny. The result was my series of books and the refining of my teaching method. Here was where my fate and destiny came together as I realised I had trodden this path many lives before.

As can be seen in the diagram for this chapter, it is only when the lower sefirot come under an inner discipline that the higher centres can be consciously activated. For most people moments of insight are rarely like a comprehensive vision within an esoteric system. Such an insight can only come either from very intense interior work on the psyche or as the result of many lives of effort. This result can be seen in people with a strong sense of vocation, like the doctor who knew she had to be a healer when still a young girl or the gifted engineer who made ingenious gadgets as a boy.

The realisation of what one is 'called forth, created, formed and made for', as the Bible says, is to recognise one's destiny. Every one has a place and purpose in the Universe, be it low or high in the scale of humanity. Destiny can take many forms. For example, without the entrepreneurs vast industries could not come into being, employing people of every level. I knew an old Irish street sweeper who found his place in giving wise advice to the many people who stopped and talked to him. Many people of destiny are quite unnoticed. Not everyone has to be a great actor, inventor, saint or prophet. Society is full of people whose gifts are taken for granted, like the master cook or gardener, the reliable lawyer or town planner.

In my case, my pre-natal memory of being born to carry out a certain mission began to come into my mind. Gradually all that had happened began to integrate and point to a precise direction which opened up more and more vistas. This became increasingly obvious as doors I did not even know were there opened and I met people from all over the world who were part of the esoteric community. They didn't just help seekers to find their path but kept a balance against the pursuit of materialism, as formal religion had become less spiritual and more political. I began to become aware that it was my generation's task to aid in this global operation.

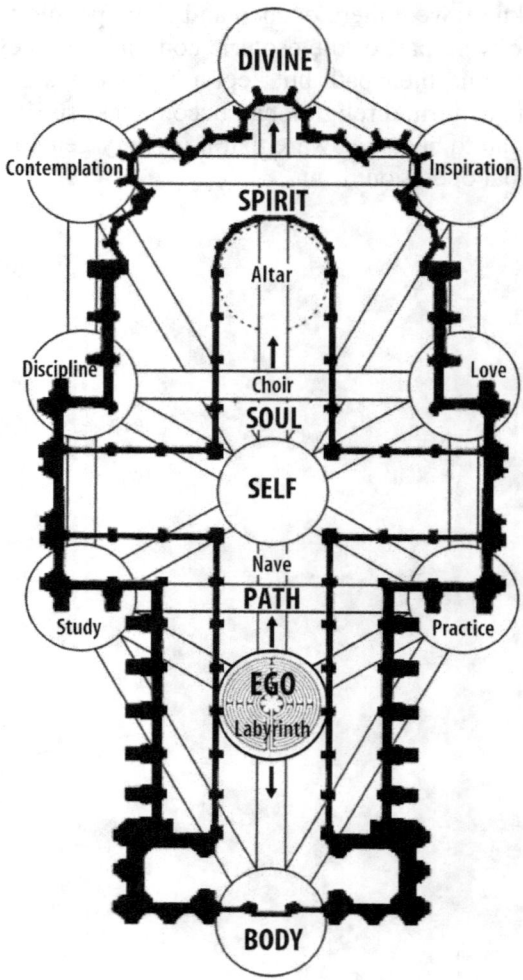

FIGURE 92—CONNECTION
This combination of the Tree and the ground plan of Chartres Cathedral was the discovery of my oldest friend, whose mission was to explore sacred geometry. Here we brought our two disciplines together, revealing that whoever designed and built Chartres had access to esoteric knowledge. It is known that one of the teachers associated with the medieval school of Chartres spent some time studying in Spain and he, no doubt, met with the Sufis and Kabbalists there. Just across the street from the Cathedral was the Jewish quarter. It is highly probable that the enlightened priests of the Chartres school had discussions with the local rabbis and the Masons who built Europe's finest Gothic cathedrals based on the model of Solomon's Temple. (Tree of Chartres discovered by Prof Keith Critchlow).

46. *Academy*

I have known my oldest close friend for nearly sixty years. We met at St. Martin's School of Art and have run parallel lives in different careers. He was a gifted painter but his love of geometry led him to become one of the world's leading experts in the field. He was particularly interested in sacred geometry and included it in buildings he designed. In time he became a professor at the Prince of Wales's Institute, which set out to preserve and develop traditional sacred and secular arts and crafts. His love for medieval cathedrals, especially Chartres, has resulted in the discovery of the Tree of Life design in the floor plan of Chartres, as seen in the illustration to this chapter. He also came to believe that there must have been some co-operation with the local Jewish college, across the road from the cathedral, because the proportions are too close to be coincidental. We both concluded that, with the master masons who built the cathedral, it was the work of a school of the soul.

My old friend is a Platonist by nature but has connections with the Hindu tradition, as well as an interest in Kabbalah. My earliest memory of him does not belong to this lifetime but to ancient Alexandria where I can remember us, I the Jew and he the Greek, having a discussion in the shade of the portico of the museum and library there. We have known each other over many centuries as brothers, in different but co-operative soul-groups. I recognised him as a companion when I first met him and we have remained friends over the years, without any sense of rivalry because we shared the same inner values.

He, together with an eminent English poetess with an international reputation, a scholar and expert on William Blake, founded the Temenos Academy. This was composed of about forty or more Fellows who were academics, writers, artists, poets and philosophers, as well as business and government people from all over the world. This was possible because the famous poetess, who lived to her mid-nineties, knew everyone worth knowing. She and I met through my old friend. We hit it off immediately because she was a Sun Gemini and I have the Moon in that sign. Besides her interest in Kabbalah, which she had studied when young, she loved Jewish humour. Indeed, she would sometimes phone me, when she was depressed, to cheer her up in order to get her perspective on life back.

I also had a distant memory of her as the daughter of a minor French aristocrat in southwestern France at the time of the Cathars. I was then a Jewish artist and book-seller who often travelled between Spain and Italy, through her area. Her father was a book lover and I talked about esoteric ideas as she, then about nineteen, listened in. In this present life we often spoke about reincarnation. During one of these conversations I suggested to her that she might have been William Blake, as she knew far more about his life than any academic study could unearth. For example, there was no obvious connection between Blake and a certain contemporary poet, as there were no letters. The reason why, she explained, was that they lived just a street or two away from each other and had no need to write. When I saw her just three minutes after she died I was very struck by the close physical resemblance she had to Blake. They certainly had much in common. She left me an original Blake print of Job in her will.

It was she who invited me to become a Fellow of the Temenos Academy. She wanted me to be on its council but I refused this rôle, as I said I would be much more useful if I was not involved in its inevitable politics. Charles, Prince of Wales was the patron of the Academy. This meant that I entered quite a different social dimension. I was now indirectly involved with history, in that Temenos had an influence on how the Prince saw and acted in the world as an archetypal figure. He portrayed many ideas in his speeches about education, climate and religion that had a universal view not usually found in politics or the Royal scene.

Prince Charles supported Temenos because, he said, it opened up a new dimension for him in that he became acquainted with different aspects of philosophy, religion and mysteries. As a sign of commitment he invited Temenos to hold concerts by various unique performers in St James's Palace which I, as a Fellow, attended. We were also privileged to visit his country house, Highgrove. At the reception he gave each person his full attention in conversation about their subject. I was moved by his discipline and intelligence.

One of the perks of being a Fellow of the Temenos Academy was that I got to meet, in private, some very interesting people. One was the Dalai Lama. During this encounter, I observed a remarkable man who had been placed in his position because, it was believed, he was the reincarnation of the previous Dalai Lama. Not an easy task, because he was subject to the cultural projection of being a god-like king by Tibetans while, at the same time, being regarded as a dangerous symbol by the Chinese Communist regime. I perceived that it was his strong sense of humour and Buddhist values that kept him sane and also prevented him from being inflated by the temptation of power. He was a fine example of someone able to handle both secular and sacred rôles on the world stage and remain a very human individual.

Another interesting person I met through Temenos was a well-known American Jewish philosopher and expert on China. I had read his books and was impressed by his knowledge and feel for the culture. I believe that, like me, he had been in China in a previous life. However, what was of note was that he picked me out of a group at a Temenos conference even though we had never met in this life. His face and demeanour were certainly familiar to me. Before I could compliment him on his work, he said how my books had been an inspiration to him in the 1970s. In our line of the 'Work' we are allowed 'sixty seconds of vainglory a year'. I used up at least half my quota at that moment. We then began to exchange Jewish jokes until each discovered which ones the other had not heard. It was like meeting another brother. This was confirmed during his lecture when a very devout Catholic made a negative and inaccurate comment about Judaism at what was meant to be an ecumenical occasion. He looked across the audience at me with the saddest of expressions before politely responding.

Another significant encounter, through Temenos, was with a famous modern Islamic scholar who teaches in an American university. He was born a month after me in 1933 and just a few days before my oldest close friend, the professor. We appeared to be members of a specific soul-group, sent down at around the same time to carry out a particular mission, each within their own tradition. While I did not feel a personal kinship with this remarkable man, there was a sense that he was a companion of the Light. We talked briefly over a lunch and made a connection. His books have much in common with mine, which is to be expected as our birth charts are very similar. This encounter gave an interesting insight into the workings of fate within the Divine Plan.

At a more social level, as a Fellow of the Academy Rebekah and I were invited to represent Temenos at one of the Queen's summer tea parties at Buckingham Palace. This was along with 5,998 other people. These guests were easy to recognise as we approached the Palace gates. All the women had smart hats, which is obligatory, while

the men wore formal suits or military uniforms. These attires did not, however, hide the wide differences in class and character to be seen in the Palace gardens. Here was a perfect cross-section of Britain and its Commonwealth of Nations. Over this very formal gathering hovered the spirit of the Old Empire as the military bands played English, Scottish, Welsh and Irish folksongs as well as marches and popular melodies. The collective imperial entity was still there, although not as strong as it was when I was a boy. The Queen's entrance and gradual progress through the disciplined crowd revealed much about the archetype of Monarchy. Few presidents could ever command such love and respect. This event was strangely moving for me, the descendant of a poor Russian Jewish migrant. I said to Rebekah, 'What would my grandparents say, to see their grandson having tea at the Tsarina's Palace'.

FIGURE 93 (Left)—HISTORY
England became a nation at noon on December 25th 1066 when William the Conqueror was crowned in Westminster Abbey. He built the Tower of London to assert his authority over the City and act as his palace there. Here began the line of the British Royal family. I met Prince Charles through the Temenos Academy, of which I am a Fellow. I perceived the heavy burden he bore. His interest in the Academy was that its members were made up of distinguished scholars, poets and musicians, as well as people in the political, scientific and business world. It was a great privilege to be asked to be one of their company. (Illustration for unpublished novel by the author).

47. Orient

I have been to Japan several times to teach. It is even more removed from Western civilisation than the Middle East, despite its modernisation. Japan is on a set of islands and, like Britain, only partly belongs to the nearby continent. It has, beneath its facade of advanced technology, the influence of China, whose civilisation it adopted in the first centuries of the Common Era, but behind this is an essentially Japanese nature of Virgo-Scorpio that reveals itself in all sorts of ways. The most obvious is the well-kept and neat countryside. On the face of it, the landscape is serene but there is the ever-present possibility of an earthquake. Likewise, the Japanese persona of politeness can be dropped when the samurai spirit is evoked, as has been seen in the times of war. While we may not know exactly when a nation was born, as with the United States, its zodiacal character can be discerned by a skilled astrologer.

I had direct insight into the nature of the Japanese when we were doing a group meditation in Tokyo. As we ascended in the exercise into the higher realms, the floor started to go up and down. It was only for a few seconds but, as I had been in an earthquake in Mexico, I knew it meant danger. However, no one moved. When the swaying of the building ceased, it was as if nothing dramatic had occurred. The Japanese were quite unperturbed while the Westerners present were very disturbed. This was very characteristic of the Scorpionic stoicism and the Virgoan self-control.

FIGURE 94 (Left)—JAPAN
On visiting Japan I saw how the people are greatly influenced by its terrain. On the surface the rural landscape is tranquil; so, too, are the many sacred places and temples. But then there is the daily shudder of an earth tremor and the periodic quake that can devastate an area. The Japanese are quiet, polite and highly disciplined. This is their Virgo aspect. However, there is also an innate Scorpio tendency that can suddenly erupt, epitomised by the Samurai cult. Here a warrior wipes his sword clean after a battle, while his hair is groomed and scented so as not to offend a person who might cut his head off. This combination of Virgo precision and Scorpionic interest in the unknown drew many to Kabbalah as it explained much about Shintoism, the religion of Japan. (Redrawing from a Japanese print by the author).

On one of my visits I went to visit Hiroshima. This city had been rebuilt completely after the atomic bomb had devastated it. As I stood under the exact spot where the nuclear device had exploded I had a psychic sense of tens of thousands of death cries. Going down to the river shore nearby, I picked up stones that had been softened by the explosion. These distorted rocks, in a way, were more shocking than the skeletal wreck of a building nearby that had been preserved as a memorial. In the museum devoted to the disaster, there was a marble step of a bank that had been roughened by the atomic bomb blast, except for where a man had been. His presence had been preserved in a polished stone shadow. This, I thought, was an awesome karma for the wanton Japanese destruction of Nanking, where tens of thousands of Chinese civilians had been killed, in that the Japanese had had to learn a bitter lesson, even as Europe had in two World Wars. The law of retribution is very exact at the national as well as the personal level.

The Virgo aspect of Japan was seen in the serene gardens in a monastery in the old capital Kyoto. This was an area in which the bare earth was raked into lines that swirled around very precisely placed rocks. The effect was utterly serene in the silence that pervaded the site. Here the heart and mind could become still and silent in contemplating Eternity as represented by this miniature cosmic landscape. Similar shrines were to be found everywhere in Japan, even in the busy cities. In her garden my hostess had added to its exquisitely laid out terrain the Tree of Life, made up of stones.

Mount Fujiyama is the icon of Japan. This at present dormant volcano is perfectly symmetrical and most feminine, in contrast to the highly masculine active volcano of Popocatépetl, forty miles from Mexico City. Lady Fuji, as she is called, which is at a similar distance from Tokyo, is seemingly quiescent. However, as I climbed up her side I felt that she might erupt at any moment, sending out blazing ash to fall upon the lush flanks of the mountain below. Due to a lack

---

FIGURE 95 (Left)—CHINA
Although China was communist when I went there, I was struck by how the society was still essentially Confucian. By this is meant that it was more oriented towards social order than the mysteries of religion. For example, the Chairman of the Party was virtually an emperor with the Marxist cadres making up a political aristocracy, just like the old mandarin system of government. On the basis of this contradiction and the periodic cycle of revolutions, I concluded that China was an Aquarian nation. My visit evoked many memories of my sojourn there in the Middle Ages. Little had changed. (Emperor Mao Tse Tung, drawing by the author).

of time I did not get to the crater. But there I believe I might have had an illumination at that point where Earth and sky meet in perfect harmony. Perhaps I will make it in my next incarnation.

The China experience was quite different. I went there on a private visit. The flight out was worthwhile in itself, as I had a bird's eye view of Constantinople and the area of Russia where my paternal grandfather had come from. I have collected old maps for years, because they are fascinating objects, but there is nothing to compare with seeing the reality laid out below from an aircraft. To see the cedars of Lebanon and the ancient land of Mesopotamia, the homeland of my ancestor Abraham, was deeply moving. Long-forgotten memories were stirred up, some pleasant and some not. The psyche is full of such deeply buried experiences.

Upon coming into Beijing, I felt I had never been to this city before even though the field-force of China was very familiar to me. This suggested that such recalls were not just imagination. I had no sense of recollection in Brazil, Finland or Canada, as I had clearly never been to these places before. So it was with the present Chinese capital. The visit to the Forbidden City was most interesting but it had no memories for me, even though the great palaces, temples and courtyards were marvels of style and power. This great civilisation appears to be Aquarian in character. On the one hand it is fixed in its rigid social order but this is periodically shattered by sudden rebellions. As seen, when Chinese society is put on the Tree, there is not much difference between the old mandarin system and the modern communist party regime with its communist emperor. The devastating Cultural Revolution started by Mao Tse Tung is typical of an Aquarian revolt against any system, in this case his own. This contradiction is truly Uranian, the radical planet that rules Aquarius.

As we moved slowly by train through the landscape, west towards the old capital of Xi'an, I began to feel more at home. However, I perceived that the 'old' China was in the process of disappearing. There were still the traditional Chinese farms, with their outer and inner courtyards, but they were now empty and derelict. Beside these ruins were high-rise blocks of dull and uniform apartment buildings and factories and cities surrounded by smoke. When we got to the city of Xi'an, the western gateway at the end of the Silk Road, I recognised the defensive towers and walls. This feeling was repeated when I visited the foreign quarter, where merchants from the Middle East and even from the distant West lived. This section was as familiar to me as medieval London or Toledo.

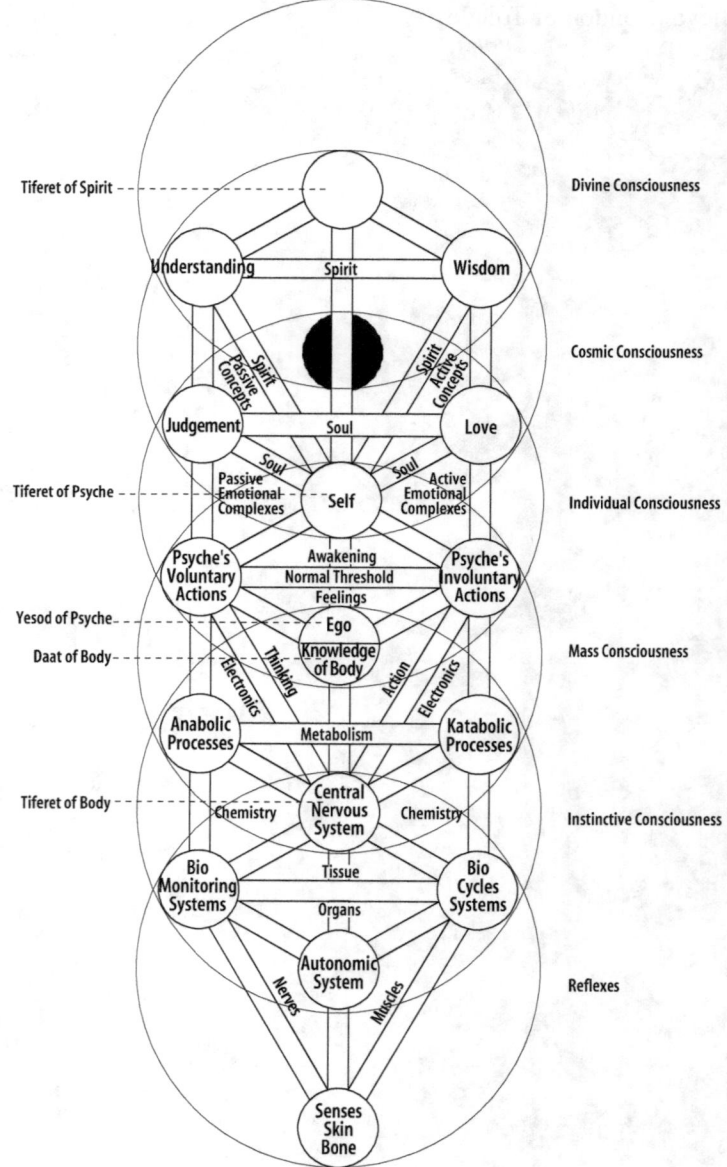

48. Home

Because Rebekah and I are both frugal by nature, our resources began to accumulate and we could afford to move. Here Providence had stepped in. The housing market suddenly dropped its prices and we were able to buy a fair-sized apartment with one large room, two smaller ones, a kitchen and bathroom. The main space became the social area where the group could meet. My study was in the corner of the main room, while Rebekah had one of the small rooms and her own kitchen. However, for some reason, neither of us felt it was to be our permanent home. While it was acceptable for several years, new noisy neighbours made us decide we must move on.

Again Heaven intervened. A student of mine saw, in a very pleasant tree-lined street nearby, a small Victorian house for sale. I called the estate agent but he said that it was already under offer. However, there was one just opposite that was about to go on the market. Rebekah went out to investigate and by 'chance' encountered the owner, who recognised her as a potential buyer and showed Rebekah around. Because there was as yet no 'For Sale' sign outside the house, nobody could know it was available. The timing of Providence, as usual, was impeccable. Rebekah then came home and told me that it might be the house we had prayed for. Besides plenty of space for our needs, it had a garden with a Russet apple tree and an old vine facing the southwest. When I heard this I began to shake. Russet apples are Rebekah's favourite fruit and the southwestern sky was perfect for my telescopes. The biblical phrase came into my head that 'Every man

---

FIGURE 96 (Left)—SCIENCE
One of the most interesting aspects of updating Kabbalah was to relate the Tree to science. The medieval Kabbalists did not have the access I had to the vast amount of information about the material world. My personal library was probably many times larger than theirs. As regards psychology, they may have known as much but the terms they used have long been outdated. Here, the body and psyche are seen as an integrated system. The lower part of the mind is greatly influenced by instinct while the body is conditioned by evolution. Upon death they separate but while the body soon disintegrates the psyche retains all it has experienced. Science has yet to recognise this. (Diagram by the author).

FIGURE 97—IMAGINATION

This image, by the French artist Doré, of the ultimate state of consciousness before entering the Divine Realm is used in a special exercise. This is to flash the picture from a projector on and off on to a screen, until it is established in the eye as an after-image. Through imagination this becomes an icon, or visual device, by which the psyche could enter the World of Formation and then go on into the realm of Creation, before encountering the luminous reality of Emanation. Here the student and his inner teacher view the entrance to the Divine Light. In this exercise it is possible, if only for a moment. (Doré's illustration for Dante's Divine Comedy, *19th century engraving).*

should sit under his own vine'. We went to see it in the evening, by formal appointment with the agent. By the time he arrived the owner had taken us through the house, saying she had tried to sell it three years before but there were no buyers until we came. I made an offer on the spot. The house was clearly meant for us.

Finding the right builder to do the necessary renovation was equally miraculous. Rebekah got the telephone number of a friend's builder. She arranged a meeting with him and started making plans. We discovered later that we had, in fact, got a different man although with the same name. This happened because the last two digits of the telephone number had been reversed by mistake by Rebekah. However, this builder was not only very competent but he was far cheaper. We also had a sense that someone from the group, who had passed away, was helping in the process as an invisible supervisor. He had been a surveyor and had promised to check any property I would buy.

Rebekah and I now had a real home and a place where we could work and have the Thursday night meetings in the large main room, which could accommodate up to fifty people. There was room for a projector and a screen, which was very useful for putting up diagrams and images. My study was on the first floor and it quickly took on the alchemical atmosphere of my earlier studies. The loft was converted into Rebekah's study, with a red staircase leading into this 'higher World'. The kitchen was remodelled according to her wishes in blues, reds and greens of the old Scandinavia. I designed the garden to look like a medieval courtyard, with old bricks laid out in lines to represent infinity and a circle of the four Worlds. At the centre was an elegant pedestal, made up of four breadboards and a large staircase post, painted to look like terracotta, for a brass Armillary sphere of the Heavens and the Earth. Other houses shut out the streetlights, enabling my telescopes to view the sky as clearly as is possible in a great city.

The house was filled with many esoteric pictures besides telescopes, maps and stones from all over the world. There were also the scrolls depicting Jacob's Ladder and the Tree and a large Zodiac wallboard, as well as terrestrial and celestial globes, a brass astrolabe and an armillary sphere. All these objects had a special significance, like two old-fashioned watches, the gold one representing Eternity and a stop-watch the ever-moving moment. From the ceiling of the big room hung a figure of Gabriel, along with the suspended globes of the Sun, Moon and Earth, and a circular sky map from whose centre hung a

FIGURE 98—STUDY
This is the room I have been building up over my life. It is full of symbolic and sacred objects. Besides books, it has a work bench and a place for tools. There are also globes of the Earth, the Moon and the celestial spheres as well as Chinese, Indian and Western versions of the Heavens. Microscopes and telescopes of various magnifications are there, so too are cameras, a fax machine and even a laptop, which is hidden away when not in use. A small silver bird, representing the Holy Spirit, hangs from a large circular map of the stars, glued to the ceiling. I hope and pray this room will be there in Paradise, if I ever get there. It has been my moveable study for over fifty years. (Photograph by Peter Dickinson).

glass jewel symbolising the 'Dew of Heaven'. There was also a large painting of the kabbalistic universe and a 'Ladder of Being' composed of a piece of copper representing metals, a crystal symbolising the mineral world, with a cluster of corn heads for the plant kingdom and a fish, cat and owl for the respective animal levels. Above these came a meditating human figure and an angel. Above this column was a Holy God Name in the form of Adam Kadmon.

Besides taking care of the house and the domestic routines, Rebekah took on the task of editing my texts. Her grammar was better than mine as she had had to learn it when studying English. Her comments were always to the point and with the intuition of a poet she could clear away any excesses. I always wrote everything including much useless information in my first draft as this was the creative part of writing. Then came the critical phase, after which she polished up the texts and made suggestions. I took all these comments seriously, as one does not get a personal assistant who is also a Kabbalist when dealing with a conventional publisher. Her help was invaluable when preparing the revised editions for the Kabbalah Society. She worked with a computer, whereas I only used a pencil and rubber as I found even a typewriter got in the way of the flow of words and ideas.

Besides writing and pondering the mysteries of Existence each day, I would talk to people who came to see me. Some wanted me to look at their birth charts and others sought advice about a personal or spiritual problem. Over the years I became more and more like an old rabbi, except that I was also being asked by Buddhists, Christians and even academics for a kabbalistic view of their particular situation.

The house is where we both wish to spend the rest of our lives. For us it was a miracle as neither had expected such a gift. Indeed, both of us had contemplated a respectable form of poverty but here we were in a place that seemed to have been designed for our lives and work. I felt like an old pioneer who had been through hard times creating, out of a wilderness, a thriving farm. At long last I could sit on the verandah and enjoy the fruits of my labour and the gifts that Heaven had given.

FIGURE 99—CONTEMPLATION

I face this wall when I meditate with my eyes open. It is full of symbols that stimulate the soul. Besides the Trees and pictures there are two watches, one of gold, which represents Eternity, the other a stopwatch symbolising the passing moment. Below the calligraphy of the Holy Name is Fludd's kabbalistic head while to the right, above an old map of the world, is the Zodiac. Above this is a meteorite and fire-formed and water-made stones, as well as a fossil and a man-made image of the Heavens. In front of an anatomical model is a 17th century globe and armillary sphere together with significant objects, one of which is a silver Torah decoration from a synagogue burnt by the Nazis. (Photograph by Peter Dickinson).

49. Reflection

Upon reaching the age of seventy I had my first real birthday party since my Bar Mitzvah at thirteen. The people invited to celebrate it in an old 17th century house were those who had played some part in my life and development. Not all were close friends but individuals who had shown me something vital at a critical point in my life, in a one-off conversation or by being what they were. One was a lady who had not had an easy life but one which she had endured with great dignity. Another was an old friend, whom I had known as a student, who had followed his star.

There were people who did not come, as it might have been a painful reunion for them. One was an old sweetheart who had married for security and had paid a heavy price for her comfort. Another was a man who I knew was envious of my work and would not have been very happy at the party. Perhaps the saddest omission was one of my great loves, the Anima lady who had rejected me but some years later made it clear she wanted me to return. Then there were those who could not come because they were too far away, had lost contact or had died. I picked up one or two of the dead who came to the party, if only to see a gathering of old friends.

The importance of friendship became manifest when I saw how those present were the human threads in the weave of my life. Most had lost the bloom of youth but not the spirit that still followed the path of truth. This was confirmed by one of the waitresses, a student hired for the evening, who said she had rarely encountered such an interesting crowd of people who talked about psychology, philosophy and mysticism instead of their jobs, children, and holidays.

This eighth decade marked a new phase in my life. I had some problems since my publishers had been taken over by a young man who wanted to make the company move more towards the New Age and self-help type of publication. I warned him that the long-established reputation for serious esoteric work would be eroded if he went ahead. He took no heed and his list moved out of the niche of a specialist market into a more popular mode.

Having seen the way this venerable publisher was going I became concerned, especially when it turned down my latest book. This was extraordinary as they had published eleven of the Kabbalah series so far. The books were slow to sell but after thirty years they still brought in a steady income for the publisher. Over one hundred thousand copies of my books in fourteen different languages had been sold. For the new publisher it was not a quick enough return on even the small reprint layout.

In a discussion with my American friend, the managing director of the Kabbalah Society which we had jointly founded, he offered to buy all the rights back. This was an offer I could not refuse, especially as he sold them to me for the grand sum of one pound. We then set up, with three members of the London group who had just gone into book production and publishing on their own account, the task of producing the Kabbalah series as a revised set. Here was Providence at work. Now began a most exciting and creative period as I had a professional knowledge and experience of book design and in this case I had no one to tell me what I could and could not do. Again, as Heaven's timing would have it, an old friend, whose ancestor had become rich by capturing a ship in the 18th century and left the family a great deal of money, had left the Bet El Trust a substantial legacy. This enabled us to finance the new editions.

So, suddenly I had to put my writing aside and concentrate on rewriting some texts and adding many new diagrams, based upon what I had learnt since I had written the original books. I also had the pleasure of including my favourite pictures. Most of these were black and white engravings from the 15th to the 19th century which depicted certain kabbalistic ideas with great precision when matched with an appropriate caption. These illustrations gave the books a traditional look which appealed to my Capricornian nature, with a modern text that came from my Geminian Moon.

FIGURE 100 (Left)—YAD
Yad *is a Hebrew term meaning 'Hand'. Such a pointer is used in the synagogue when reading from the scrolls of the Torah. I made this one from a telescopic tube, the end of a garden hose and a hand I made from a sheet of brass. The engraving of Creation is from a book I bought from a junk shop when I was a student. I thought it would be useful one day. This day came fifty years later when the Kabbalah Society published the revised editions of my books. It seems that my soul knew that this battered old volume was part of my Fate. The Yad has four sections which represent the Worlds of Jacob's Ladder.* (Pointer and engraving. Photograph by Peter Dickinson).

FIGURE 101—FATE
Here I am as an old gentleman, having lived out my fate according to my birth chart. I see now in hindsight how accurate it is. And yet I could have missed living out my fate if I had chosen to work in the family firm where there was a tempting degree of personal and financial security. However, it would not have been a fulfilled life as I could never have explored my potential. Free will is a crucial factor in life. Had I not chosen to follow the path of a Kabbalist I would never have enjoyed life, despite its dark times, so much. I therefore thank my stars. (Author's birth chart).

There was, however, a price to be paid for all this super-effort. While I have enjoyed excellent health for most of my life, the strain of overwork at seventy-plus manifested in a jump in my blood pressure. I had a warning omen, in having my attention sharply drawn to a man I passed in the street who had had a stroke. I was being told to slow down. One night, while lying in bed feeling my heart beating fiercely, I experienced a shimmering presence descending upon me and centring on my solar plexus. A wheel of power then began to vibrate with great force, sending out waves throughout my body. As I observed all this, I became aware of one of my old teachers, a physician now long dead, who was present and supervising what appeared to be some kind of operation. From then on I slowly began to recover. It seemed that I was still of use on Earth and this was very reassuring in a period in which several old friends and colleagues were dying off. Death is always something that is supposed to happen to other people. While the idea of becoming disembodied did not frighten me, the thought that I would not complete my mission did. I had had, over the years, a constant dream of dying before it was done.

This episode made me reflect on the Kabbalah Society and what might happen after I have gone. We now had groups all around the world, some we knew of, others we did not. Their work was based upon my books. I knew that, like all schools of the soul, ours would eventually decline unless someone came along who had a destiny similar to my own. I had deliberately not allowed any formal organisation in the school as I knew from experience this would make the structure crystallise. Moreover it would tempt someone, sooner or later, to use an inevitable pyramid of rank as a base for power. The groups were designed to be loosely associated, so that if one failed or became corrupt it would not affect the Society as a whole. As yet there is no obvious candidate to take my place but, no doubt, if the school is to complete its mission, then such a person will come. If not, then the Society will dissolve, at least leaving a body of knowledge that will be useful for future generations.

This brings me to the conclusion of this book; but not, I hope, to the immediate end of my life. What I can say at this point is that I set out to make a clear exposition of the metaphysical and psychological system of Kabbalah and its methods in an intelligible way that people can make practical use of. A set of the books has been sent to the Kabbalah department of the Hebrew University in Jerusalem. What they do with them will be most interesting. I suspect only a future generation of students will take them seriously when I am dead and gone, for by that time I might even be seen as kosher or respectable.

I have yet one more book to complete. This is *A Kabbalistic View of History*. I have been working at this on and off for the last twenty years. It is such a vast canvas that I kept losing control of its essential form because I had to seek out the thread of Providence from thousands of incidents. The seeming chaos of history is recorded mostly by individuals who had a biased view according to their culture and whether they were winners or losers in the battle between animal level people in the personal and general struggle for survival. Only around one per cent of the world's population is interested in spiritual evolution. Fortunately they have an enormous influence, as seen in the examples of Buddha, Moses, Plato and Zoroaster who created civilisations. I shall continue to work on this epic until I get it as right as I can.

Now at seventy-six I will continue my mission until I am called to the World Beyond. There, I hope, I will find myself with my companions of the light, as well as an ethereal version of my Earthly study where I can read all the books I did not have time for in life. While I await such a transition, there is still much to do to 'aid God to behold God' in the Mirror of this World.

Summer 2009
Z'ev ben Shimon Halevi

www.ingramcontent.com/pod-product-compliance
Lightning Source LLC
Chambersburg PA
CBHW050207130526
44590CB00043B/3028